THANX, ERNIE
MEL HALL
2013

THE ILLUSTRATED CATALOG OF

RIFLES AND SHOTGUNS

THE ILLUSTRATED CATALOG OF
RIFLES AND SHOTGUNS

DAVID MILLER

CHARTWELL
BOOKS, INC.

This edition published in 2012 by
CHARTWELL BOOKS, INC.
A division of BOOK SALES, INC.
276 Fifth Avenue Suite 206
New York, New York 10001
USA

Designer: Philip Clucas MSIAD

ISBN-13: 978-0-7858-2929-4

Printed and bound in India

The publisher would like to thank and acknowledge
the following for their help in publishing this book:
Patrick F. Hogan, The Rock Island Auction Company
and Patrick Reardon for access to his Civil War
firearms collection.

Contents

Introduction

The development of the Longarm, that being a long smooth-bored barrel mounted on a wooden stock which could be fired from the shoulder using both hands, led to it becoming in common use by infantry from the 14th century onwards. This coincided with it gradually becoming more effective, more accurate, and above all, more reliable. Development went in fits and starts, however, with long periods where nothing much changed.

By the time of the American Civil War smoothbore flintlock arms were still in evidence but the pressure of the war made demands on technology which fast-forwarded the development of the longarm by many years. The need for superior accuracy to inflict maximum damage on the other side led to the development of the rifled barrel which enabled troops to pick off the enemy at greater ranges before the opponent's guns became effective. The need for more reliable ignition led to the widespread adoption of the percussion cap. Other developments like the Minie bullet which expanded in the bore of the barrel to give a more effective gas seal also increased range and velocity. Multi-shot firearms like the lever–action Henry Rifle (see page 21) and the Spencer Repeating Carbine (page 37) also came into use on the Union side giving them a tremendous advantage.

During the Frontier period (1870-1900) the rifle developed alongside the shotgun (which is also covered in this book), to the point where at the end of the era the first semi-automatic rifles and shotguns appeared, mostly by courtesy of one man – John M. Browning.

Two World wars saw both weapons used martially – the shotgun such as the Stevens Model 620 (page 237,) in a close combat role, and the rifle used as the main weapon of the infantry like the Mauser K98 (page 104) but with special versions developed for sniping and elite forces units.

Arriving in the modern period we can see state-of-the-art automatic "Assault" rifles like the Colt M16 (page 135) and sophisticated modern sporting weapons – both rifles like the Remington Nylon 66 (page 170) and shotguns like the Mossberg Model 500 (page 221) that have benefited from the pressure of military development. At the same time we show examples of guns which are still shot for pleasure that ignore all trappings of modernity like the traditional English style side by side shotgun, the Gamba London (page 215) and high quality traditional single- shot bolt-action hunting rifles like the Weatherby Mark V series (page 187).

Baker Rifle

Designed by Ezekiel Baker and first selected for service in 1800, the Baker was the first general issue rifled weapon to enter British service. A muzzle-loading flintlock piece, it fired a tight-fitting ball that had to be firmly rammed into the barrel. A wooden mallet was originally issued to assist in this task. It enabled riflemen to operate in open formations and pick off their targets at longer ranges than was possible with smoothbore muskets.

Type: Muzzle-loading flintlock rifle
Origin: Tower Armouries, England
Caliber: .62   **Barrel length:** 30.25in

Beach

Claudius H. Beach was a gunsmith at Marshall, Michigan and is known to have been active in the years 1868-77,but probably set up business before that date and finished later. This percussion sporting rifle has a cast steel barrel from which the original rear sight has been removed and replaced by an adjustable sight mounted on the tang. This weapon is clearly marked with the maker's name, but has no date.

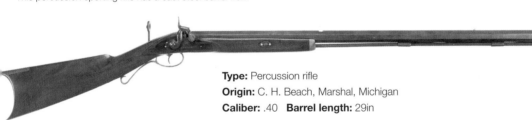

Type: Percussion rifle
Origin: C. H. Beach, Marshal, Michigan
Caliber: .40   **Barrel length:** 29in

Brown Bess Short Land Pattern Musket

From about the 1730 onwards, the British Army was equipped with a series of simple, effective flintlock muskets, known by the soldiers' nickname of "Brown Bess." This was never a formal title, and the term covered a multitude of variations in caliber, muzzle length and lock detail. The Short Land Pattern shown here entered service from about 1763 onwards, becoming the standard issue arm and a popular gun with soldiers for the next 100 years or so.

Type: Muzzle-loading flintlock musket
Origin: Tower Armories, England
Caliber: .75   **Barrel length:** 42in

Brown Bess Mortimer 3rd Model

The Brown Bess was also manufactured by a number of contractors, and this one has the markings of H.W Mortimer and Co. of London. The marking states: "H.W. Mortimer Gunmaker to his Majesty". Henry Walkgate Mortimer was born in 1753 and received this Royal Appointment from George III in 1783. He also made guns for the East India Company and was gunmaker to the British Post Office, making mail coach Blunderbusses and Pistols. He died in 1811.

Type: Muzzle-loading flintlock musket
Origin: H.W. Mortimer and Co of London, England
Caliber: .75   **Barrel length:** 39in

Bodenheimer Half-Stock Percussion Rifle

William Bodenheimer, Senior, arrived in Lancaster, Ohio in 1817 and set up business as a gunsmith. His son, William Bodenheimer, Junior, joined his father in 1849 and took over before his father's death in 1876. This fine rifle is one of their products, a traditional half-stocked percussion rifle, the style of which dates back to the early nineteenth century. Like so many rifles of the period it carries the maker's name but no date.

Type: Percussion rifle
Origin: William Bodenheimer, Lancaster, Ohio
Caliber: .33   **Barrel length:** 39.5in

Charleville Musket

The first French standardised model musket appeared in 1717 and this was followed by a series of modifications over the ensuing century .The weapon seen here was made in France at the government-owned Manufacture de Charleville.The three barrel bands suggest that it is a Model 1728, and was among the weapons supplied to the United States' Continental Army in 1778, during the Revolutionary War. Such French flintlock muskets served as the pattern for the Springfield M1795.

Type: Muzzle-loading flintlock musket
Origin: Manufacture de Charleville, Charleville, France
Caliber: .36   **Barrel length:** 44.5in

Enfield Pattern 1853 Rifle Musket (3-Band)

By 1853 the British Government were waking up to fact that to keep up with the French their infantry needed a standard issue rifled arm. Captain Claude Minie had developed an elongated lead bullet, which fitted the barrel and was therefore easily loadable. On firing a plug at the rear of the projectile was forced forward, expanding its thin lead rim, forming a tight gas seal as the bullet traveled up the barrel. The British developed an improved version with a hollow base where the expanding gases behind the bullet flared out the rim the form the all-important gas seal. The Enfield Pattern 1853 was designed to use this ammunition.

Type: Muzzle-loading percussion rifle
Origin: Enfield, England and Tower Armories, England
Caliber: .577
Barrel length: 39in

Relatively light, well made, popular and effective, it used metal bands to fix the barrel to the stock. The standard infantry rifle with the 39in barrel used three such bands, hence the "3-Band" designation.

Many were made at the Royal Ordnance Factory in Enfield, London, while others were made by various contractors, even though marked Tower Armouries. We show here another contract rifle made by Parker Field.

Britain's Volunteer regiments were equipped with worn out guns from the Crimea so many better off recruits purchased their own weapons from one of the many London gunmakers who produced contract versions of the Enfield.

Harper's Ferry Model 1795 Musket

Harper's Ferry is named after Robert Harper, an English immigrant, who established a watermill there in 1748. It was selected by George Washington himself, as the site for a national gun foundry this being duly authorized by Congress in 1794, with production starting in 1796. Shown here is a Model 1795 manufactured in 1815 and is in original condition, complete with its ramrod and 16 inch bayonet.

Type: Muzzle-loading flintlock musket
Origin: Harper's Ferry Armory, Harper's Ferry, Virginia,
Caliber: .69   **Barrel length:** 44.5in

Harper's Ferry Model 1803 Rifle

The Model 1803 was the first weapon to be officially accepted as a standard design by the U.S. Army .It was intended for use by "riflemen" and efforts were made to reduce the weight. Since riflemen were not expected to engage in hand-to-hand combat it was not equipped with a bayonet. The original barrel of the Model 1803 was 33 inches long but in 1814 this was increased to the 36 inches seen here.

Type: Muzzle-loading flintlock rifle
Origin: Harper's Ferry Armory, Harper's Ferry, Virginia,
Caliber: .54   **Barrel length:** 36in

Harper's Ferry Model 1816 Musket

The Harper's Ferry Model 1816 was manufactured from 1817 to 1844 with three minor variations. From 1832 on barrels were "bright" until production ended in 1844, and it's this production that is identified as the Type III shown here. In the 1850s many were altered by the "bolster" conversion to percussion firing and some of these were altered yet again during the Civil War, with rifled barrels, sights and a "patent breech."

Type: Muzzle-loading, flintlock musket
Origin: Harper's Ferry Armory, Harper's Ferry, Virginia.
Caliber: .69   **Barrel length:** 42in

Pomeroy Muskets

Lemuel Pomeroy ran his arms factory at Pitfield, Massachusetts from 1809 onwards. It appears to have been reasonably successful as he had a staff of 33 and received regular government contracts. The weapon seen here is a Pomeroy version of the popular U.S. Model 1816 musket and bayonet, produced in response to a contract for 5,000 such weapons. Many such guns would have survived to be converted to percussion ignition at the outset of the Civil War.

Type: Breech-loading musket
Origin: L. Pomeroy, Pitfield, Massachusetts
Caliber: .69   **Barrel length:** 42in

Quackenbush Safety Rifle

Henry M. Quackenbush, of Herkimer, New York, designed and manufactured his first air pistol in 1871 and his business grew so rapidly that several moves to ever-larger premises were required. He produced a line of air pistols and air rifles, and in 1886 he produced his first .22 rifle design. The .22 rifle seen here is elegant in its simplicity, having reduced the individual components to the essential minimum.

Type: Bolt-operated, single shot rifle
Origin: H.M. Quackenbush, Herkimer, New York
Caliber: .22   **Barrel length:** 22in

Siebert Plains Rifle

Charles Siebert (1839-1915) started to work for his brother, Christian, at the age of twelve in his brother's gunshop in Columbus, Ohio. He then moved to Circleville, about 30 miles South of Columbus and also in Ohio, where he established his own business. This classic plains rifle is unusual in having a round barrel, since most small-town gunsmiths of the period did not have the necessary tools for turning a round barrel.

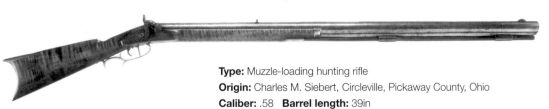

Type: Muzzle-loading hunting rifle
Origin: Charles M. Siebert, Circleville, Pickaway County, Ohio
Caliber: .58   **Barrel length:** 39in

Allen and Wheelock Drop Breech Rifle

A single shot breechloader produced from 1860 to 1871, some saw military service in the Civil War as privately procured weapons. It has a part round, part octagonal barrel between 23 and 28 inches long. The breech block drops down when the trigger guard is lowered, ejecting the case and allowing a fresh round to be inserted. Made in a variety of calibers-.22 through .44, all rimfire. Total production 1500-2000.

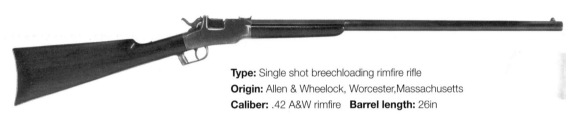

Type: Single shot breechloading rimfire rifle
Origin: Allen & Wheelock, Worcester,Massachusetts
Caliber: .42 A&W rimfire   **Barrel length:** 26in

Ball Lever Action Carbine

Although this gun was delivered too late for action it is generally considered a Civil War weapon. The carbine is a 7 shot rimfire repeating arm, operated by a lever which doubles as the trigger guard. The left hand side of the receiver has a robust saddle-ring or a sliding lug. It has a two-piece walnut stock with a three-quarter length forend fastened by two barrel bands.

Type: Repeating cartridge carbine
Origin: Lamson & Co.,Windsor, Vermont,
Caliber: .50 rimfire   **Barrel length:** 20.5in

Bridesburg Model 1861 Rifle Musket

This Model 1861 rifle musket was manufactured by the Bridesburg Machine Works that was owned by Alfred Jenks and his son, Barton, who at the outbreak of the Civil War, were well-established and successful manufacturers of cotton and wool milling machines. They built a new factory in 1863 to house some 150 workers who produced around 5000 US Government pattern muskets per month.

Type: Percussion service musket
Origin: Bridesburg Machine Works,Pennsylvania
Caliber: .58   **Barrel length:** 40in

Bridesburg Model 1863 Rifle Musket

The Model 1863 was effectively a Model 1861 with some minor improvements to the hammer and muzzle retaining bands in the Type I and further modifications to the rearsight and spring retainers for the barrel bands in the Type II.

Bridesburg were one of several manufacturers who made contract rifles during the Civil War. By the end they had produced just under 100,000 rifles for the Federal Government.

Type: Percussion service musket
Origin: Bridesburg Machine Works,Pennsylvania
Caliber: .58   **Barrel length:** 40in

J.F. Brown Target/Sniper Rifle

This weapon is of a type used by sharpshooters in the Civil War when it represented the very latest technology. The weapon was made by J.F. Brown of Haverhill Massachusetts. The telescopic sight was manufactured by L.M. Amadon of

Bellows Falls, Vermont, who was one of the pioneers of such devices. Both Amadon and Brown were famous in their time for the high quality of their products.

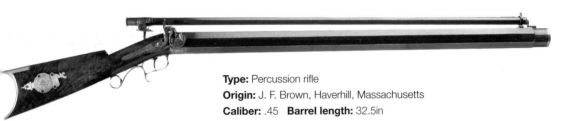

Type: Percussion rifle
Origin: J. F. Brown, Haverhill, Massachusetts
Caliber: .45   **Barrel length:** 32.5in

Burnside Carbine

The prolific Burnside carbine remained in production from 1857 to 1865. Designed by Ambrose E. Burnside, who formed the Bristol Firearms Co. in Rhode Island, and later

improved by one of his gunsmiths, George P. Foster. Finally Burnside had sold his interests in the company, going on to greater things as the commander of the Army of the Potomac.

Type: Percussion breechloading carbine
Origin: Bristol Firearms Co., Providence, Rhode Island
Caliber: .54   **Barrel length:** 21in

Colt Model 1855 Revolving Carbine

A reasonably rare weapon that was produced in .36, .44 and .56 inch caliber and in barrel lengths of 15, 18, 21 and 24 inches. Only 4,435 were produced and their manufacture lasted from 1856-64. The .56 caliber version had a five shot cylinder and the .36 and .44 calibers were graced with six shots. This would have given the weapon a distinct advantage over single shot carbines of the day.

Type: Percussion revolving carbine
Origin: Colt Armaments Manufacturing Co,Hartford, Connecticut
Caliber: .56 **Barrel length:** see text

Colt Special Model 1861 Musket

Samuel Colt claimed that the "Colt Special", combined the best features of the Springfield Model 1861 musket and the Enfield Pattern 1853, although it was, in reality, a Model 1861 simply re-engineered in order to make it suitable for manufacture on the Enfield machinery Colt had already bought from the bankrupt Robbins & Lawrence. Colt won his orders and deliveries started in September 1862. Colt's production total was 131,000 weapons.

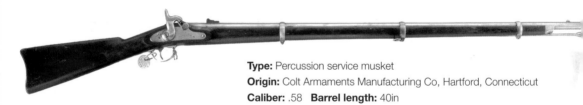

Type: Percussion service musket
Origin: Colt Armaments Manufacturing Co, Hartford, Connecticut
Caliber: .58 **Barrel length:** 40in

Cook and Brother Carbine

A muzzle-loading carbine from the early Civil War period based on the Enfield 1853 Pattern carbine, made by Ferdinand and Francis Cook, who set up shop in New Orleans in 1860.Over 1,500 guns of this type were produced. Stocks were either walnut or maple but some were pecan wood which was readily available in the South. Furniture was brass with a cast iron ramrod with flat button tip operated by a swivel joint.

Type: Percussion carbine
Origin: Cook & Brother, New Orleans, later Athens, Georgia
Caliber: .58 **Barrel length:** 21 in

Cosmopolitan Carbine

This forerunner to the Gwyn & Campbell Carbine was made in the same factory at Hamilton, Ohio. An order for 1,140 units for the State of Illinois was placed through the U.S Ordnance Dept. in December 1861 and delivered the following July. Virtually the whole batch was issued to the 5th and 6th Illinois Cavalry. The 6th Illinois Cavalry, commanded by Benjamin Grierson, took part in "Grierson's Raid" in April-May 1863.

Type: Percussion carbine
Origin: Cosmopolitan Arms Co., Hamilton, Ohio
Caliber: 52　**Barrel length:** 19in

Dickson Nelson & Co Rifle

Dickson, Nelson and Co manufactured rifles for the Confederacy based on the U.S. Model 1841. Also known as the Shakanoosa Arms Company, its founders William Dickson and Owen O.Nelson manufactured arms in first in Adairsville,Georgia (1862-63), Macon (1863-64) and finally Dawson,Georgia (1864-1865). The gun shown has a raised tang rear sight and sling swivels on the trigger guard and forend. Its lock date is 1865 and the stock is made of dark cherry wood with brass mountings.

Type; Percussion rifle
Origin: Dickson Nelson & Co, Georgia
Caliber: .58　**Barrel length:** 33in

Enfield Pattern 1853 Cavalry Carbine

A Carbine version of the Pattern 1853 Enfield was also made for cavalry and artillery issue. As can be seen the gun uses the same lock mechanism as its larger brethren, and is distinguished by its short 21 inch barrel, secured by just two barrel bands and a swivel ramrod. Many of these guns were ordered by the Confederate States, although fewer than 5,000 of them actually got through the blockade.

Type: Muzzle-loading percussion carbine
Origin: Enfield, England
Caliber: .577　**Barrel length:** 21in

Enfield Rifles in American Service

When the Civil War started both sides looked to overseas to make up the shortfall in their infantry weapons. While a range of longarms was procured, the most popular foreign arm quickly became the Enfield Pattern 1853.

Along with the Springfield Model 1861, the Enfield was one of the the most numerous longarms in the war, and in fact, while nominally .577 caliber, it could also fire the .58 Springfield ammunition. When the war was a growing certainty the Chief of Ordnance of the Confederacy, Colonel

Josiah Gorgas, was only too aware of the fact that manufacturing industry in the South could not supply enough arms to properly equip his forces. He sent his agent Caleb Huse to England and other European countries to buy arms. Because of the bad feeling over the War of Independence and that of 1812, and perhaps closer cultural affinities with the Southern States, England particularly wished to support the Confederate war effort. Huse managed to procure over 400,000 of the Pattern 1853 series.

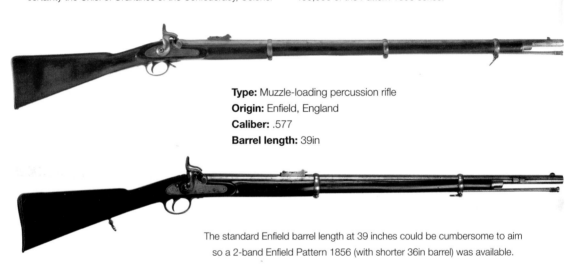

Type: Muzzle-loading percussion rifle
Origin: Enfield, England
Caliber: .577
Barrel length: 39in

The standard Enfield barrel length at 39 inches could be cumbersome to aim so a 2-band Enfield Pattern 1856 (with shorter 36in barrel) was available.

Fayetteville Confederate Rifle Type I

After the Confederate raid on the Harper's Ferry Armory in the spring of 1861, captured components, gunmaking tools and equipment were removed to the Confederate Armories at Richmond and Fayetteville. Most of the production at

Fayetteville was based on the design of the Model 1855 rifle.The early production Type I (shown here) had a hump on the lockplate which was shaped to accept the Maynard taped primer system which the Confederates didn't have access to.

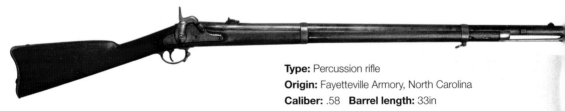

Type: Percussion rifle
Origin: Fayetteville Armory, North Carolina
Caliber: .58   **Barrel length:** 33in

Fayetteville Confederate Rifle Type II

A later production Fayetteville Type II with the "low hump" lockplate and a hammer with a distinctive S shaped contour. The earlier Type I had a lock plate with a higher hump to the same profile as the Maynard Tape Primer system (see previous entry.)This particular gun shows the results of over-enthusiastic cleaning and sanding at some point in its history. The most collectible examples are stamped C.S.A.on the brass buttplate tang.

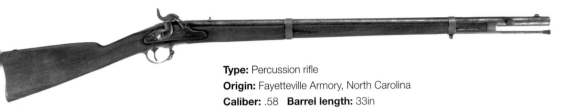

Type: Percussion rifle
Origin: Fayetteville Armory, North Carolina
Caliber: .58   **Barrel length:** 33in

Gallager Carbine

Designed by Mahlon J. Gallager from South Carolina, this gun was used extensively in the Civil War. Patented July 17th 1860, almost 18.000 were produced at the Richardson and Overman factory in Philadelphia. It was single shot breechloader in .50 inch caliber loaded by activating the trigger guard to slide the barrel forward allowing access to the breech. The patchbox was a luxury which other manufacturers avoided in order to keep costs down.

Type: Breech-loading percussion carbine
Origin: Richardson & Overman, Philadelphia.
Caliber: .50   **Barrel length:** 22.25in

Gibbs Carbine

Shown here is one of the rarest Civil War carbines to have survived. An order for 10,000 was placed by the federal government with the New York, Phoenix arms factory, owned by W.F Brooks and W.W. Marsden. The factory was destroyed in the New York Draft Riots of 1863, at which time only 1,052 guns had been completed. The action is similar in operation to that of the Gallager with the barrel sliding forward to access the breech.

Type: Breech-loading percussion carbine
Origin: William F. Brooks, New York
Caliber: .52   **Barrel length:** 22in

Greene Carbine

This carbine was produced in limited quantities at the Chicopee Falls factory of the Massachusetts Arms Co. The gun is a .54 caliber single shot breechloader using the Maynard tape primer ignition system. The 22 inch barrel swung down and to the right to allow access to the breech, and the sling was mounted on the trigger guard. 300 were made and some are known to have been issued to the 6th Ohio Cavalry.

Type: Breech-loading percussion carbine
Origin: Massachusetts Arms Co., Chicopee Falls, Massachusetts
Caliber: .54   **Barrel length:** 18in

Greene Bolt Action Rifle

The first bolt-action rifle purchased by the U.S. government, some 900 were delivered during the Civil War. Patented by Lt. Col. J. Durrell Greene, it used a twisted oval section bore which imparted a spin in the same way as rifling.

The hammer was underneath, in front of the trigger guard. After locking the bolt, the firer still had to insert a percussion priming cap on the nipple beneath the stock.

Type: Single-shot, bolt-action percussion rifle
Origin: A. H. Waters,Millbury, Massachusetts
Caliber: .53   **Barrel length:** 35in

Gwyn & Campbell Carbine

Also known as the "Union Carbine" or the "Grapevine Carbine," it was manufactured by Edward Gwyn and Abner C. Campbell of Hamilton, Ohio, and was the successor to the Cosmopolitan. Made between 1863-64, 8,202 of these carbines were widely issued to the Union Cavalry regiments. The example shown is the Type 1, identified by its serpentine hammer and spur at the rear of the trigger guard which acts as a lever latch to open the breech.

Type: Percussion breech-loading carbine
Origin: Edward Gwyn and Abner C. Campbell, Ohio
Caliber: .52   **Barrel length:** 20in

Harper's Ferry Model 1841 "Mississippi Rifle"

When production of the Hall breech-loading rifle ended in 1841, the Harper's Ferry factory was converted to manufacture the U.S. Model 1841 rifle. Some 25,000 were produced there between 1846 and 1855. The Model 1841 will always be known as the "Mississippi rifle" in memory of the troops who used it during the Mexican-American War, particularly at the Battle of Buena Vista against Santa Anna's Mexican army in1847. Jefferson Davis's 1st Mississippi

Rifles, armed with the new gun turned the tide for the outnumbered US troops, and it has been known ever since been known as the "Mississippi rifle" in their honor.

Type: Muzzle-loading, percussion rifle
Origin: Harper's Ferry Armory, Virginia,
Caliber: .54
Barrel length: 33in

This example is dated 1850 and appears to be in original condition and complete except for the sling swivels.

Another Model 1841, though not in as complete condition, because although the swivels and sling are present the ramrod is missing.

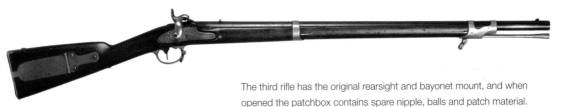

The third rifle has the original rearsight and bayonet mount, and when opened the patchbox contains spare nipple, balls and patch material.

Harper's Ferry Model 1842

No less than 106,629 of these Model 1842 smoothbore muskets were made between 1844 and 1855, the example seen here having left the factory in 1851. Its battered appearance shows that it has seen much hard service, but not so immediately obvious is that, for some reason, two-and-a-half inches have been cut off the muzzle. A lot of Model 1842s were modified after leaving Harper's Ferry particularly during the Civil War when many guns were rifled.

Type: Muzzle-loading, percussion musket
Origin: Harper's Ferry Armory ,Virginia,
Caliber: .69   **Barrel length:** 42in

Harper's Ferry Model 1855 Percussion Rifle Musket

Over 59,000 of these Model 1855 rifle muskets were made at the Harpers Ferry and Springfield Armories, and most saw extensive service during the Civil War. It was the first issue firearm to fire the .58 expanding Minie bullet, and also used the Maynard Tape Priming system instead of individual percussion primer caps. In April 1861 Harper's Ferry was overrun by Confederate forces and the production equipment seized to make rifles for the South.

Type: Muzzle-loading, percussion musket
Origin: Harper's Ferry Armory, Virginia,
Caliber: .58   **Barrel length:** 40in

Harper's Ferry Model 1855 Percussion Rifle

A development of the Model 1855 rifle musket, the Model 1855 Rifle had a shorter barrel (at 33in) fixed to the stock by only two bands instead of three. It kept the same Maynard primer mechanism and used the same .58 Minie bullet. Only 7,613 of these rifles were made before the Harper's Ferry Armory was destroyed in 1861.The Model 1855 was the last muzzle-loading rifle to be adopted by a significant national armory.

Type: Muzzle-loading, percussion rifle
Origin: Harper's Ferry Armory, Virginia,
Caliber: .58   **Barrel length:** 33in

Henry Rifle

Invented and patented by B. Tyler Henry (1821-1898), the Henry rifle was chambered for the .44 Henry cartridge, with a fifteen-round, tubular magazine in the butt. It had an octagonal 24 inch barrel with no foregrip, but with a walnut buttstock and a brass butt-plate. Some 14,000 of these rifles were made between 1861 and 1866, of which the early examples had iron frames and the remainder, as seen here,

brass frame. The gun was significant in the Civil War because of its superior firepower. A drawback was that the shooters forehand gripped the bare barrel which became hot in action.

Type: Tubular-magazine, lever-action rifle
Origin: New Haven Arms Co. Connecticut
Caliber: .44 Henry   **Barrel length:** 24in

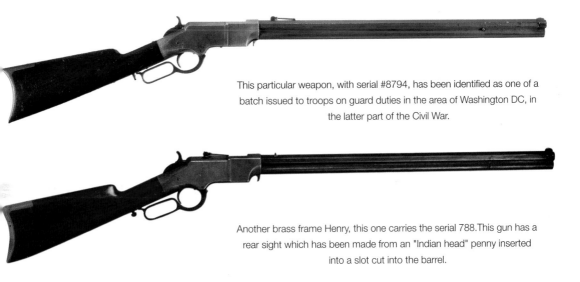

This particular weapon, with serial #8794, has been identified as one of a batch issued to troops on guard duties in the area of Washington DC, in the latter part of the Civil War.

Another brass frame Henry, this one carries the serial 788. This gun has a rear sight which has been made from an "Indian head" penny inserted into a slot cut into the barrel.

Jenks "Mule Ear" Carbine

The original model was designed by William Jenks who signed a contract with the navy in 1841 for the supply of 4,250 of his breech-loading carbines. They were named "Mule Ear" because of the distinctive shape of the

breechlever and sidehammer, this being the only sidehammer weapon ever to see service in the U.S. forces. The initial order was subcontracted to sword manufacturer N.P.Ames but after 1845 all production was at Remington's factory.

Type: Percussion Carbine
Origin: Remington, Ilion, New York
Caliber: .54   **Barrel length:** 24in

Joslyn Model 1862 and 1864 Carbines

The Joslyn turned out to be one of the most prolific of Civil War arms, being produced from early in the War through to spring 1865. It evolved during that time from percussion cap ignition to .52 rimfire ammunition in the early 1862 model, with the nipple giving way to the firing pin. The Model 1862 accounted for about 3,500 of the total run of 16,500 with the Model 1864 accounting for the bulk of the production, of which some 8,000 units were official Federal government purchase and 4,500 privately purchased through military outfitters like Schuyler, Hartley & Graham in New York.

Type: Single-shot cartridge carbine
Origin: Joslyn Firearms Co., Connecticut
Caliber: .52 rimfire   **Barrel length:** 22in

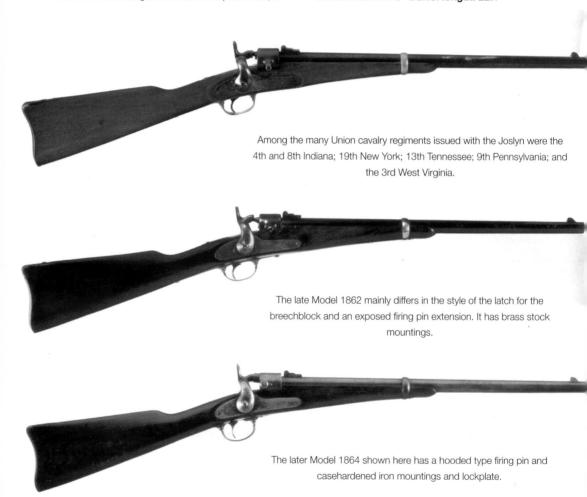

Among the many Union cavalry regiments issued with the Joslyn were the 4th and 8th Indiana; 19th New York; 13th Tennessee; 9th Pennsylvania; and the 3rd West Virginia.

The late Model 1862 mainly differs in the style of the latch for the breechblock and an exposed firing pin extension. It has brass stock mountings.

The later Model 1864 shown here has a hooded type firing pin and casehardened iron mountings and lockplate.

Justice Rifled Musket

P.S. Justice began manufacturing rifles and rifle muskets as the Civil War broke out in 1861, one of many new manufacturers trying to meet the demand for weapons from Union forces. Justice rifles were not of particularly high quality, but were some of the first wartime production to get into the hands of the fighting men. Most were assembled from a mixture of existing components, and this rifle has some parts dated 1829.

Type: Percussion rifle musket
Origin: P.S. Justice, Philadelphia
Caliber: .69   **Barrel length:** 39in

Lee Single-Shot Carbine

A few hundred of these carbines were made in Milwaukee, Wisconsin from 1864-65. The mechanism was unusual, in that the centrally mounted hammer formed part of the barrel lock. When unlocked, reloading was achieved by pivoting the rear of the barrel out to the right. Ammunition was .44 rimfire. A further order was placed for 1,000 and the barrels, made by Remington, were produced in the wrong caliber leading to rejection of the order.

Type: Single-shot cartridge carbine
Origin: Lee Firearms Co., Milwaukee, Wisconsin
Caliber: .44 rimfire   **Barrel length:** 21 in

Lindner Carbine

This carbine was a .58 inch caliber single shot breech-loader activated by turning a sleeve on the barrel through 180 degrees, allowing the spring loaded breechblock to pop up ready for loading. The first type was produced in two contracts totaling 892 guns, and were marked "Edward Lindner's/ Patent /March 29, 1859" on the breech only. They were used by the 1st Michigan Cavalry and the 8th West Virginia Mounted Infantry.

Type: Percussion breech-loading carbine
Origin: Edward Lindner, New Hampshire
Caliber: .58   **Barrel length:** 20in

Lindsay Two-Shot Musket

There were many attempts to find a means of delivering more than one shot from the same weapon without reloading. John Parker Lindsay of New York City was one of those who devoted much effort to solving this problem and patented a system in which two chambers fed into a single barrel, the two shots being fired consecutively. He received a government order on December 17, 1863 for 1,000 muskets to this design.

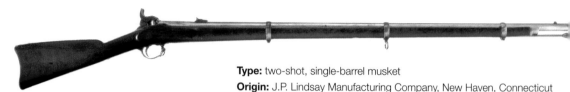

Type: two-shot, single-barrel musket
Origin: J.P. Lindsay Manufacturing Company, New Haven, Connecticut
Caliber: .58 **Barrel length:** 41 in

Lorenz Model 1854 Rifle Musket

This weapon was designed by Lieutenant Lorenz of the Imperial Austro-Hungarian Army. When the Civil War broke out purchasers from both the Union and the Confederacy scoured Europe looking for firearms, and as the Lorenz was then being replaced by a Model 1862 rifle in Austro-Hungarian service, many thousands were readily available. As a result, the Model 1854 musket was used by both sides; the Union bought some 225,000 and the Confederacy approximately 100,000.

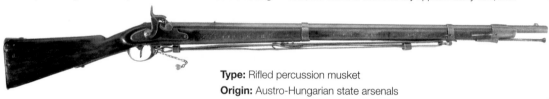

Type: Rifled percussion musket
Origin: Austro-Hungarian state arsenals
Caliber: .54 or .58 **Barrel length:** 39in

Marlin-Ballard Carbine

Charles H. Ballard invented and patented the "dropping-block" action in 1861. In this system, the breechblock, which contained the hammer, trigger mechanism and the associated springs, was pushed down by the operating lever and moved away from the chamber. In its original form the empty cartridge was ejected by the use of a large stud which projected below the fore-end. Civil War production of the carbine was approximately 6,600 units made by Ball & Williams.

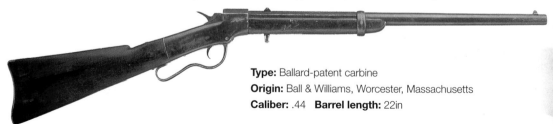

Type: Ballard-patent carbine
Origin: Ball & Williams, Worcester, Massachusetts
Caliber: .44 **Barrel length:** 22in

Maynard Carbine

Manufactured by the Massachusetts Arms Co. of Chicopee Falls, the gun was designed by Dr Edward Maynard, inventor of the tape primer ignition system which this weapon utilized. The Company is worthy of mention in that many famous names are featured in the original board of directors of 1851, including Horace Smith and Daniel B. Wesson (later to form Smith and Wesson), Joshua Stevens (later J. Stevens Arms Co.) and J.T. Ames (Ames Mfg. Co.). The company entered the longarms market in 1855 with the manufacture of the Greene breech-loading carbine, followed by the first Maynard Carbines in 1858-59.

Type: Percussion, breech-loading carbine
Origin: Massachusetts Arms Company,
   Chicopee Falls, Massachusetts
Caliber: .50   **Barrel length:** 20in

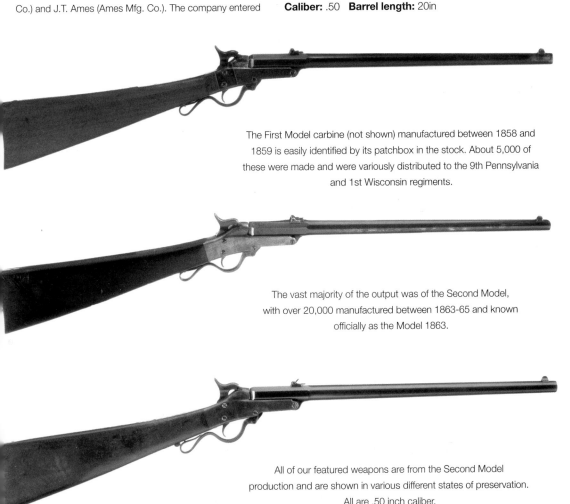

The First Model carbine (not shown) manufactured between 1858 and 1859 is easily identified by its patchbox in the stock. About 5,000 of these were made and were variously distributed to the 9th Pennsylvania and 1st Wisconsin regiments.

The vast majority of the output was of the Second Model, with over 20,000 manufactured between 1863-65 and known officially as the Model 1863.

All of our featured weapons are from the Second Model production and are shown in various different states of preservation. All are .50 inch caliber.

Merrill Carbine

A simple and effective breechloader, a total quantity of 14,495 carbines were made by H. Merrill of Baltimore, Maryland. The majority of the production was accounted for by Federal government purchase but some weapons did reach the Confederacy. The Second Model was in part inspired by the pressures of wartime production saving both time and cost which accounts for the missing patchbox .There were improvements too, like the copper-faced breech plunger that sealed the percussion cartridge in the breech allowing less gas to escape. The Second Model also had modifications to the breech lever latch, making it a rounded button as opposed to a flat knurled type.

Type: Percussion breech-loading carbine
Origin: H. Merrill, Baltimore, Maryland
Caliber: .54   **Barrel length:** 22.25 in

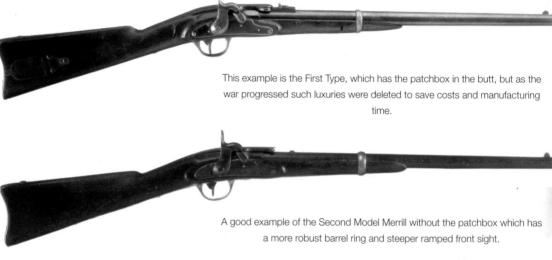

This example is the First Type, which has the patchbox in the butt, but as the war progressed such luxuries were deleted to save costs and manufacturing time.

A good example of the Second Model Merrill without the patchbox which has a more robust barrel ring and steeper ramped front sight.

Right: Merrill Carbines did get into Confederate hands as this rare cartridge box marked "Merrill's Carbine C.S Laboratory, Richmond,VA" shows.

Miller Model 1861

William H. Miller and George W. Miller, both of West Meriden, Connecticut patented a "Conversion Block" which enabled an existing muzzle-loader to be converted to a breech-loader. The contract to carry out the conversion to government

pattern Model 1861 muzzle-loaders was placed with the Meriden Manufacturing Company and the work was carried out between 1865 and 1867. The example shown here is a converted Model 1861, with a 39 inch barrel.

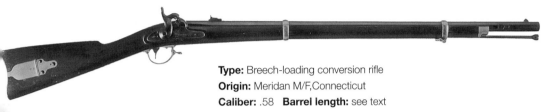

Type: Breech-loading conversion rifle
Origin: Meridan M/F, Connecticut
Caliber: .58 **Barrel length:** see text

Miller Parkers' Snow Rifle

Parkers' Snow were one of the manufacturers of the Model 1861 rifle musket, and this weapon was originally made for a Civil War contract. From 1865 onwards, some 2,000 of the Parkers' Snow rifles were converted to the patented breech-

loading system developed by the Miller Brothers (see above). By releasing a catch on top of the barrel, the breech assembly could be hinged upwards to allow a new round to be loaded.

Type: Percussion conversion rifle
Origin: Parkers' Snow and Co., Meridien, Connecticutt
Caliber: .58 centerfire **Barrel length:** 31.5in

Palmer Bolt Action Carbine

W. Palmer patented the design of this breech-loading arm in December 1863 making it a weapon of the Civil War era, but Lamson were only contracted to make them late in the War with delivery being made in June 1865 after the fighting had

stopped. Only about 1,000 are known to have been manufactured although the carbine is significant in being the first metallic cartridge bolt-action weapons to be issued to U.S. troops.

Type: Single-shot bolt-action carbine
Origin: E.G. Lamson and Co., Vermont
Caliber: .54 rimfire **Barrel length:** 20in

Peabody Carbine

Developed during the Civil War, but ultimately arriving too late for service, the unfortunate Peabody was sold off to foreign powers such as Mexico, Canada, France and Spain. This meant that although all U.S. military interest ended with the war, this fairly conventional rimfire breech-loader went on to provide its makers - The Providence Tool Company of Providence, Rhode Island - with a healthy income in the 1870s.

Type: Single-shot breech-loading carbine
Origin: Peabody and Providence Tool Company, Rhode Island
Caliber: .50 rimfire   **Barrel length:** 20in

Peabody Rifle

Development of this rifle began in the early Civil War years and it was tested by the army but ultimately coming to late to see service. Despite this the gun was produced in large numbers in the 1860s and 1870s for foreign contracts in a variety of calibers, including .43 Spanish, .45 Peabody, .45-70, .50 and .50-70. The standard barrel was 30 inches. Over 112,000 units of the rifle and the carbine were made.

Type: Single-shot breech-loading rifle
Origin: Peabody and Providence Tool Company, Rhode Island
Caliber: .43 Spanish   **Barrel length:** 30in

Remington Model 1841 Mississippi Rifle

In 1845 Remington negotiated the purchase of a contract for 5,000 Model 1841 Mississippi Rifles held by John Griffiths of Cincinnati. This deal also included machinery, although it's not clear if this was actually supplied. Remington delivered the first batch of Model 1841s in 1850, and used this success to gain subsequent government contracts for these and other military weapons. One of the giants of American gunmaking was now in business.

Type: Percussion rifle musket
Origin: E. Remington and Sons, Ilion, New York
Caliber: .69   **Barrel length:** 42in

Remington Model 1816 Maynard Conversion

The Maynard Tape Priming system was fitted to many obselete military muskets, including this Model 1816. It is one of a batch of about 20,000 that had Maynard locks supplied by Remington, who bid for the work in an attempt to keep their skilled gunmakers employed and to remain in the frame for future government contracts. The actual conversions were carried out from 1856-58 by the Frankford Arsenal, Philadelphia, who also rifled the smoothbore barrels.

Type: Muzzle-loading, percussion musket
Origin: see text-
Caliber: .69   **Barrel length:** 42in

Remington Model 1863 "Zouave" Rifle

Remington was awarded the contract to produce some 12,000 of this well made percussion rifle. Similar to the standard Model 1863, it was slightly shorter and had only two barrel bands. It is not known with any certainty why the name "Zouave" was given to this weapon, as there are no records to suggest it was issued particularly to these regiments with their unusual colorful clothing. As can be seen from the two examples we show, many surviving Zouave rifles are in excellent condition, implying that most, if not all were never issued to Federal Troops during the Civil War.

Type: Muzzle-loading, percussion rifle
Origin: E. Remington and Sons, Ilion, New York
Caliber: .58   **Barrel length:** 33in

This gun was part of a contract placed on December 13th 1863 for 2,500 rifles which were promptly delivered by Remington between December 23rd 1863 and January 8th 1864.

Remington was paid $17.00 per rifle including the bayonet for the Zouave rifle. Despite this the gun was nicely turned out with brass furniture and patchbox, which many other weapons of the period lacked.

Richmond Muskets

During the Confederate raid on the Harper's Ferry Armory in April 1861, captured parts and gunmaking equipment were moved to Richmond and Fayetteville to begin production of rifles and muskets. The Richmond Armory produced thousands of weapons from 1861 to 1865, in larger numbers than any other Confederate longarm. Most were based on the Model 1855 and 1863 rifles. Confederate production didn't use the Maynard system, but as the captured lockplate dies were set for the Model 1855 and its Maynard Tape primer lock, early Richmond lockplates followed the same shape, giving them a high profiled hump.

Type: Percussion rifle
Origin: Richmond Armory, Richmond, Virginia
Caliber: .58
Barrel length: 40in

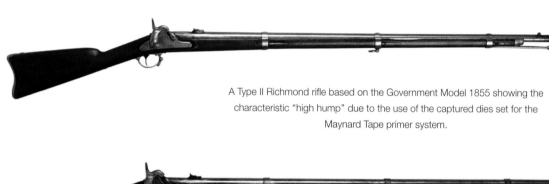

A Type II Richmond rifle based on the Government Model 1855 showing the characteristic "high hump" due to the use of the captured dies set for the Maynard Tape primer system.

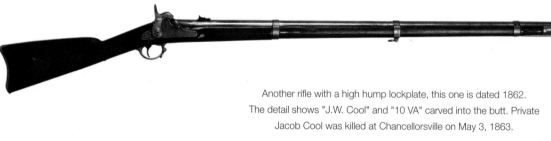

Another rifle with a high hump lockplate, this one is dated 1862. The detail shows "J.W. Cool" and "10 VA" carved into the butt. Private Jacob Cool was killed at Chancellorsville on May 3, 1863.

Later modifications produced the Type III seen here which can be recognized by the lower profile hump on the lockplate.

This Richmond musket is dated 1862 and the butt is carved with the owner's name- James Clay- who served with the 18th Virginia and took part in Pickett's Charge at Gettysburg.

Robinson Sharps Carbine

Made in Richmond, Virginia between 1862 and 1864 and based on the Hartford-made Model 1859 Sharps, this weapon generally lacked the refinement and quality workmanship of the original. Approximately 1,900 First Type guns were produced by Robinsons between 1862-63, The Confederate Government took over the Robinson factory in March 1863 and introduced the Second Type, which was identical to the First except for the markings on the breech ("Richmond, VA.").

Type: Percussion breech-loading carbine
Origin: Richmond, Virginia
Caliber: .52 **Barrel length:** 21in

Robins, Kendall and Lawrence Model 1841 Mississippi Rifle

The firm of Robins, Kendall and Lawrence had a contract to produce some 10,000 of the Model 1841 Mississippi Rifle, and this well kept example was produced in 1847. The lock is marked "Windsor VT/1847" and with this dating it may have seen service in the Mexican War for which the gun was named. Many surviving Model 1841s were subsequently bored out to .58 caliber to give further service in the Civil War.

Type: Percussion rifle
Origin: Robins, Kendall and Lawrence, Windsor, Vermont
Caliber: .54 **Barrel length:** 33in

Sharps 1852 Saddle Ring Carbine

After working for other manufacturers, including John Hall at Harpers Ferry, Christian Sharps eventually set up his own company in 1851, in co-operation with Robbins and Lawrence, in Windsor, Vermont. Robbins and Lawrence made the weapons, while Sharps provided technical advice and marketed them from the Sharps Rifle Manufacturing Company, in Hartford, Connecticut. Sharps developed a range of single-shot breechloading rifles and carbines that were to be heavily used by soldiers in the Civil War and after, and by sportsmen and hunters. This is one of Sharps' earlier designs, and is a neat ,52 caliber cavalry carbine which used the Sharps patent pellet primer mounted on the lockplate.

Type: Single-shot, breech-loading percus¬sion carbine
Origin: see text
Caliber: .52   **Barrel length:** 21.5in

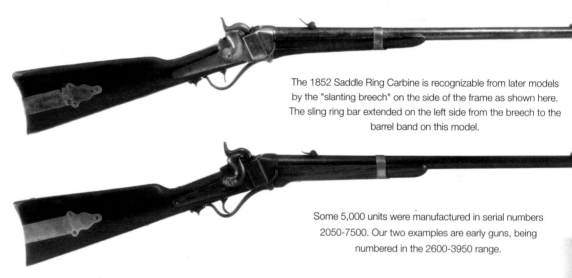

The 1852 Saddle Ring Carbine is recognizable from later models by the "slanting breech" on the side of the frame as shown here. The sling ring bar extended on the left side from the breech to the barrel band on this model.

Some 5,000 units were manufactured in serial numbers 2050-7500. Our two examples are early guns, being numbered in the 2600-3950 range.

Sharps New Model Rifle

As a result of experience with the Model 1852, the Sharps Company updated the design to what is known as the straight breech, or New Model rifles and carbines. As far as the carbine series goes, some 98,000 were made of Models 1859, 1863, and 1 865, although they can be regarded as a single type. The Model 1863, which we are illustrating, was produced both with and without a patchbox (twice as many without).

Type: Single-shot, breech-loading percussion rifle
Origin: Sharps, Hartford, Connecticut
Caliber: .52   **Barrel length:** 30in

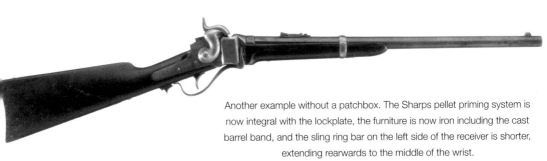

Another example without a patchbox. The Sharps pellet priming system is now integral with the lockplate, the furniture is now iron including the cast barrel band, and the sling ring bar on the left side of the receiver is shorter, extending rearwards to the middle of the wrist.

Sharps New Model Rifles

Sharps rifles were chosen as the issue arm for Hiram Berdan's Sharpshooters. Berdan himself made various unauthorized modifications to the gun such as the replacement of the single trigger with the double-set trigger. The initial order for 2,000 guns (supplied at $42,50 each) was delivered to the grateful Sharpshooters in 1862.The guns carried the serial numbers 54374 to 57567, but this range also includes around 1,300 Sharps M1859 carbines and a number of single trigger non-Berdan M1859 rifles. The guns were light (at 8 pounds, 12 ounces), compact (47 inches long overall), accurate, and capable of firing up to nine rounds per minute.

Type: Single-shot, breech-loading percus¬sion rifle
Origin: Sharps, Hartford, Connecticut
Caliber: .52
Barrel length: 30in

A standard Model 1859 with the single trigger. Limited numbers of these weapons were issued to regular army and navy units.

A modified gun with double-set trigger as used by the U.S. Sharpshooters in the Civil War.

Sharps & Hankins Model 1862 Carbine

In 1853 Christian Sharps severed all connections with the Sharps Rifle Manufacturing Company in Hartford, Connecticut. He returned to Philadelphia and set up as C. Sharps & Company and set about manufacturing a breechloading, single shot pistol. In 1862 he formed a partnership with William Hankins to produce weapons for the Civil War, and began manufacture of this sliding barrel action carbine. A total of 8,000 were made between 1862-65.

Production was mainly centered on the navy type, which had the unusual feature of a leather-covered barrel to prevent corrosion.. An army type was made in small numbers (around 500.)

Type: Breech-loading, metallic cartridge, military carbine
Origin: Sharps and Hankins, Philadelphia, Pennsylvania
Caliber: .52 rimfire   **Barrel length:** 24 in and 19 in.

Sadly for Christian Sharps the new gun was nowhere near as iconic as the one he had previously designed.

The Navy issue carbine had fixings for a leather barrel sleeve of which surviving examples with the leather in good shape are all too rare.

The cavalry carbine version had a shortened 19 inch barrel and a saddle ring. It was mainly associated with the 11th New York Volunteer Cavalry.

Smith Carbine

Originally patented by Gilbert Smith of Buttermilk Falls, New York, around 30,000 Smith carbines were made between 1861-65 in Massachusetts. Manufacture took place at the American Machine Works plant in Springfield, at the American Arms Co., and the Massachusetts Arms Co., both located in Chicopee Falls. The gun's agents, Thomas Poultney and D.B.Trimble of Baltimore managed to sell substantial quantities to the government but some guns were sold commercially through New York military outfitters Schuyler,Hartley & Graham .The gun is loaded by releasing the catch in front of the trigger, allowing the barrel to pivot downward to give access to the breech.

Type: Single –shot percussion breech-loading carbine
Origin: see text
Caliber: .50 **Barrel length:** 21.6 inches

The Smith was mass-produced by three contractors and surviving examples are not hard to find. They are serial numbered 1 on up.

Note the barrel release catch at the front of the trigger guard-when released the gun virtually folds in half.

As a collector's item this Smith carbine is in only "Fair" condition because the walnut stock has suffered through the years and lets the gun down somewhat.

Spencer Model 1860 Rifle

Christopher M. Spencer was born in 1841 and initially made his weapons at South Manchester, Connecticut, until moving to Boston in about 1862. His Model 1860 rifle was similar to the Model 1860 carbine, but with a longer, 30 inch, barrel and a full-length stock extending almost to the muzzle, with an iron tip and secured by three barrel bands. There were two almost identical variants, one for the navy (1,000 produced in 1862-4) the other for the army (11,450 produced in 1863-4). The gun was a 7-shot repeater, the magazine tube being housed in the center of the buttstock.

Type: Magazine-fed repeating rifle
Origin: Spencer Repeating Rifle Co., Boston, Massachusett
Caliber: .52 **Barrel length:** 30 in

This Model 1860 has brass studs on the stock which may indicate Native American ownership at some point after the war. Many weapons from the conflict found their way out West.

Only 11,000 units were completed in time to take part in the Civil War and the gun really developed its full potential after the hostilities ceased. This is a Model 1870 Army rifle.

This is one of a very small batch made for an army trial immediately following the Civil War. It is chambered for the .46 round and has a 31 inch barrel; it is fitted with the Stabler magazine cut-off which converted the gun to single–shot firing.

Spencer Repeating Carbine

The gun is loaded via a tubular magazine housed in the buttstock, and rounds are fed into the breech by cranking down the trigger guard lever. Many soldiers were also equipped with the Blakeslee Cartridge Box, a wooden box containing between 6 and 13 metal tubes pre-loaded with 7 rounds. By placing the end of the reloading tube against the open end of the tubular magazine and dropping the cartridges through, the carbine could be reloaded in a matter of seconds. The Spencer fired a .52 inch caliber rimfire straight copper cartridge. The case was .56 inches in diameter, so the cartridge is often referred to as the No. 56.

Type: Magazine-fed repeating carbine
Origin: Spencer Repeating Rifle Co., Boston, Massachusetts
Caliber: .52
Barrel length: 22 in

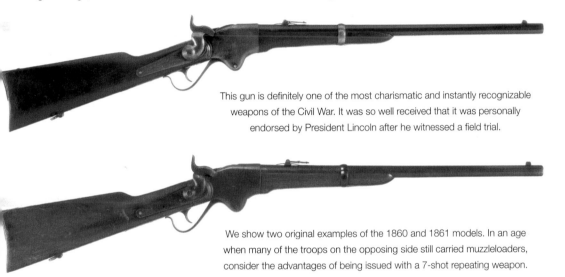

This gun is definitely one of the most charismatic and instantly recognizable weapons of the Civil War. It was so well received that it was personally endorsed by President Lincoln after he witnessed a field trial.

We show two original examples of the 1860 and 1861 models. In an age when many of the troops on the opposing side still carried muzzleloaders, consider the advantages of being issued with a 7-shot repeating weapon.

Springfield Model 1855 Rifle Musket

A fine example of the U.S.Model 1855 made at the Springfield Armory. fitted with the Maynard Tape primer system. Rifles such as this saw extensive service during the Civil War. See earlier entry for the Harpers Ferry Model 1855 on page 20. As the war progressed this weapon became increasing obsolete and was branded unreliable; particularly the Maynard Tape Primer system which failed in the frequently damp conditions encountered in the field.

Type: Percussion rifle musket
Origin: National Armory, Springfield, Illinois
Caliber: .58   **Barrel length:** 40in

Springfield Model 1861 Rifle

Over one million of this percussion rifle were produced during the Civil War years, and together with its British Enfield counterpart they armed over 40 per cent of the fighting men in that conflict. This "Springfield Rifle" was well-balanced, reasonably light, reliable and deadly effective in the right hands. Unlike the Model 1855 it no longer made use of the Maynard system, but instead returned to the more conventional but reliable separate brass primer caps. Thousands of Model 1861s were also made by individual contractors, and a selection of these are shown here.

Type: Percussion rifle musket
Origin: National Armory, Springfield, Illinois
Caliber: .58   **Barrel length:** 40in

The gun bearing this lock was produced in Bridesburg as part of the 98,000 order placed with Alfred Jenks. This was one of the largest single orders of the war.

This lock is from a contract gun by J.T Hodge and A.M.Burton, at the Trenton Locomotive and Machine Co. Trenton New Jersey.

Here is a lock of a gun from the Jenks contract made in Philadelphia by John Rice.

This lock belongs to a gun which is part of a batch of 15,000 produced by Parkers' Snow of Meriden.

Springfield Model 1863

The Model 1863 Rifle Musket was a combination of improvements on the Model 1861 Rifle Musket. Among noticeable changes on the Model 1863 Rifle Musket Type I are the beveled contours on the hammer shank and the lack of barrel band retaining springs with split type bands. The addition of finishes such as hardening and bluing is also a departure from previous U.S. armory practise. Unlike the Model 1861, no known government contracts were given for the Model 1863, but it is evident though that some of the 1861 contractors made modifications in their production to conform to this newer Springfield adaptation.

Type: Percussion rifle musket
Origin: National Armory, Springfield, Illinois
Caliber: .58
Barrel length: 40in

This example is Model 1863 Type I with the minor improvement to the hammer.

The Type II had further modifications to the rear sight and spring retainers for the barrel bands.

Starr Percussion Carbine

A carbine designed by Ebenezer T. Starr, son of Nathan Starr, Jr. and made in Yonkers, New York by the Starr Arms Company between 1862-65. The weapon features a pull down trigger guard/lever to open the breech, single brass barrel band and walnut stock without patchbox. In government tests this gun came out ahead of the Sharps, although this was certainly not reflected in the ordering pattern: 20,000 of the Starr against nearly 100,000 for the Sharps.

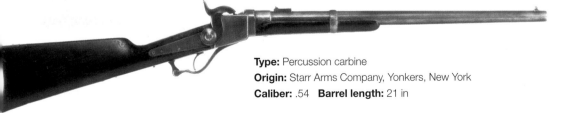

Type: Percussion carbine
Origin: Starr Arms Company, Yonkers, New York
Caliber: .54 **Barrel length:** 21 in

Starr Cartridge Carbine

This carbine used .52 caliber rimfire ammunition but was entirely similar to its percussion predecessor except for a less serpentine hammer. Timing was unfortunate, in that the final delivery of the 5,000 units made came right at the end of the Civil War, two weeks after Jefferson Davis had been captured by Union Cavalry. The return to peacetime spelled the end of the Starr Arms Co. and they went out of business in 1867.

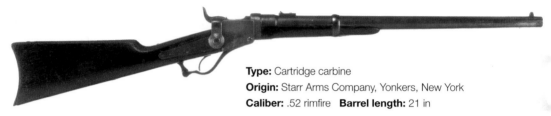

Type: Cartridge carbine
Origin: Starr Arms Company, Yonkers, New York
Caliber: .52 rimfire   **Barrel length:** 21 in

Triplett & Scott Carbine

Louis Triplett of Columbia, Kentucky, and a co-worker named Scott were awarded a patent in December 1864 for a "magazine or self-loading fire¬arm." As a result, their home state of Kentucky placed an order for 5,000 of these rifles which were made by the Meriden Company. The carbine shown here had a 22 inch barrel and the rifle version had a 30 inch barrel. Both were chambered for the .50 Spencer round.

Type: Magazine-fed, repeating rifle and carbine
Origin: Meriden Manufacturing, Meriden, Connecticut
Caliber: .50 Spencer   **Barrel length:** see text

Warner Carbine

James Warner patented this breechloader in 1863, and it entered production with the Massachusetts Arms Co. in 1864. Only 1,500 of this simple but effective single-shot weapon were produced. Brass frames always make for an eye-catching gun and this one is no exception. The breech is accessed by lifting the hinged block and extraction is by a slide at the rear underside of the forestock. There is a single saddle ring without a sliding bar.

Type: Breech-loading cartridge carbine
Origin: Massachusetts Arms Co., Massachusetts
Caliber: .50 rimfire   **Barrel length:** 20in

Wesson Military Rifle

Frank Wesson was the brother of Daniel and uncle to Edwin Wesson, all of whom made their names in the gun trade. He had a small gunmaking business in Worcester, Massachusetts where he made rifles and pistols including the Two-Trigger Rifle shown here with a full octagonal, 26 inch barrel, and chambered for .38 Rimfire, which was presented, to Captain Joseph Walker, an extremely courageous officer of the United States 1st New York Engineer Corps.

Type: Tip-up, breech-loading carbine
Origin: Frank Wesson, Worcester, Massachusetts
Caliber: .38RF **Barrel length:** 26in

Whitney Model 1841 Mississippi Rifle

A fine version of the ubiquitous Mississippi Rifle made by Whitney from 1843-55 and was the first contract taken up by Eli Whitney Jr. after he took over the company from the Blakes. It may have only had a 33 inch barrel, but as it was developed to fire the Minie expanding bullet it was effective and accurate at long ranges. A folding rear sight aided marksmanship. Over 26,500 were delivered.

Type: Single-shot percussion rifle
Origin: Whitneyville Armory, New Haven, Connecticut
Caliber: .54 **Barrel length:** 33in

Whitney 1861 Navy Percussion (Plymouth Rifle)

This rifle was developed at the instigation of Rear Admiral John Dahlgren, an Ordnance officer for the US. Navy. Much of the development was undertaken on board the ordnance trials ship USS Plymouth, hence the name given to the rifle. Whitney delivered 10,000 of these rifles from 1861-64 and they proved to be accurate and effective. Note the large leaf type folding rear sight graduated to 1000 yards which is unique to this gun.

Type: Single-shot percussion rifle
Origin: Whitneyville Armory, New Haven, Connecticut
Caliber: .69 **Barrel length:** 34in

Colt-Burgess

The Colt-Burgess was the only attempt by Colt to compete in the lever-action market, using a patent held by Andrew Burgess, of Owego, New York. There were two versions, a rifle with a 25.5 inch barrel and a fifteen-round tubular magazine and a carbine with a 20.5 inch barrel and a twelve-round magazine. The Colt-Burgess was only in production from 1883 to 1885 during which time 3,775 rifles and 2,593 carbines were completed.

Type: Tubular magazine, lever-action rifle
Origin: Colt, Hartford, Connecticut
Caliber: .44-40   **Barrel length:** 25.5in

Colt Lightning

The Colt Lightning was the first slide-action rifle to be manufactured by Colt and was produced in three frame-sizes. The small-frame version was available only in .22 caliber with a 24 inch barrel, while the medium frame version (rifle with a barrel length of 26 inches and carbine-barrel length 20 inches) was available in .32-20,.38-40,and .44-40 calibers. The large-frame version (includes rifle with a barrel length of 28 inches and carbine-barrel length 22 inches) was chambered for .38-56 up to .50-95. The largest round for the large-frame rifle was the .50-95 Express and earned the nickname "Express model" for all caliber versions.

Type: tubular magazine, slide-action rifle
Origin: Colt ,Hartford, Connecticut
Caliber: see text
Barrel length: see text

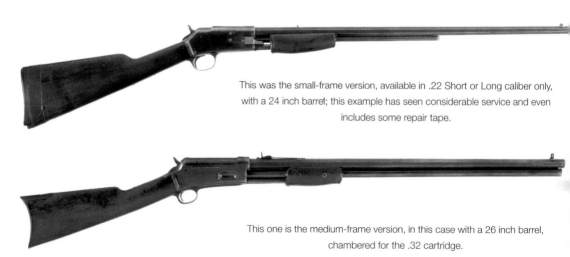

This was the small-frame version, available in .22 Short or Long caliber only, with a 24 inch barrel; this example has seen considerable service and even includes some repair tape.

This one is the medium-frame version, in this case with a 26 inch barrel, chambered for the .32 cartridge.

Dimick Plains Rifle

Horace E. Dimick established his business in St Louis in 1849, where he produced Plains rifles and derringers, and the weapon seen here is inscribed with his name. This half-stock weapon has a very heavy barrel which is rifled, according to the wording of his patent, "...by a system of straight grooves, extending from the base of the bore to about the position of the trunnions, and twisting from thence to the muzzle."

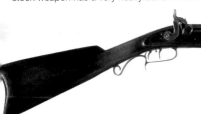

Type: Plains rifle
Origin: H. E. Dimick, St Louis, Missouri
Caliber: .58   **Barrel length:** 32.5in

Marlin-Ballard Number 2 Sporting Rifle

The Marlin-Ballard Number 2 was produced at New Haven between 1876 and 1891. It was made in four calibers (.32, .38 rimfire, .38 centerfire, and 44) and in three barrel lengths (26, 28 and 30 inches). The weapon shown here is .44-40 caliber with a 30 inch barrel, and mounts a tang-mounted vernier rearsight and a foresight with a gold-plated protector. This gun was resigned as an ideal long range hunting rifle.

Type: Ballard-action, single-shot rifle
Origin: Marlin, New Haven, Connecticut
Caliber: .44-40   **Barrel length:** 30in

Marlin-Ballard Number 4 Rifle

The Martin-Ballard Number 4 hunting rifle was produced between 1876 and 1891 in a number of calibers, and this example is in .44-75 Everlasting. Various barrel lengths from 26 to 30 inches were offered, but the purchaser of the rifle seen here made a special order for an extra-long, octagonal 32 inch barrel, although it is still fitted with the usual Rocky Mountain foresight. There is also a barrel-mounted, ramped rearsight and a tang mounted vernier sight.

Type: Ballard-action, single-shot rifle
Origin: Marlin, New Haven, Connecticut
Caliber: .44-75 Everlasting   **Barrel length:** 32in

Marlin-Ballard Number 8

Produced between 1884 and 1890 the Number 8 was among the most popular of the Marlin-Ballard rifles. It featured a part-round, part-octagonal barrel, either 28 or 30 inches in length, and was chambered for .32-40 or .38-55 cartridges. The example shown here has a 30 inch .38-55 caliber barrel, with a globe foresight and vernier tang-mounted backsight. It is fitted with a Swiss butt and while there is checkering, there is no engraving.

Type: Ballard-action, single-shot rifle
Origin: Marlin, New Haven, Connecticut
Caliber: .38-55   **Barrel length:** 30in

Marlin Model 1881 Lever-Action Rifle

The Model 1881 was Marlin's first lever-action rifle, with some 20,000 produced between its introduction in 1881 and its withdrawal in 1892. It featured a smoothly-operating lever action fed from a tubular magazine under the barrel. Five calibers were offered (.32-40, .38-55, .40-60, .45-70 and .45-85) and three lengths of barrel (24, 28 and 30 inches). The standard barrel was octagonal, but a round one was available on special request.

Type: Lever-action, repeater rifle
Origin: Marlin, New Haven, Connecticut
Caliber: .40-60   **Barrel length:** 24in

Marlin Model 1889 Lever-Action Rifle

This was the first of Marlin's lever-action rifles to be fitted with side-ejection and proved very popular with some 55,000 sold between 1889 and 1899. As usual it was offered in a variety of calibers and barrel lengths; the example seen here is chambered for the .32 cartridge and has the shortest, 24 inch, barrel. There was also a variety of finishes and this is the deluxe version with checkered and highly-polished walnut furniture.

Type: Lever-action, repeater rifle
Origin: Marlin, New Haven, Connecticut
Caliber: .32   **Barrel length:** 24in

Marlin Model 1891

The Marlin Model 1891, designed by L.L. Hepburn, was the company's first rifle to fire the .22 round and its direct descendants are still in production today, some 120 years later. The Model 1891 was unusual from the start in that it was capable of accepting any of the .22 Short, .22 Long or .22 LR without adjustment. The barrel was a standard 24 inches long and octagonal in profile, and was fitted with iron sights.

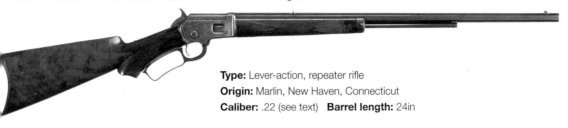

Type: Lever-action, repeater rifle
Origin: Marlin, New Haven, Connecticut
Caliber: .22 (see text)   **Barrel length:** 24in

Marlin Model 1892

Next was the Model 1892 (seen here) is a side-loading "second variation" model, stamped with patent dates of 1878, 1889 and 1890 " plus that of 1892. The Model 1892 incorporated some minor improvements over the Model 1891 which included a blued receiver (which is clearly visible), an improved ejector, a wider firing pin and improved safety features, one piece sear and trigger. Around 45,000 Model 1892s were made between 1895 and 1916.

Type: Lever-action, repeater rifle
Origin: Marlin, New Haven, Connecticut
Caliber: .32   **Barrel length:** 24in

Marlin Model 1897

Next came the Model 1897 which was an improved Model 1892, but with different barrels {24, 26 or 28 inches) and firing .22 rimfire only. It was a takedown weapon and some 125,000 were sold between 1897 and 1917, when production had to stop to enable the company to concentrate on more war-like weapons.

Type: Lever-action, repeater rifle
Origin: Marlin, New Haven, Connecticut
Caliber: .22 rimfire
Barrel length: see text

Marlin Model 97

This gun is basically a late production model of the Model 1897, which was characterized by its flattop receiver as opposed to the earlier Model's rounded top. Other options were available at this time, including a bicycle rifle which had a barrel length of 16 inches with a full magazine. The later guns were finished in casehardened hammer, receiver ,and lever with a blued barrel and magazine. Walnut stocks were standard.

Type: Lever-action, repeater rifle
Origin: Marlin, New Haven, Connecticut
Caliber: .22 rimfire
Barrel length: 16,24,26,28in

Marlin Model 1893

The Model 1893 was the first Marlin weapon specifically designed for smokeless cartridges, which had only recently been introduced at that time. It was offered in five calibers, while the barrels could be either round or octagonal, and varied in length between 24 and 32 inches. The weapon seen here is in .38-55 caliber with the 30 inch barrel and was shipped from the factory in November 1896.The gun has a custom stock which is heavily checkered.

Type: Lever-action, repeater rifle
Origin: Marlin Firearms Company, New Haven, Connecticut
Caliber: see text   **Barrel length:** 24in

Marlin Model 93

Some 900,000 Model 1893s were manufactured marked ''Model !893'' up to 1905 and this was shortened to ''Model 93'' thereafter. This example is the Carbine version with a 20 round inch barrel which retained a full magazine, heavier barrel retaining bands, a carbine style buttplate and saddle rings on the left side of the left side of the frame. Calibers are 25-36,30-30,32 special,32-40,and 38-55.

Type: Lever-action, repeater rifle
Origin: Marlin Firearms Company, New Haven, Connecticut
Caliber: see text   **Barrel length:** 24in

Marlin Model 1894

The Model 1894 was very similar to the Model 1893, but with a shorter action; the example seen here is in .25-20 caliber and has a 24 inch round barrel (barrels range from 24-32inches.) The shorter action of the Model 1894 was possible due to the shorter cartridges that it used, providing a more compact gun with a full magazine capacity. Some 250,000 Model 1894s were produced between 1894 and 1935.Other calibers were 32-20,38-40,and 44-40.

Type: Lever-action, repeater rifle
Origin: Marlin Firearms Company, New Haven, Connecticut
Caliber: see text   **Barrel length:** 24in

Marlin Model 94

As with the Models 1893/93, from 1905 onwards the designation was shortened from Model 1894 to Model 94, as in the example shown here, which is chambered for the .38-40 round and has a 24 inch barrel. Another distinguishing feature is that the crescent style rifle buttplates were used until 1906 ,after which they changed to the "S" shape which are made without a heel or tang.

Type: Lever-action, repeater rifle
Origin: Marlin Firearms Company, New Haven, Connecticut
Caliber: see text   **Barrel length:** 24in

Marlin Model 1895

The Model 1895 was a large weapon designed for big game hunting, being produced in .33 W.C.F, .38-56, .40-65,.40-70, .40-83, .45-70 and .45-90 calibers, with barrel lengths from 26 to 32 inches. This rifle is in .45-70 caliber with a 26 inch barrel, and, age apart is in "as sold" condition. As a collector's item this gun, one of 18.000 manufactured between 1895 and 1917 is now considered relatively rare and certainly desirable.

Type: Lever-action, repeater rifle
Origin: Marlin, New Haven Connecticut
Caliber: see text   **Barrel length:** see text

Marlin Model 1895 Custom Model

This Model 1895, however, has been altered on at least one and possibly more occasions. A .40-65 caliber weapon, the barrel has been shortened and is now only 22 inches long, with a new and much larger foresight blade, while the factory-mounted rear sight has been removed and a new sight added at the rear end of the receiver. It is also using a half magazine such as the one fitted to the Model 1895 Lightweight Rifle.

Type: Lever-action, repeater rifle
Origin: Marlin, New Haven Connecticut
Caliber: see text   **Barrel length:** see text

Marlin Model 1894 Cowboy

The Model 1894 Cowboy returned to production in 1969, chambered for the .44 Magnum. Since then a wide variety of Model 1894s has appeared, chambered for rounds varying in caliber from .22 through .38 Special. This example is chambered for the .45 Long Colt round and is intended to meet the requirements of the Cowboy Action Shooting sport. The weapon weighs 7.5 pounds and the tubular magazine holds ten rounds.

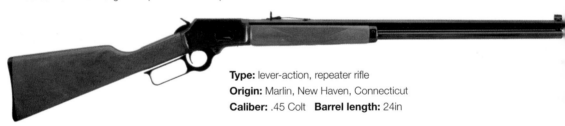

Type: lever-action, repeater rifle
Origin: Marlin, New Haven, Connecticut
Caliber: .45 Colt   **Barrel length:** 24in

Maynard Model 1873 Target Rifle

This Model 1873 target rifle incorporates a number of Dr Maynard's patents. It is a tipping-barrel breechloader, which uses a brass cartridge with a wide, thick rim (also a Maynard patent) to provide the gas-seal at the rear of the chamber as well as enabling the empty case to be extracted easily. It has a 30 inch, part-octagonal barrel with a fixed foresight and two-position rear sight, there is also a folding peep sight on the tang.

Type: Tipping-barrel, percussion, breech-loading target rifle
Origin: Massachusetts Arms Company, Chicopee Falls, Massachusetts
Caliber: .35-30   **Barrel length:** 30in

Merrimack Arms Ballard Rifle

Merrimack Arms manufactured Ballard-patent weapons between 1867 and 1869 and this rifle was produced early in that period. It has an octagonal, 26 inch long barrel, with the forearm and stock made from fancy American walnut. The forearm tip and the crescent-shaped butt-plate are made of case steel. The foresight is a "Martin's Magic Globe" with a long cylindrical hood to expose a glass tube with a gold pinhead post for low light conditions.

Type: Ballard-action rifle
Origin: Merrimack Arms Company, Newburyport, Massachusetts
Caliber: .44   **Barrel length:** 26in

Miller Farm Kentucky Rifle

This gun comes from Miller Farm near Savannah, Illinois, and fought in the Black Hawk War and along the Illinois frontier. It was used in the defense of Apple Fort and at the Battle of Bad Axe River August 1, 1832. The percussion lock bears the names Whitmore, Wolfe & Dunn, who are known to have operated in Pittsburgh from the early 1850s to at least 1872, which suggests that they converted it to percussion ignition.

Type: Flintlock rifle (originally)
Origin: Not known
Caliber: .44   **Barrel length:** 40in

Needham Model 1861 Conversion

Another breechloading conversion to the Model 1861 rifle, this one has an unusual history. The basic rifle is a "Bridesburg" Model 1861, originally made by Alfred Jenks and Son, of Philadelphia, and procured after the Civil War by the Fenian Brotherhood, an Irish-American secret society. One of their more outlandish plans was an attempt to invade Canada from the United States and hold it against the British while using their possession to bargain for Irish independence.

Type: Breech-loading rifle conversion
Origin: Alfred Jenks and Son, Philadelphia
Caliber: .58 centerfire   **Barrel length:** 40in

Remington Springfield M1870 Rolling Block

The original concept for this style of breechloader was developed by Joseph Rider. Known as the split breech or "rolling block" system, it was simple to use, reasonably quick to operate, and extremely rugged and reliable. The firer simply had to pull back the hammer to cock it, then rotate the breech-block downwards to open it and eject the spent case. A new round was loaded then the block simply thumbed back upwards to lock the breech.

Type: Breech-loading rifle
Origin: E. Remington, Ilion, New York
Caliber: .50 70   **Barrel length:** 33in

Remington No. 1 Sporting Rifle

Remington based a whole range of guns on the first variant of the rolling block action, subsequently known as the No. 1 action. Therefore the weapon shown here is a No.I Sporting Rifle, which was made in a range of calibers, using both rimfire and centerfire cartridges, including .40, .44, .45, and .50 centerfire. Rimfire calibers include .44 and .46. Standard barrel lengths were 28 inch and 30 inch.

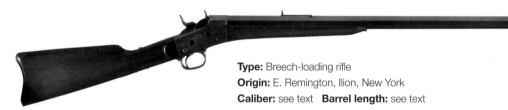

Type: Breech-loading rifle
Origin: E. Remington, Ilion, New York
Caliber: see text   **Barrel length:** see text

Remington No. 1½ Sporting Rifle

In 1885 Remington offered this lighter and smaller version of the No.I action, with thinner receiver and less overall weight than the earlier design. It was intended for lower-powered ammunition, and was available in a range of calibers, including .22, 25, .32 and .38 rimfire, together with .32, .38 and .44 centerfire. The later No. 2 Remington was even lighter, with a smaller frame.At least 4,200 No1½ Sporting Rifles were made over a ten-year period.

Type: Breech-loading rifle
Origin: E. Remington & Sons, Ilion, New York
Caliber: see text   **Barrel length:** 24 to 28in

Remington Hepburn No.3 Rifle

Lewis L. Hepburn worked for Remington in the early 1870s, and there developed this falling block system. Hepburn's breech is lowered and raised by operating a lever on the right side of the receiver, making for a very strong action, capable of handling the most powerful centerfire black powder cartridges. Barrel lengths were available in 26, 28 and 30 inches, while a massive selection of calibers and cartridges could be catered for.

Type: Breech-loading falling block rifle
Origin: E. Remington & Sons, Ilion, New York
Caliber: see text   **Barrel length:** see text

Remington Keene Repeating Rifle

In their attempt to regain the military market, Remington worked with designer John W. Keene to develop this bolt-action magazine fed rifle, designed to compete with the Winchester Model 1873. First sold in 1879, a variety of rifles and carbines were eventually produced, using a range of calibers. In the event, few were sold to the government. Shown here is a sporting rifle variant, with a magazine holding up to nine, 45-70 cartridges.

Type: Bolt–action tubular magazine rifle
Origin: Remington Arms Co,Ilion ,New York
Caliber: .45-70   **Barrel length:** 24in

Remington Light-Baby Carbine

The Remington Arms Company was ever vigilant to find new gaps in the arms market and did so with the following gun. Sold as a lightweight sporting rifle, The "Light Baby" Carbine followed the style of Remington's heavier rolling block military saddle-ring carbines. It was sold from 1892 to 1902, and fired a light .44-40 cartridge (also fired by many Remington revolvers.) At only 5 pounds it was easily handled, and some 3,480 were sold.

Type: Breech-loading carbine
Origin: Remington Arms Co., Ilion, New York
Caliber: .44-40   **Barrel length:** 18in or 20in

Remington Lee Rifle

James Parish Lee was one of the most important weapons designers of the late 19th Century. In 1879 he patented a new bolt-action rifle firing .45-70 cartridges. In 1881 he entered into an agreement with Remington to manufacture his weapons. The Lee is important, in that it introduced the bolt-action/box magazine combination. The rifle shown here is a Model 1882 made for a U.S. Army contract. Firing the .45-70 black powder round, it has a 32in barrel.

Type: Bolt-action box magazine rifle
Origin: Lee Arms Company and E. Remington & Sons, Ilion, New York
Caliber: see text **Barrel length:** see text

Remington No. 4 Rolling Block Rifle

A lightweight rolling block carbine introduced in 1890 and weighing only 41b 4oz. Known as a "boy's rifle", it quickly became one of the most popular sporting guns produced by any American manufacturer, and by 1901, some 157,595 were sold. In that year Remington introduced a "takedown" version, where the barrel could be easily detached from the frame for cleaning and storage. And from 1906 it was also available in a smooth-bore shotgun configuration.

Type: Lightweight rolling block rifle
Origin: Remington Arms Co., Ilion, New York
Caliber: .22 and .32 rimfire, .25-10 Stevens **Barrel length:** 18in or 20in

Remington Model 1897 Military Rolling Block Rifle

Remington revisited the military application of the rolling block system in 1896, where they redesigned it with stronger materials to make use of high-powered small-bore cartridges fired by smokeless propellant. The New Model Small-bore Military Rifle was redesignated the Model 1 897 after a few years, and over 28,000 were made, including 7,702 in 7mm for the Mexican Government who had been a good customer of Remington during the final years of the nineteenth century.

Type: Rolling block rifle
Origin: Remington Arms Co., Ilion, New York
Caliber: 30-40 and 7mm Spanish **Barrel lenqth:** 30in

Savage Model 1899

In the late 1800s European arms manufacturers switched to bolt actions, but lever actions retained their popularity in the United States, mainly because a skilled shooter could fire up to fifteen well-aimed shots within one minute. Such qualities were especially important in the where large areas, particularly in what was then still the "Wild West," were lawless and citizens needed a weapon for self-defense as well as for hunting. The Model 1899 was much improved version of the Model 1895 and turned out to be one of those fortunate designs with a combination of features which got things just right and, as a result, over one-and-a-half million have been produced since. In the early years the Model 1899 was chambered for 0.30-30, 0.25-35 and 0.32-40.

Type: Lever-action sporting rifle
Origin: Savage Arms ,Utica, New York
Caliber: .303 Savage
Barrel length: see text

The original version, the Model 1899A, appeared in two versions: one with a 26 inch barrel, which was manufactured from 1899 to 1927, and the other with a 22 inch barrel (known as the Model 1899A Short) from 1899 to 1922. This is a .30-30, 26 inch version manufactured in 1903, with plain metalwork, furniture and iron sights.

Shown here is also a Model 1899A manufactured in 1903, but is the deluxe version with checkered patterning on the fore-end and pistol grip, and with a tang sight in addition to the barrel-mounted iron sights. It has a 26 inch barrel chambered for .303 Savage.

This Model 1899A Short has a 22 inch barrel, in this case chambered for the .303 Savage, although it was also made in other calibers.

Savage Model 1899

Production of the Savage Model 1899 was suspended in 1917 due to war work, but once the conflict was over production restarted with the Model 99A, which was essentially a minor variant of the pre-1917 weapon and remained in production until 1936. A whole variety of sub-models were produced until 1942 when commercial production was again suspended so that the factory could once again concentrate on war work. Production recommenced in 1946 and in 1960 the one millionth production Model 1899/99 was presented to the National Rifle Association.

Type: Lever-action sporting rifle
Origin: Savage Arms Corporation, Utica, New York
Caliber: .303 Savage
Barrel length: 26in

The first post-World War One version to appear was the Model 99A, seen here with a 26 inch octagonal barrel and chambered for .303 Savage.

A Model 99H carbine with a 20 inch barrel chambered for the .30-30 round and with an owner-added tang sight.

The example seen here is chambered for .250-300 with a 20 inch barrel, and has had a tang sight and a recoil pad added.

Savage Model 1895

Many people know the Savage Model 1899 yet the Model 1895 is largely forgotten. The rifle was made by Marlin and about 5,000 were completed between 1895 and 1899. It had an eight-round magazine and weighed 8.7 pounds. There was a cocking indicator, which was viewed through a hole in the top of the breechblock; it showed "C" when the action was cocked and "S" when the striker was down.

Type: Lever-action sporting rifle
Origin: Savage Arms Corporation, Utica, New York
Caliber: .303 Savage   **Barrel length:** 26in

Savage Model 1903

The Model 1903 was introduced in 1903 and remained in production until 1922. It was a .22 slide-action weapon with a 24 inch octagonal barrel, open, iron sights and a seven-round detachable magazine mounted beneath the frame, in front of the trigger guard.. The example shown here is a standard model, but there were also gallery and some very rare factory-engraved models.

Type: slide-action sporting rifle
Origin: Savage Arms Corporation, Utica, New York
Caliber: .22 LR   **Barrel length:** 24in

Savage Model 1914

Development of the Savage .22 rifle continued from the Model 1903 (previous entry) through the Model 1911 bolt-action and 1912 semi-automatic. Next came this Model 1914, which returned to slide-action, albeit with an altered slide mechanism and much longer slide handle. It had a 24 inch octagonal barrel. A factory-engraved Model 1914 with gold inlays,a pearl pistol-grip cap, and in mint, unfired condition, was sold at auction in 2002 for $33,600.

Type: Slide-action sporting rifle
Origin: Savage Arms Corporation, Utica, New York
Caliber: .22   **Barrel length:** 24in

Sharps Cartridge Conversions

After the Civil War, many Sharps carbines and rifles were converted to fire metallic cartridges. This fine example of a carbine has been modified to take .50-70 centerfire, although there were some that were made for .52-70 rimfire. Many such guns arrived in the West; perhaps Civil War veterans bringing their weapons with them or those guns looted from battlefields sold cheaply for the price of a bottle of whiskey.

Type: Single shot, breech-loading cartridge carbine
Origin: Sharps,Hartford, Connecticut.
Caliber: .50-70 centerfire **Barrel length:** 21.5in

Sharps Model 1874 Military Rifle

Although known as the Model 1874, this series of weapons began production in 1871. They come in a bewildering array of calibers. The main difference between this model and the earlier Sharps is that the lock is no longer a modification of the earlier Sharps primer design, but is made as new for cartridge use. The one shown here is a military rifle, and is a hybrid, with parts salvaged from older models.

Type: Breech-loading, metallic cartridge, military rifle
Origin: Sharps,Hartford, Connecticut
Caliber: .45-70 **Barrel length:** 30in

Sharps Model 1874 Military Carbine

Sharps regularly produced military carbine versions of their weapons; the British Army, for example, took a number of the Model 1855 carbine. Thus, the company also made a carbine version of the Model 1874, seen here, with a 21 inch barrel. It is not known whether any military sales were made, but, if not, they would certainly have found ready buyers on the civil market.

Type: Breech-loading, metallic cartridge, military carbine
Origin: Sharps,Hartford, Connecticut
Caliber: .44 **Barrel length:** 21 in

Sharps Model 1874 Sporting Rifle

Sharps were very popular with the sporting shooters and some 6,000 of the Model 1874 sporting rifle were sold. Because of its high velocity and accuracy the gun found a use in the West as the main weapon responsible for the slaughter of the herds of buffalo that roamed the plains. Know as the "Sharps Buffalo Gun," the large caliber version (the 50-90) were used to finally devastate the herds in the late 1800s. The classic barrel length was 30 inches but the guns were also with shorter barrel lengths, some would have been modified after they left the factory.

Type: Breech-loading sporting rifle
Origin: Sharps, Hartford, Connecticut
Caliber: .45-70 **Barrel length:** 30in

This one is chambered for .45-70 and the 28 inch octagonal barrel is stamped "Old Reliable" suggesting that it was made at Bridgeport in or after 1876.

This one has a 28.75 inch barrel and there are signs that it was shortened to this length, possibly by 1.25 inches and the foresight reinstalled above the new muzzle. A Kentucky-style brass butt-plate has also been fitted.

Sharps Model 1874 Mid-range Rifle

Sharps made three types of the Model 1874 which were optimized for competitive shooting. One was for the Creedmoor competitions, which were shot at very long ranges (150 made), the second for long range (425 made) and the third, seen here, for medium-range (102 made). In this case, "medium" meant 300 to 600 yards, and the weapon had a 30 inch barrel with a wind-gauge, spirit-level foresight and a leaf rearsight mounted on the barrel.

Type: Target rifle
Origin: Sharps,Hartford, Connecticut
Caliber: .44-90 **Barrel length:** 30in

Sharps Borchardt Rifles

Hugo Borchardt took out a patent in 1876 on a hammerless, dropping block mechanism, which offered significant improvements to the original Sharps' dropping block mechanism of 1848, being more efficient as well as stronger and quicker acting. This resulted in a series of Sharps-Borchardt rifles which enjoyed a brief vogue in the late 1870s, with some 10,000 military and 12,500 sporting rifles being made. However by then the whole notion of a single-shot

dropping block rifle was faced with stiff competition from repeating lever and bolt action rivals that it didn't prevail. Production ceased when Sharps went out of business in 1881

Type: military/sporting rifle
Origin: Sharps Rifle Manufacturing Company, Hartford, Connecticut
Caliber: 45-70   **Barrel length:** see text

This Sharps-Borchardt military rifle was chambered for the US government .45-70 round with a 32 inch barrel, full-length fore-end and two barrel bands.

This sporting rifle is also chambered for the .45-70 round, but has a 30 inch barrel with a modern globe foresight. The original barrel-mounted rear sight has been removed and replaced by a vernier sight on the tang.

Sharps Borchardt Zischang-Built Schutzen Rifle

This Schutzen rifle is based on a carefully selected Sharps-Borchardt action, which was streamlined and considerably improved by Zischang. The fully octagonal barrel is 31.5 inches long and mounts a wing-gauge, spirit-level foresight, as well as a Stevens #605 .87 inch diameter telescopic sight.

There is also a Zischang-made mid-range vernier rear sight mounted on a specially-fitted pedestal above the pistol grip. Zischang has also fitted double set triggers and a unique two-finger lever, both to his own design.

Type: Schutzen rifle
Origin: A.O. Zischang, Syracuse, New York
Caliber: .32-40   **Barrel length:** 31.5in

TAMING THE FRONTIER **59**

Spencer Model 1865 Carbine

Spencer also produced a later Model 1865, chambered for a .50 cartridge and with a slightly shorter 20in barrel. Many were also fitted with the Stabler cut-off, a device which blocked the magazine. If careful, aimed, fire was needed, the user could block the magazine and feed single cartridges in to the breech, one at a time. The magazine could thus be kept full until rapid fire was needed, whereupon the firer simply slid the cut-off aside and let loose. The gun was extensively used in the Indian Wars and in a close fight like that at Beecher's Island its improved ballistics and repeating action proved decisive.

Type: magazine-fed repeating carbine
Origin: Spencer Repeating Rifle Co., Boston, Massachusetts
Caliber: .50
Barrel length: 20in

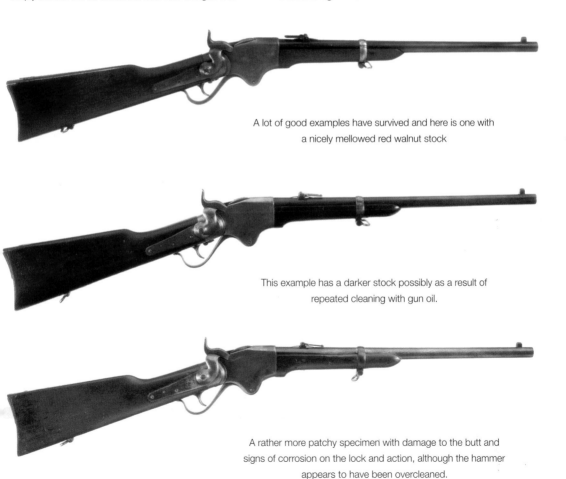

A lot of good examples have survived and here is one with a nicely mellowed red walnut stock

This example has a darker stock possibly as a result of repeated cleaning with gun oil.

A rather more patchy specimen with damage to the butt and signs of corrosion on the lock and action, although the hammer appears to have been overcleaned.

Spencer Model 1867 Rifle

This is a Model 1867 military rifle with a 30 inch barrel and six-groove rifling, a full stock forend and three barrel bands. It is marked on the breech M1867. The gun is fitted with the Spencer patent cut-off in place of the Stabler device which effectively converts the weapon to single shot firing. The gun is chambered for .50 caliber rimfire cartridges.

Type: Magazine-fed repeating carbine
Origin: Spencer Repeating Rifle Co., Boston, Massachusetts
Caliber: .50   **Barrel length:** 30in

Spencer Sporting Rifle

After the Civil War, Spencer attempted to produce weapons for the civilian market, but with limited commercial success. Spencer's productivity during the war ultimately proved to be his undoing. After the war there was a vast surplus of Spencer arms available to the public. Spencer had produced himself right out of the market. By 1869 the Spencer Repeating Rifle Company was in bankruptcy. This hunting rifle is chambered for .44 and has a 26 inch barrel.

Type: Magazine-fed repeating sporting rifle
Origin: Spencer Repeating Rifle Co., Boston, Massachuset
Caliber: .44   **Barrel length:** 26in

Springfield Spencer Conversion Rifle

This rather curious conversion that started life as a Spencer Carbine made by the Burnside Rifle Company of Providence, Rhode Island. The urgent needs arising from the Indian Wars led to 1,215 of these carbines being selected for conversion to rifles, which was done at the Springfield Armory. This involved taking the Spencer action virtually unchanged and fitting a new rifled barrel, sights, foregrip and a ramrod. The butt-stock was unchanged.

Type: Carbine converted to rifle
Origin: National Armory, Springfield, Illinois
Caliber: .50 Spencer   **Barrel Length:** 32.5in

Springfield Allin "Trapdoor" Rifles

By the end of the Civil War, the US Army had realized that the infantry urgently needed a breech-loading rifle, but funds were urgently needed to rebuild the country after the devastation of war and government funds were short. In addition, there was a huge surplus of muzzle-loaders left over from the war. This problem was overcome by Edwin S. Allin, the Master Armorer at the Springfield Armory who devised and patented the "trapdoor" mechanism where the weapon was opened by means of a front-hinged lifting block on the top of the breech, which was raised to enable a new round to be loaded. Some 30,000 existing rifles and carbines were modified in what was known as the "Allin conversion," but once that program had been completed new rifles and carbines were designed from scratch incorporating the Allin "trapdoor." The first of these was the US Model 1868 which was followed by the Models 1873, 1879, 1880, 1884 and 1889, each of which incorporated only minor changes over its predecessor.

Type: Breech-loading single-shot rifle
Origin: National Armory,Springfield.Illinois
Caliber: .45-70
Barrel length: 32.5in

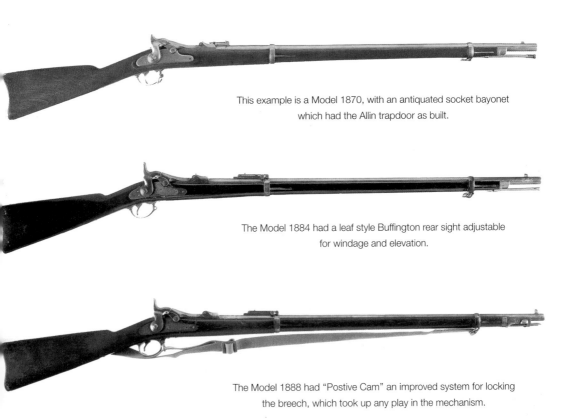

This example is a Model 1870, with an antiquated socket bayonet which had the Allin trapdoor as built.

The Model 1884 had a leaf style Buffington rear sight adjustable for windage and elevation.

The Model 1888 had "Postive Cam" an improved system for locking the breech, which took up any play in the mechanism.

Springfield "Officer's Model " 1875 Rifle

A superb example of a high quality piece, one of only 477 made at the Springfield Armory. They were intended for private sale to military officers for hunting purposes. Many officers stationed in the West during the Indian campaigns were keen hunters including Custer. The gun had extensive scrolling engraved on the lock, hammer, breech-block, receiver, barrel band, buttplate, heel, and trigger guard. Other special details were the single set trigger, and the sporting style of the stock including the single ferrule under the barrel and the forend cap slotted to accept the cleaning rod. It uses the same Allin trapdoor system and ammunition as issue rifles.

Type: Breech-loading single shot cartridge rifle
Origin: National Armory, Springfield, Illinois
Caliber: .45-70
Barrel length: 26in

The right side of the rifle shows the high level of finish including the brass forend cap, barrel band and wooden cleaning rod.

The left side view with the sights extended. The gun has a fixed front sight and a leaf style rear sight on the barrel with an additional vernier sight fixed onto the tang.

Springfield Indian Carbine

This carbine was created by taking a Springfield musket, which would have had a barrel 44 inches long, and shortening it to 21.75 inches long. The forearm was suitably shortened and held in place by a single barrel band, covered by a length of cloth, sewn with sinew. In common with most Indian weapons of this period, the woodwork has been decorated with patterns of brass tacks.

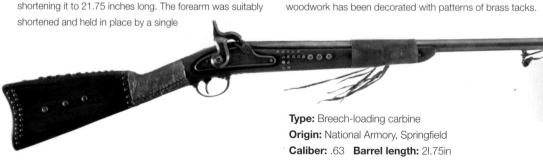

Type: Breech-loading carbine
Origin: National Armory, Springfield
Caliber: .63   **Barrel length:** 2l.75in

Springfield Model 1879

The Model 1873 Cavalry Carbine and its successor the Model 1879 were both made as original Allin trapdoor models. They were also the standard weapons of the US Cavalry in the Indian Wars of the 1870s and 1880s. They were single shot weapons and many soldiers were unwilling to give up their Spencer rifles when facing a foe armed with Winchesters and Spencers. The issue of single shot weapons was deliberate attempt to reduce the imagined overuse of ammunition. The replacement of the 7th Cavalry's Spencers with this gun is one of the causes cited for the rout at Little Big Horn.

Type: Trapdoor carbine
Origin: National Armory, Springfield
Caliber: .45-70
Barrel length: 22in

Shown here is a very early production example of the original Model 1873

This one is a saddle-ring version of the Model 1879.

Here we have a particularly fine Model 1879, completed in 1880, which appears to have been neither issued nor fired.

Springfield Chaffee Reese Rifle

This bolt-action rifle was designed by Reuben S. Chaffee and General James Reece, both of Springfield, Illinois. Five rounds of ammunition were held in a tubular magazine in the butt, which were fed forward by an oscillating rack, which was engaged by pulling the bolt to the rear. A prototype was made and submitted to the Army, as a result of which a trials batch of some 750 was made at the Springfield Armory in 1884.

Type: Bolt-action, magazine-fed rifle
Origin: National Armory, Springfield, Illinois
Caliber: .45-70 **Barrel length:** 27.9in

Springfield Model 1892 Krag Rifle

The U.S. Army held a competition to find a bolt-action, magazine rifle, which would be suitable for service as the basic infantry weapon. Fifty weapons were subjected to trials, which eventually narrowed down to a choice of three: Krag No.5, Lee No. 3; and Mauser No. 5 which were virtually equal in all respects. The army finally settled on the Krag and the weapon was put into production as the "U.S. Magazine Rifle, Caliber .30, Model 1892."

Type: Bolt-action, magazine-fed rifle
Origin: Krag and Jorgensen, Norway and Springfield Armory, Illinois
Caliber: .30-40 **Barrel length:** 30in

Springfield M1896 Krag Cavalry Carbine

The Model 1896 Cavalry Carbine, seen here was a development of the Krag infantry rifle having the same action and sights, but the barrel was only 22 inches long and the forearm was much shorter; a bar-mounted saddle-ring was on the left side, as usual. Issued in 1896/7, the Model 1896 carbine had a rather short service life, being withdrawn from regular units in 1901 and passed on to militia units.

Type: Bolt-action, magazine-fed carbine
Origin: Springfield Armory, USA.
Caliber: .30-40 **Barrel length:** 22in

Springfield Model 1896 Krag Rifle

This was the rifle that equipped most of the U.S. Infantry and Marine Corps units during the Spanish-American war. There were eventually some forty official modifications to the Model 1892 and these were all incorporated into a new production version, the Model 1896. This new version also introduced a completely new backsight with a continuously curved base, which was graduated from 250 yards up to a maximum of 600 yards.

Type: Bolt-action, magazine-fed rifle
Origin: National Armory, Springfield, Illinois
Caliber: 30-40   **Barrel length:** 30in

Springfield Model 1898 Krag Rifle

The M1898 was the result of a major review of the earlier models; the new pattern was approved in March 1989, although it did not actually reach the troops until October 1899. The most significant aspect of this was the introduction of a new high velocity cartridge, which gave the weapon a theoretical range of 2,000 yards, but the new round lasted only a few months when it was discovered that it caused breakages in the bolt locking-lugs.

Type: Bolt-action, magazine-fed rifle
Origin: National Armory, Springfield, Illinois
Caliber: 30-40   **Barrel length:** 30in

Springfield Model 1899 Krag Carbine

The Model 1898 cavalry carbine like the Model 1898 rifle was intended to use the new high velocity bullet but when it proved too powerful for the bolt to handle the gun was withdrawn with only about 5,000 completed. Attention then turned to the Model 1899 cavalry carbine, which was derived from the Model 1898 carbine, but with the fore-end lengthened by about three inches and fitted with the Ml896 rear sight.

Type: Bolt-action, magazine-fed carbine
Origin: National Armory, Springfield, Illinois
Caliber: .30-40   **Barrel length:** 22in

Stevens Ideal Single-shot Model 44

The "Ideal" single-shot rifle used a falling-block action, activated by a lever which combined its function with that of trigger-guard. There were many choices of caliber and barrel length. The first in the series was the Model 44, with some 100,000 produced between 1896 and 1933, the gun was joined in 1903 by the Model 044 (seen here) which was similar in appearance but had an improved action.

Type: single-shot rifle
Origin: J. Stevens Arms Co., Chicopee Falls, Massachusetts
Caliber: .28-30   **Barrel Length:** 26in

Stevens Ideal Single-Shot Model 45

The Model 45 was in production from 1896 to 1916 and was available in a wide range of calibers from .22 rimfire up to .44-40. All had a Swiss-style buttstock. Most Model 45s were fitted with Beach sights but this example is fitted with a Stevens designed telescopic sight, which is 28 inches long. It is fitted with a 23.75in octagonal/round barrel, chambered for the .22 round.

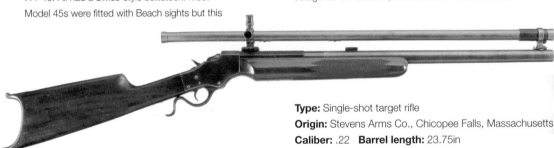

Type: Single-shot target rifle
Origin: Stevens Arms Co., Chicopee Falls, Massachusetts
Caliber: .22   **Barrel length:** 23.75in

Stevens Model 49 "Walnut Hill" Single Shot Rifle

This fine target rifle uses the same action as the Model 44 with a Loope lever, and a special- order 34 inch full octagonal barrel. It has a Swiss –style heavy steel buttplate, and a stock carved from English walnut with cheek pieces and a pistol grip. The rear sight is a Stevens mid-range vernier peep sight. It ahs a distinctive finish with rose, amber and blue hues.

Type: Single-shot target rifle
Origin: Stevens Arms Co.,Chicopee Falls, Massachusetts
Caliber: .32-40   **Barrel length:** 34in

Stevens Model 414

The Model 414, also known as the "Armory Model," was produced between 1912 and 1932 in .22 caliber only. It had the same action as the Stevens Model 44, with a Rocky Mountain foresight. It was usually fitted with a Lyman receiver sight, but this example has a Malcolm scope on saddle mounts. The forearm and short, large diameter handgrip is unusual.

Type: Single-shot, bolt action target rifle
Origin: |. Stevens Arms Co., Chicopee Falls, Massachusetts
Caliber: .22 Short   **Barrel length:** 26in

Stevens Model 425

From 1910 until the start of war production in 1917, Stevens produced 26,000 high-powered hunting rifles in the 400-series: Models 425, 430, 435 and 440. These were lever-action weapons, all with a 22 inch barrel, but chambering either .25, .30-30, .32 or the .35 cartridge. The significance of the numbering was the higher the number, the higher the specification. The example shown here is a Model 425, chambered for .35 Remington and with simple iron sights.

Type: Single-shot, lever-action hunting rifle
Origin: Stevens Arms Co., Chicopee Falls, Massachusetts
Caliber: .35 Remington   **Barrel length:** 22in

Ward-Burton Model 1871 Carbine

Up to the beginning of the Civil War the average life of an issue firearm was 10-40 years. In the immediate period after the war there was a scrabble to adopt breech-loading weapons. New models were issued and replaced within a year or two. Guns like the Ward-Burton carbine, of which only 316 were made at Springfield, came and went in a flash. This has the distinction of being the first bolt-action carbine to be issued to the U.S.cavalry

Type: Bolt-action, magazine-fed carbine
Origin: National Armory, Springfield, Massachusetts
Caliber: .50   **Barrel length:** 22in

Winchester Model 1866

When Henry became Winchester in 1866 a new gun was marketed under the Winchester name which bore a lot in common with the Henry rifle that had distinguished itself so clearly during the latter days of the Civil war. The new gun addressed some of the design faults of the Henry. The barrel's tendency to heat up under heavy fire was cured by fitting a forend grip. The magazine reloading problem was cured by fitting a loading gate in the side of the action. The Model 1866 was an immediate success with 170,000 being

produced from 1866 to 1898. They were split into three types: carbine with round barrel; sporting rifle with round or octagonal barrel; and musket with round barrel.

Type: Tubular magazine ,lever-action rifle
Origin: Winchester Repeating Arms Co,
   New Haven, Connecticut
Caliber: .44 Henry
Barrel lengths: 20, 24.4, and 27in

This one is a sporting rifle with a 24.4 inch barrel of which 28,000 were made.

This is the saddle ring carbine with a 20 inch barrel which accounted for 127,000 of the total production of the Model 1866. This was known as the "Yellow Boy" carbine because of the color of the brass receiver.

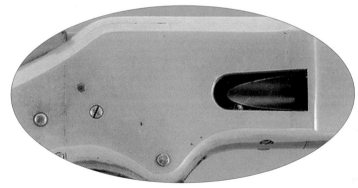

Right: A close up of the detail of the right side of the brass receiver showing the loading port that transformed the gun's usability over the original Henry.

Winchester Model 1873

Developed from the successful Model 1866 the Model 1873 had a stronger iron (later steel) frame, a dust cover over the action, and most importantly was available in the same caliber as the new Colt 1873 .

This meant that for the serious Western user that they could service both firearms from the same ammunition supply, such as a wagon or saddle bag. Both guns earned the title: The Gun(s) That Won The West. The same versions: a carbine, rifle and musket were offered and the total production from 1873 to 1919 was 720,000 units. A .22 rimfire version was launched in 1884 but it was not popular.

Type: Tubular magazine, lever-action rifle
Origin: Winchester Repeating Arms Co,
New Haven, Connecticut
Caliber: .44-40   **Barrel lengths:** 20, 24.4, and 27in

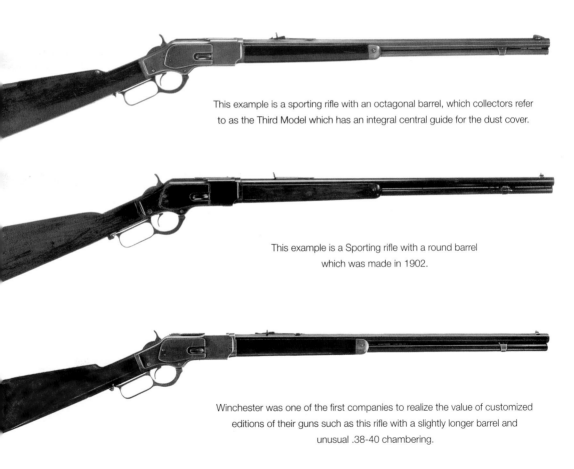

This example is a sporting rifle with an octagonal barrel, which collectors refer to as the Third Model which has an integral central guide for the dust cover.

This example is a Sporting rifle with a round barrel which was made in 1902.

Winchester was one of the first companies to realize the value of customized editions of their guns such as this rifle with a slightly longer barrel and unusual .38-40 chambering.

Winchester Model 1873 Carbine and Musket

A standard Model 1873 Saddle ring carbine with a 20 inch round barrel; it was made in 1889.

This gun is a late production (1909) Model 1873 Trapper's Carbine with a shortened 16.25 inch barrel

This one is the musket version with a 30 inch round barrel and its associated spike bayonet.

Winchester Model 1876

The Model 1876 incorporated changes necessary to handle the more powerful cartridges then coming into use; .40-60 WCF; .45-60 WCF; .45-77 WCF; and .50-95 Express. The main change was a larger and more robust receiver in all variants, but, in addition, the carbine's barrel was lengthened to 22 inches and the musket's to 32 inches, while in both the forearms were lengthened to cover the full length of the tubular magazine.

Type: Tubular magazine, lever-action rifle
Origin: Winchester Repeating Arms Co,New Haven, Connecticut
Caliber: see text   **Barrel lengths:** see text

Winchester Model 1885

The Model 1885 was the first patent of John M. Browning's that Winchester would buy and was also the first single-shot to be manufactured by the company. In all, the company made 139,725 Model 1885s between 1885 and 1920, but there were so many variations that it is difficult to detail common variants. It has been calculated that Winchester offered the Model 1883 in 45 centerfire and 14 rimfire calibers, in a wide variety of barrel lengths, either round or octagonal, to match the caliber, and finishes and extras to match the purchaser's pocket.

Type: Single-shot breech-loading rifle
Origin: Winchester Repeating Arms Co,
    New Haven, Connecticut
Caliber: see text
Barrel lengths: see text

A standard Winchester Model 1885 High Wall sporting rifle, with a 30 inch. .38-55 caliber barrel. It has a wind gauge foresight and Lyman tang-mounted elevating peep sight; both are by Lyman. It will be observed that the frame angles upwards rather sharply to leave only the hammer spur visible - this is the "High Wall."

Close examination of this one shows that in this case the frame continues forward and upwards at the same angle as the top of the wrist, thus leaving the hammer and breech visible - this is the "Low Wall."

This example is a takedown model, one of the many options with the Model 1885.

Winchester Model 1885 Express Rifle

Express rounds and the associated rifles were designed for a very high muzzle velocity and use at comparatively short ranges - 200 yards or less - so that the round followed a more-or-less flat trajectory and also killed game as cleanly and quickly as possible. Note that all three rifles are of the High Wall variety and all are simple weapons with shotgun butts and iron sights - there was no time for telescopic sights in the type of shooting these weapons were intended for. The Model 1885's designer, the legendary John M.Browning, was himself a keen hunter and it is likely that is just the sort of purpose that he had in mind for the gun.

Type: Single-shot breech-loading rifle
Origin: Winchester Repeating Arms Co,
  New Haven, Connecticut
Caliber: see text   **Barrel lengths:** see text

This one is chambered for the .40 Express round; it has a 30 inch round barrel and a case-hardened finish, with walnut stock.

Shown here is a rifle with a 30 inch part round/part octagonal barrel and chambered for the rather larger and heavier .50-111 Express.

Another one fitted with a 30 inch round barrel, it is the only known example to be chambered for the British-made .50 Eley Express.

Winchester Model 1886 Rifle

The Model 1886 was introduced to use the more powerful centerfire cartridges then becoming available. As always, there was an immense range of options for the potential purchaser to choose from. There were the three basic configurations -Rifle, Musket and Carbine - with the Rifle being sub-divided into Sporting, Fancy Sporting, Takedown, Extra Lightweight and Extra Lightweight Takedown. There were also ten different calibers, ranging from .33 WCF to .50-110 Express, with the government .45-70 being the most popular. Then there were choices to be made on barrel lengths. It remained in production for 49 years (1886-1935), during which time some 160,000 were made.

Type: Lever-action rifle
Origin: Winchester Repeating Arms Company,
  New Haven, Connecticut
Caliber: see text
Barrel length: see text

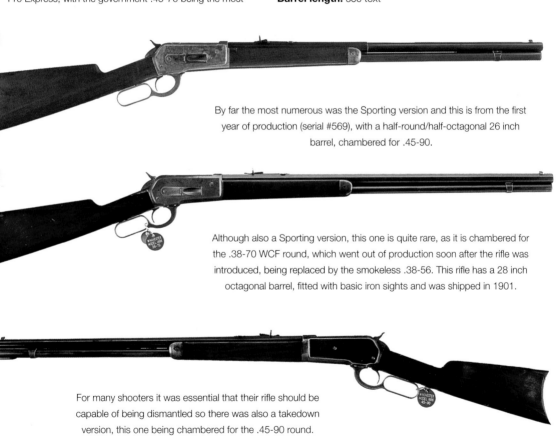

By far the most numerous was the Sporting version and this is from the first year of production (serial #569), with a half-round/half-octagonal 26 inch barrel, chambered for .45-90.

Although also a Sporting version, this one is quite rare, as it is chambered for the .38-70 WCF round, which went out of production soon after the rifle was introduced, being replaced by the smokeless .38-56. This rifle has a 28 inch octagonal barrel, fitted with basic iron sights and was shipped in 1901.

For many shooters it was essential that their rifle should be capable of being dismantled so there was also a takedown version, this one being chambered for the .45-90 round.

Winchester Model 1890

The Model 1890, designed by the brothers John and Matthew Browning, was Winchester's first-ever slide-action rifle and achieved world-wide popularity, with a total of 775,000 produced between 1890 and 1932. All Model 1890s had 24 inch barrels and were available in either .22 Short, .22 Long, or .22 WRF chamberings, with .22 LR being added in 1919 (the .22 WRF was developed specially for the Model 1890). The gun had a tubular magazine holding between 11 and 15 rounds depending on the type of ammunition used. Popular with small-game hunters ,the gun at just $16 was widely used in fairground shooting booths.

Type: Slide-action rifle
Origin: Winchester Repeating Arms Company, New Haven, Connecticut
Caliber: .22 (see text)   **Barrel length:** 24in

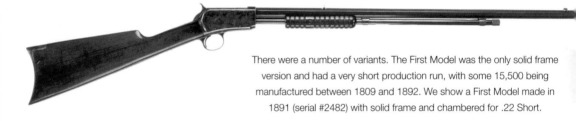

There were a number of variants. The First Model was the only solid frame version and had a very short production run, with some 15,500 being manufactured between 1809 and 1892. We show a First Model made in 1891 (serial #2482) with solid frame and chambered for .22 Short.

All subsequent Model 1890s had takedown frames; the Second Model being divided into case-hardened and blued frame versions. The picture is of the Second Model case-hardened version, also chambered for the .22 Short.

This later version Second Model has blue finish on the action; it is chambered for .22 WRF. The Third Model also had a blued frame and very minor differences in the breech locking system.

Winchester Model 1892

The Model 1892 was, in essence, an updated Model 1873 employing a slightly smaller version of Browning's Model 1886 action. It was available in five calibers - .218 Bee, .25-20, .32-20, .38-40 and .44-40 - and various barrel lengths appropriate to the caliber; there was also a choice of magazine sizes in some models. There were five variants; Sporting Rifle, Fancy Sporting Rifle, Carbine, Trapper's Carbine and Musket. More than one million Model 1892s were sold, with the production run extending from 1892 to 1932 for most models, and to 1941 for carbines.

Type: Lever-action rifle
Origin: Winchester Repeating Arms Company,
New Haven, Connecticut
Caliber: see text
Barrel length: see text

A Model 1892 Sporting Rifle in exceptionally good condition, this has a 24 inch round barrel and is chambered for .44 WCF; it has the standard sights and a full-length magazine.

A .25-20 caliber Model 1892 Saddle-Ring Carbine with a 20 inch round barrel.

The Trapper's Carbine version with a 14 inch barrel.

Winchester Model 1894

The Model 1894 was the first Winchester to be designed from the outset to use smokeless powder cartridges and has proved immensely popular; it was the first sporting rifle to exceed one million sales, the total by 1963 was some 2 million and today the figure stands at about 7 million. With a production run already in excess of 110 years it is not surprising that there have been a bewildering number of variations, with the company's catalog listing fourteen on offer in 2005. In general, however, there have been the usual five basic variants: Sporting, Fancy Sporting, Extra Lightweight, Carbine and Trapper's Carbine.

Type: Lever-action rifle
Origin: Winchester Repeating Arms Company, New Haven, Connecticut
Caliber: see text **Barrel length:** see text

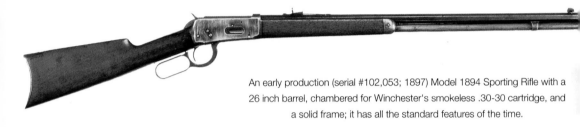

An early production (serial #102,053; 1897) Model 1894 Sporting Rifle with a 26 inch barrel, chambered for Winchester's smokeless .30-30 cartridge, and a solid frame; it has all the standard features of the time.

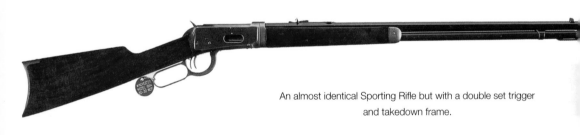

An almost identical Sporting Rifle but with a double set trigger and takedown frame.

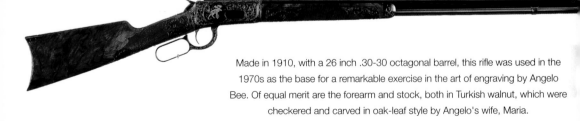

Made in 1910, with a 26 inch .30-30 octagonal barrel, this rifle was used in the 1970s as the base for a remarkable exercise in the art of engraving by Angelo Bee. Of equal merit are the forearm and stock, both in Turkish walnut, which were checkered and carved in oak-leaf style by Angelo's wife, Maria.

Winchester Model 1895

John Browning's Model 1895 was the first Winchester lever-action to feature a box magazine, in this case a non-detachable type with a five-round capacity. It was designed to meet the requirements of the new high-power smokeless cartridge and was made in nine calibers. It received the highest possible endorsement when it was adopted by Theodore Roosevelt as his favorite hunting rifle. Some 426,000 were produced between 1895 and 1931. As with previous models, it was produced in Sporting Rifle,

Fancy Sporting Rifle, Carbine and Musket variants, with some interesting examples in the latter category including a version for the Army for use in the Spanish American War.

Type: Lever-action, box magazine-fed rifle
Origin: Winchester Repeating Arms Company,
   New Haven, Connecticut
Caliber: see text
Barrel length: see text

A very early production Model 1895 with the flat-sided receiver, which characterizes the first 5,000 (actual serial of this weapon is #3797). It has a 28 inch .30-30 caliber barrel and clearly shows the unmistakable profile created by the external magazine.

Another Model 1895 Rifle, in this case chambered for the British government .303 cartridge (although this is not a military weapon). It has a 28 inch round barrel and a Lyman sight mounted on the receiver.

A musket version supplied to the U.S. Army in 1898, with a 28 inch barrel and chambered for .30-40.

Winchester Model 1903

The Model 1903 was the first semi-automatic rifle to be produced by Winchester and had a 20 inch barrel chambered for the .22 Winchester Automatic Rimfire (.22 Win). This round was more powerful than conventional .22 in order to operate the blow-back system and has long since been out of production. The tubular magazine was located in the buttstock.

There were two variants: Standard with plain furniture and steel crescent butt, and De Luxe, with high quality furniture. Some 126,000 were sold between 1903 and 1932. The Model 63 was introduced in 1933 and was designed to use the much more readily-available .22 LR.

Type: Semi-automatic, tubular magazine, rifle
Origin: Winchester Repeating Arms Company,
New Haven, Connecticut
Caliber: .22 Win
Barrel length: 20in

The standard Model 1903 with the original 20 inch barrel. Note the loading port set into the side of the stock.

This one is a late production De Luxe model, with a Lyman tang-mounted rear sight and nicely rendered checkering on the forearm and pistol grip.

All Model 1903s fired the .22 Winchester round and in 1933 the company replaced the Model 1903 with the Model 63 shown here with a telescopic sight.

Winchester Model 1905

The Model 1905 was based on the Model 1903 but enlarged to enable it to handle centerfire cartridges, such as the .32 Winchester and .35 Self-Loading rounds. It also had a detachable box magazine and a 22 inch barrel. There were two variants: Sporting Rifle and Fancy Sporting Rifle. About 30,000 were made between 1905 and 1920. The Model 1907 was an improved Model 1903, but with a 20 inch barrel chambered for the new .351 Winchester Self-Loading Cartridge. In addition to the usual Sporting and Fancy

Sporting, there was also a Police version. The Model 1910 was a Model 1907 strengthened to handle the .401 Winchester Self-Loading cartridge.

Type: Semi-automatic, box magazine, rifle
Origin: Winchester Repeating Arms Company, New Haven, Connecticut
Caliber: see text
Barrel length: see text

We have here a Standard Rifle, chambered for the .32 Winchester Self-Loading (WSL) round.

A Model 1907 Standard Rifle chambered for .351 WSL.

The De Luxe version, again made for .351 WSL with nickel-plated forend cap and sling.

Arisaka Meiji 38th Year Rifle

Some shortcomings in the Meiji 30th Year rifle were thought to have been rectified in the 35th Year type, but a trials batch fielded during the Russo-Japanese war revealed yet further problems. These mainly concerned extraction and susceptibility to mud and dust, and were solved by a new and simpler bolt combined with a bolt-cover. The new design was designated the Meiji 38th Year type (1905) and entered service in 1906. This rifle was in continuous production from 1907 to 1944 and a total of well over three million were produced at the Imperial arsenals at Mishawaka, Kokura, Maiden and Nagoya.

Type: Bolt-action, magazine-fed rifle
Origin: various arsenals, see text
Caliber: 6.5 x 50mm
Barrel length: 31 .5in

Shown here is a late production 38th Year rifle with its associated bayonet and the Imperial chrysanthemum and "38th Year" markings.

This one was made at the Nagoya arsenal and clearly shows the bolt cover.

Seen here is a Meiji 38th Year rifle supplied to the Siamese (Thai) Army and marked as such.

Arisaka Meiji 38th Year Carbine

The Meiji 44th Year type carbine (1911) combined the usual Arisaka action with a much shorter, 20 inch barrel and a permanently fixed bayonet which was attached to a hinge on the nose-cap and swiveled back under the barrel when not in use. This weapon was in production from 1912 to 1942. The two examples shown here are standard production versions, showing the very neat bayonet installation. Although originally intended for the cavalry the carbine was popular with infantry involved in jungle warfare, since its shorter length made it easier to handle.

Type: Bolt-action, magazine-fed carbine
Origin: Koishigawa/Nagoya/Mukden arsenals
Caliber: 6.5 x 50mm   **Barrel Length:** 20in

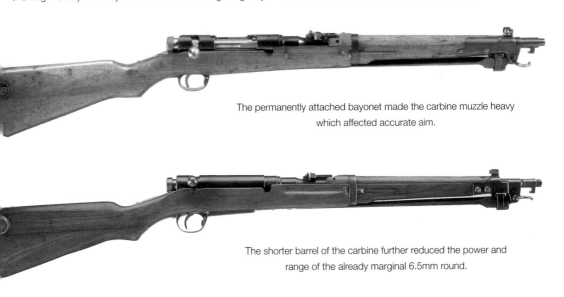

The permanently attached bayonet made the carbine muzzle heavy which affected accurate aim.

The shorter barrel of the carbine further reduced the power and range of the already marginal 6.5mm round.

Arisaka Meiji 97th Year Sniper Rifle

The Meiji 97th Year sniper rifle (1937) was the outcome of a development program that lasted well over ten years. It was based closely on the Meiji 38th Year rifle but the bolt handle was both longer and angled sharply downwards. A Toka 2.5x telescopic sight was mounted on the left side of the weapon; this position was intended to make recharging the magazine easier, but did, in fact, make holding and aiming (vital characteristics in a sniper rifle) more difficult.

Type: Bolt-action, magazine-fed sniper rifle
Origin: Kokura'/Nagoya arsenals
Caliber: 6.5 x 50mm   **Barrel length:** 30in

Arisaka Type 99 Rifle

The Meiji 38th Year rifle entered production in 1907 and remained the unquestioned standard service rifle of the Japanese forces for the following 30 years. Battle experience in the Sino-Japanese war in the late 1930s, however, showed that, once again, Japanese weapons had failed to keep up with modern trends and the 6.5mm round was no real competitor for the 7.9mm round used by the Chinese, especially at longer ranges. As a result, a new 7.7mm round

was rushed through development and successfully tested on converted 38th Year rifles. After some teething troubles the Type 99 long rifle was produced.

Type: Bolt-action, magazine-fed rifle
Origin: various arsenals
Caliber: 7.7 x 58mm
Barrel length: 26in

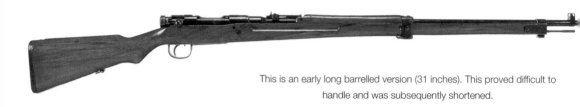

This is an early long barrelled version (31 inches). This proved difficult to handle and was subsequently shortened.

Shown here is the standard short barrelled version (26 inches) introduced in 1942.

Some type 99s were fitted with special sights and a monopod for use against aircraft.

An example of late war production.

Arisaka Type 99 Sniper Rifle

Seen here is a Type 99 sniper rifle produced at the Kokura
arsenal with a Tomioka Type 1 2.5x sight and a monopod rest.
Interestingly, the Imperial Chrysanthemum marking has been
ground out in 1945 to "spare the Emperor's embarrassment"
at the humiliation of surrender, a common feature of many
surviving Japanese World War Two weapons.

Type: Bolt-action, magazine-fed sniper rifle
Origin: Kokura and Nagoya arsenals
Caliber: 7.7 x 58mm
Barrel length: 24.25in

The right side of the Type 99 Sniper Rifle with the telescopic sight installed.
Note too the folding monopod rest under the stock forend.

This rifle was produced at Nagoya arsenal and the sight has been removed to show the
mounting bracket. Note the carrying-case for the mount and the very strong leather sling.

BSW Training Rifle

This is one of many pre-war .22 training rifles, produced under the "Kleinkaliber Wehrsportsgewehr" (small caliber, sports rifle, or KKW program weapons). It was made by engineering company Simson& Co in the German armament town of Suhl. In the late 1930s the company was forcibly taken over by the Nazi party and renamed the Berlin-Suhler- Waffenfabrik (BSW), but after just over a year in business, BSW was absorbed into the well-established Gustloff company. As with other weapons in the KKW program, this was designed to simulate the look, feel and weight of the Mauser G98 service rifle.

Type: Bolt-action sports and training rifle
Origin: Berlin-Suhler-Waffenfabrik, Suhl, Germany
Caliber: .22   **Barrel length:** 24in

Chinese Mauser

The Chinese Army purchased small numbers of Mauser rifles at various times, starting with an unknown quantity of Model 1895s in about 1896-7. The Kwangtung state arsenal then manufactured the Model 21 Short Rifle in the 1930s, which was a crude copy of the FN Modelle 30. The weapon seen here, however, was manufactured in vast numbers, perhaps as many as two million, and was a direct copy of the standard model Mauser.

Type: Bolt-action rifle
Origin: Chinese Nationalist state arsenal
Caliber: 7.9 x 57mm Mauser   **Barrel length:** 24in

Czechoslovak VZ-33 Gendarmerie Carbine

In the immediate aftermath of World War One the Czechs and Slovaks seized their independence from the collapsing Austro-Hungarian Empire and immediately set about creating a national army and the industry necessary to support it. They took over the existing Skoda works but also created a new factory at Brno, specifically to manufacture Mauser-pattern weapons, although these soon incorporated Czech improvements. The Brno factory, which had been privatized in 1924, developed the VZ-33, which appeared in 1933 as a lightweight weapon for the civil police and treasury gendarmerie. It was a development of the Mauser Model 1898 and production for home and export orders continued until the German occupation in 1939, when all production switched to the German Wehrmacht. The latter so liked this weapon that they officially adopted it as the Gewehr 33/40 and issued it to their Gebirgsjager (mountain troops).

Type: Bolt-action rifle
Origin: Ceskoslovenska Zbrojovka AS, Brno, Czechoslovakia
Caliber: 7.92 x 57mm   **Barrel length:** 18in

Our first example is an original VZ-33 made pre-war for Czech police and treasury gendarmerie

This is an export version made for Guatemala.

The Gewehr 33/40, a Czech-made VZ-33 for German mountain units was
almost indistinguishable from the standard VZ-33.

Daudeteau Rifle

The Daudeteau rifle was developed to fire a special long, round-nosed, parallel-sided round, which required a special design of chamber and barrel. Ammunition was loaded into the action by means of a curved, five-round stripper clip. The design appears to have been around for some years as the weapon seen here is dated 1879, but the only known official consideration was given in 1896 when the Daudeteau was offered to the French Navy.

Type: Bolt-action rifle
Origin: Manufacture de St Denis, France
Caliber: 6.5 x 53.5SSR Daudeteau No 12   **Barrel length:** 31.25in

Here is a shortened version with a sling, possibly part of
the order placed by the French Navy in 1896.

De Lisle Silenced Carbine

This silenced weapon was intended for use by British
Commandos and special forces in World War Two. Silencers
and baffles can reduce the muzzle report to a suitably low
level, but they can't deal with the crack of a supersonic rifle
bullet. To avoid this problem, the De Lisle used pistol
ammunition: the .45 ACP round as fired by the Colt M1911
pistol and Thompson sub¬machine gun. The stock and bolt
mechanism are modified from a standard SMLE, with a new

short barrel and integral silencer attached. A 10-shot box
magazine fitted under the receiver. The De Lisle was
apparently quite effective in its specialized role.

Type: Single-shot silenced carbine
Origin: Sterling Armament Co., Dagenham, England
Caliber: .45 ACP
Barrel length: 8.25in

Erma DSM 34 Training Rifle

ERMA was the acronym for the Erfurter Maschinewerke
Gmbh, usually known as Erma-Werke, which specialised in
submachine guns, including the famous MP38 and MP40, but
also produced .22 caliber training weapons and conversion

kits.The weapon seen here is the Deutsche Sport Modell 34
{DSM 34) Training Rifle, one of several such designs produced
by various armament firms to meet the Nazis' need for military
training for organizations such as the Hitler Youth.

Type: Training rifle
Origin: ERMA, Erfurt, Germany
Caliber: .22   **Barrel length:** 26in

FN Model 1949

A team led by Dieudonne Saive began work at the FN factory on a semi-automatic rifle in the 1930s, but escaped to England when Belgium was overrun by the Germans in 1940, to continue their work at the Royal Small Arms Factory at Enfield. As soon as their country had been freed in late 1944 the team returned to Herstal and their work lead, in the first instance, to this weapon, the Model 1949, also known as the SAFN Saive Automatique Fabrique Nationale). It was a conventionally-shaped rifle, with a full length, handguard which totally enclosed the gas cylinder, and box magazine for ten 7.92mm rounds.

Type: Semi-automatic service rifle
Origin: Fabrique Nationale (FN), Herstal, Belgium
Caliber: 7.92 x 57mm Mauser
Barrel length: 23in

Here are three examples of this rifle

Fusil MAS 36

The French Army fought World War One armed with rifles that dated back to the 1880s, and in the 1920s it became clear that a totally new weapon was required, designed around the 7.5 x 54mm rimless round. Progress was slow and it was not until 1929 that the final two designs were selected, and it was a further eight years before the winner began to reach the troops. The MAS 36 was a 7.5mm caliber weapon with a 23 inch barrel and a five-round, built-in magazine. Even though it entered service in 1937 only a relatively small number had reached units by the outbreak of war in 1939.

Type: Bolt-action service rifle
Origin: Manufacture d'Armes Ste Etienne (MAS), France
Caliber: 11mm
Barrel length: 31.5in

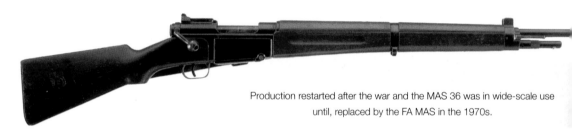

Production restarted after the war and the MAS 36 was in wide-scale use until, replaced by the FA MAS in the 1970s.

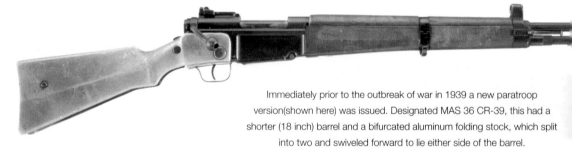

Immediately prior to the outbreak of war in 1939 a new paratroop version(shown here) was issued. Designated MAS 36 CR-39, this had a shorter (18 inch) barrel and a bifurcated aluminum folding stock, which split into two and swiveled forward to lie either side of the barrel.

Another version appeared in 1951, equipped with a permanently-attached grenade launcher. Designated MAS 36 PG-511, this had a sight for the grenade launcher, which folded back along the top of the handguard when not in use (it can be seen in this picture, just to the left of the foresight guard.)

Garand M1 Semi-Automatic Rifle

Commonly known as "the Garand," it was standardized as the MI on January 9, 1936 but a variety of problems meant that the first production weapons did not reach units until early in 1937. Even then there were further problems, particularly with the gas system, but once these were solved, production built up rapidly. Total U.S. production, which continued well into the 1950s, was just over 6 million: National Armory, Springfield - 4,617,000 (1935-57);

Winchester Repeating Arms Co - 513,580 (1940-5); Harrington & Richardson - 445,600 (1951-4); International Harvester - 457,750 (1951-4).

Type: Magazine-fed ,gas operated ,semi-automatic rifle
Origin: National Armory, Springfield
Caliber: .30-60
Barrel length: see text

Here we have a standard production M1 rifle (Serial number 647195)
which has a 22.75 inch barrel.

The M1 was also produced in a carbine version for use by officers
and senior NCOs, which had a shorter, 18 inch barrel as seen in
this one made by Winchester.

Another carbine, this time from the Rock-Ola Arsenal,
one of a number of manufacturing plants for this gun.

Garand M1 Semi-Automatic Rifle

Commonly known as "the Garand," it was standardized as the MI on January 9, 1936 but a variety of problems meant that the first production weapons did not reach units until early in 1937. Even then there were further problems, particularly with the gas system, but once these were solved, production built up rapidly. Total U.S. production, which continued well into the 1950s, was just over 6 million: National Armory, Springfield - 4,617,000 (1935-57);

Winchester Repeating Arms Co - 513,580 (1940-5); Harrington & Richardson - 445,600 (1951-4); International Harvester - 457,750 (1951-4).

Type: Magazine-fed ,gas operated ,semi-automatic rifle
Origin: National Armory, Springfield
Caliber: .30-60
Barrel length: see text

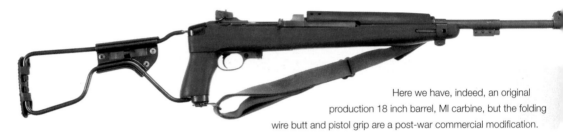

Here we have, indeed, an original production 18 inch barrel, MI carbine, but the folding wire butt and pistol grip are a post-war commercial modification.

These two are also copies of the World War Two Iver Johnson paratrooper carbine, but were manufactured commercially and do not attempt to make themselves out to be anything other than the reproductions they are. The one above was made in the 1960s/70s, note the curved magazine and additional forward handgrip.

This one was made by Universal Arms, probably in the 1970s, and has a straight ten-round magazine.

This post-war Garand, made by the Springfield Armory at Genesco, Illinois, has a 25 inch barrel and is chambered for the 7.62mm Nato round.

The Garand was also modified to make an effective sniper rifle, and these two sniper versions were developed in 1943/44 and were standardized in mid-1944, the main differences between the two being the type of scope. The M1E7 was standardized in July 1944 as the MIC, and the M1E8 in September 1944 as the MID, both with a Griffin & Howe side mount for the telescopic sight. As built, the MIC was fitted with an M73 (Lyman Alaskan) or M73B1 (Weaver 330) telescopic sight, while the MID had an M81 {cross-hair graticule) or M82 (post graticule) sight.

In the course of time, however, sights were changed, in part because of availability, but also to meet the individual sniper's personal preferences. Thus, the MIC seen here has an M82 sight. This MID has the later M84 sight. Both weapons have a leather cheek-piece laced onto the butt and the MID has the conical flash-suppressor, which later became a standard fitting on all sniper rifles.

Garand National Match target Rifle

As most service rifles are modified to meet the stringent requirements of competitive shooting, and the Garand was no exception. The first one we show is a National Match version of the MI in .30-06 caliber in which a specially selected action has been mated with a specially produced 24 inch barrel.

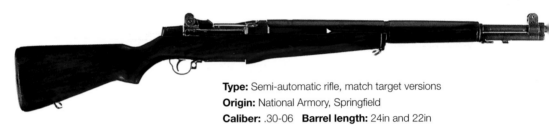

Type: Semi-automatic rifle, match target versions
Origin: National Armory, Springfield
Caliber: .30-06   **Barrel length:** 24in and 22in

Gustloff KKW Training Rifle

The Gustloff-Werke was a small weapons production facility located at Suhl in Germany. Its best known product was the VG 1-5 (Volksgerat or People's Weapon), a simple automatic rifle, intended for mass production in 1944/45. However, it also took part in the pre-war KICW program, producing this weapon which was intended to present the user with the same look and feel as the K98 service rifle, but with the minimal recoil of .22 caliber.

Type: Small caliber, single shot, training and competition rifle
Origin: Gustloff Werke, Suhl, Germany
Caliber: .22   **Barrel length:** 24in

Gustloff-Werke G43

This is a Gustloff-produced version of the Walther G43 (Gewehr 43) and was, in fact, among the first to be produced. It is stamped with the "bed" production code, which identifies the Gustloff-Werke, but there is reason to believe that this was one of a batch that was assembled at the SS-controlled Buchenwald Concentration Camp.

Type: G43 service rifle
Origin: Gustloff Werke, Suhl, Germany
Caliber: 8mm   **Barrel length:** 24in

Haenel Maschinenpistole MP44

The MP 43 was gas-operated, where gasses operate a piston which drives back, unlocking the bolt and pushing it back to begin the extraction-reloading cycle. Ammunition was fed from a 30-round detachable box magazine under the receiver. The rifle was also designed to be easy to manufacture by the use of stampings and spot welding wherever possible. The designation was changed to MP 44 in 1944.

Type: Automatic assault rifle
Origin: Haenel Waffen und Fahrradfabrik, Germany
Caliber: 7.92mm Kurz (Short)
Barrel length: 16.5in

Johnson M1941

This rifle was the brainchild of Melvin Johnson, an officer in the U.S. Marine Corps Reserve. The action of the weapon was unique and patented in 1937; it involved a combination of short recoil and a bolt with eight lugs, which rotated through 20 degrees to lock/unlock (a concept which reappeared in the 1950s in the Armalite AR-10). There was an integral ten-round rotary magazine, which could be loaded while the bolt was closed. The design included a half-length wooden stock combined with a perforated metal cooling sleeve and a long length of exposed barrel. Production ended in 1944 after some 70,000 had been produced.

Type: Automatic rifle
Origin: Melvin Johnson, Province, Rhode Island
Caliber: .30 06
Barrel length: 22in

This rifle is dated June 1941 and is believed to be one of the order for the Dutch East Indies Army that was diverted to the U.S. Marine Corps and Raider Battalions in the Far East on the outbreak of war.

Lee-Enfield SMLE

The Royal Small Arms Factory (RSAF) at Enfield, England made radical modifications to American James Lee's design for the Lee-Metford rifle resulting in a new model that was named the "Lee-Enfield." It was decided to end the existing distinction between infantry rifles and the much shorter cavalry carbines in order to produce a single weapon satisfying all requirements. The result was a new weapon, officially designated the "Rifle, Short, Magazine, Lee-Enfield."

The SMLE was in service for many years and, not surprisingly, there were many modifications and improvements. There were also sniper versions, training versions, grenade launchers and drill rifles.

Type: Bolt-action magazine rifle
Origin: Royal Small Arms Factory, Enfield, England
Caliber: .303   **Barrel length:** 25.2in

Here we see the action in the cocked position and the very substantial bayonet. This rifle is fitted with a leather sling as an alternative to the more common webbing version.

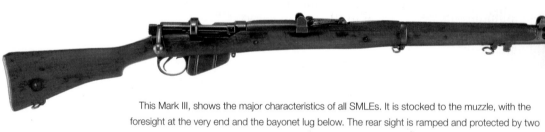

This Mark III, shows the major characteristics of all SMLEs. It is stocked to the muzzle, with the foresight at the very end and the bayonet lug below. The rear sight is ramped and protected by two "ears." The bolt lever lies conveniently placed for the firer's right hand and is seen here turned down. Forward of the trigger is the ten-round magazine.

The British Army indicated major changes by a new mark number (Mark I, Mark II, etc) and minor changes by a "star" (Mark I*, Mark I**, etc).

Lee-Enfield continued

The SMLE Mark III had a 25.2 inch barrel and an overall length of 44.6 inches. It weighed 8.7 pounds without ammunition, with a removable ten-round magazine. It was reloaded either by removing the magazine and loading rounds individually, or, with the magazine in place, using a five-round charger, which was fitted into a guide and the rounds then pushed into the magazine with the right thumb. In the open position, the bolt lever stuck out at right angles and it was pushed forward and then down, which loaded a new round and cocked the action; once fired, the bolt was raised and then pulled back to extract the empty cartridge case.

Type: Bolt-action magazine rifle
Origin: Royal Small Arms Factory ,Enfield, England
Caliber: .303
Barrel length: 25.2in

This Mark III* was produced towards the end of World War One, when quality and workmanship were being sacrificed in order to raise production rates. This led to the bindings of copper and brass wire seen here, which were intended to reduce splintering if the barrel should burst.

The only unsuccessful SMLE, the Mark 5 had the rear sight moved back to a position immediately above the trigger and an additional reinforcing band around the bodywork behind the muzzle.

The barrel and action of a combat rifle can be used to produce high quality customized target rifles for civilian use. We show a very striking weapon, still chambered for the .303 round, but with a totally new stock and butt, coupled with a Weaver telescopic sight and an integral magazine. The barrel has been reduced to 22 inches and is fitted with a new foresight.

Lee-Enfield SMLE Special Versions

As with any weapon, there were numerous special versions of the SMLE. A large number of Mark IIIs were modified to accept the "E.Y." grenade launcher; one of those shown here is a bare rifle with the bayonet lug removed, while the other has the grenade launcher fitted, together with two sheet metal reinforcing bands to reduce splintering in the event of a burst barrel. The No 36 Grenade had a circular plate screwed to its base and was then placed into the cup, whereupon a special ballistic cartridge was used to launch it. A range of up to 200 yards was claimed, although 100 yards was probably nearer the mark.

Type: Bolt-action magazine rifle
Origin: Royal Small Arms Factory ,Enfield, England
Caliber: .303
Barrel length: 25.2in

Here is the Lee-Enfield Mark III modified to accept the E.Y. grenade launcher.

This Mark III has the grenade launcher fitted and two reinforcing barrel bands to protect against a burst barrel as a result of the increased pressure caused by launching the grenade.

The Training Rifle No2 Mark IV was produced by converting the service rifle to take a .22 caliber barrel and action, while retaining the appearance and weight of the full-size rifle.

Lee-Enfield Rifle No.4

The Rifle No. 4 (always known, simply, as "the number 4") was developed from the SMLE Mark VI, which had a heavier barrel and better sights than earlier versions of the SMLE. Testing of small numbers began in the 1920s and development continued at a slow pace throughout the 1930s, but, although approved in late 1939, the first of the new Rifle No. 4 Mark Is did not reach troops until early 1942.The nose cap was removed, the stock cut back to

expose about three inches of the muzzle, and the rear sight moved to the rear of the body, all of which combined to make it look like a very different weapon.

Type: Bolt-action magazine rifle
Origin: Royal Small Arms Factory ,Enfield, England
Caliber: .303
Barrel length: 25.2in

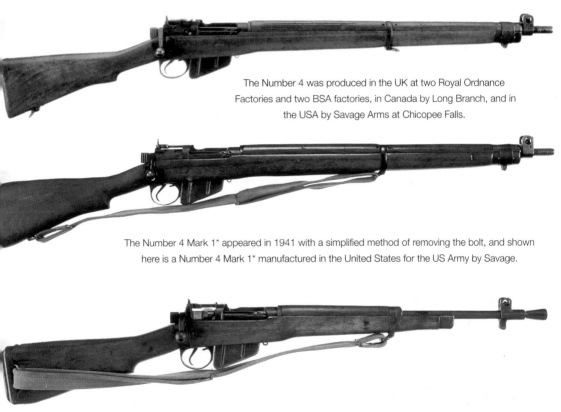

The Number 4 was produced in the UK at two Royal Ordnance Factories and two BSA factories, in Canada by Long Branch, and in the USA by Savage Arms at Chicopee Falls.

The Number 4 Mark 1* appeared in 1941 with a simplified method of removing the bolt, and shown here is a Number 4 Mark 1* manufactured in the United States for the US Army by Savage.

During World War Two the British found themselves engaged in a major campaign on the jungles of North-east India and Burma, where the existing rifles proved to be too cumbersome for jungle fighting. This led to the development of the Number 5, usually known as the "jungle carbine." This had the Number 4 action, but with a shorter barrel, a new bayonet, a rubber shoulder-pad on the butt, and a flash-suppressor.

Lee-Enfield Winchester Pattern 1914 Mark 1

In 1914 the British Army tested a new bolt-action rifle which fired a rimless .276 round; these trials were a success and it was approved for production as the Pattern 1913. But, when World War One broke out in August 1914, all British domestic production was concentrated on the Short Magazine Lee-Enfield in order to arm the rapidly expanding army. So, an order was placed with Winchester for 200,000 of a rifle based on the Pattern 1913, but modified to take the standard British .303 round. Winchester's design was accepted as the Pattern 1914 and placed in immediate mass-production with Eddystone, Remington-UMC and Winchester. In late 1916, the British reduced their orders and Winchester ended production in December of that year. The rifle seen here is a Pattern 1914 which was found in the Winchester factory in the 1960s and it would appear that it had been completed after the order had been canceled and never delivered.

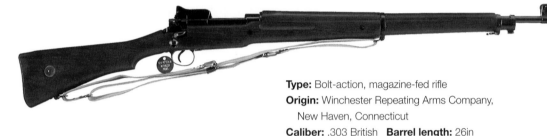

Type: Bolt-action, magazine-fed rifle
Origin: Winchester Repeating Arms Company,
New Haven, Connecticut
Caliber: .303 British   **Barrel length:** 26in

Lithgow Short Magazine Lee-Enfield

The Australian government established a State armaments factory at Lithgow in New South Wales, which commenced production in 1912. It manufactured exclusively British designs until 1956, including the Short Magazine Lee-Enfield and No. 4 Rifle, as well as Vickers and Bren machineguns. It was strategically important in that the factory was away from hostilities in Europe and production could continue without the risk of bombing capture etc. It later produced the FN-FAL under licence (1958-86) and now produces the Austrian Steyr AUG as the F88 assault rifle. Seen here are three British-designed Short Magazine Lee-Enfield (SMLE) rifles, all built by Lithgow. The first, a Mark 3, was made in 1922 and shows the general characteristics, with the bayonet boss beneath the muzzle, foresight protector, forward sling swivel ramped rear sight, ten-round box magazine and bolt-action (the bolt in the picture is in the cocked position, a breach of normal safety rules}.

Type: Bolt-action, service rifle
Origin: Australian Government Arms Factory,
Lithgow, NSW, Australia
Caliber: .303 British   **Barrel length:** 25in

This example is a Mark 3 built in 1922.

This example is a Mark 3 built in 1942.

Shown here is a rifle built in 1944 and then exported to South Africa which used British equipment in those days.

Ljungman AG-42B Rifle

Designed by Erik Eklund, the Ljungman semi-automatic rifle was accepted for service by the Swedish Army in 1942 and served until replaced by the German Heckler & Koch G3 in the mid-1960s. The Ljungman employed a gas system which was most unusual at the time, in which the gas was tapped at a point about two-thirds of the way down the barrel and then directed back down through a cylinder to an extension of the bolt carrier, thus delivering its thrust direct to the bolt and avoiding the use of a piston. Similar systems were later used in the French M1949 and the AR-10 and AR-15 developed by Eugene Stoner. The Ljungman served in the Swedish Army as the AG-42B, but was not a universal rifle, being issued instead on the basis of several per infantry squad, the remaining riflemen carrying Mauser-type weapons.

Type: Semi-automatic rifle
Origin: Husqvarna
Caliber: 6.5 x 55mm **Barrel length:** 24in

Mannlicher-Carcano M1891

The Mannlicher-Carcano Model 1891 was manufactured at the State arsenals at Terni and Brescia. The design was periodically updated, the most significant being in 1938 when fears that the 6.5 x 52mm bullet was insufficiently powerful leading to the development of the Model 1891/38 chambered for a new 7.35 x 52mm cartridge. Modifications to existing rifles had only just started when World War Two broke out and it was quickly decided that it would be too complicated to change to a new rifle and a new round, so the few 7.35mm rifles already converted were withdrawn and issued to the militia.

Type: Bolt-action, rifle
Origin: Fabbrica Nazionale d'Armi, Terni and Brescia, Italy
Caliber: 6.5x52mm
Barrel length: see text

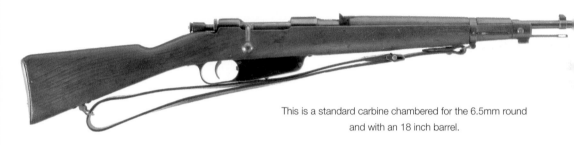

This is a standard carbine chambered for the 6.5mm round and with an 18 inch barrel.

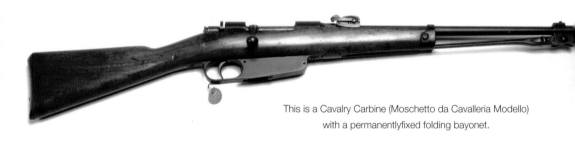

This is a Cavalry Carbine (Moschetto da Cavalleria Modello) with a permanentlyfixed folding bayonet.

This is the Carcano Model 1938 Short Rifle which was a development of the M1891 built to take the 7.35mm cartridge.

Mauser Gewehr M1898

The Gewehr 98 (G98) was the most successful bolt-action rifle ever made, having been produced in vast numbers and used, in one form or another, by most armies around the world. Also known as the Kar 98 or K98, it was a strong and reliable weapon employing Mauser's forward-locking lugs and a five-round magazine whose bottom was level with the stock. As originally produced, the bolt handle stuck out at right angles from the weapon, which was clumsy and liable to catch on clothing, but this was eventually changed to a turned-down design.

Type: Bolt-action, single-shot rifle
Origin: Mauser, Oberndorf, Germany
Caliber: 8mm   **Barrel length:** 29in

The example here is an early model with the sticking-out bolt, the type used by German forces throughout World War One.

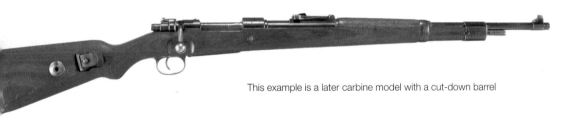

This example is a later carbine model with a cut-down barrel

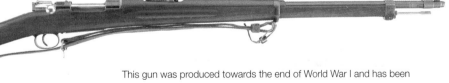

This gun was produced towards the end of World War I and has been modified for trench warfare. It has a cover to keep out the mud, a 20-round magazine and a large rear sight graduated to just 0-100 metres.

Swedish Mauser Rifle and Carbine

Sweden's first orders for Mauser weapons were for carbines for the cavalry and horse artillery. Designated Karabin M/1894, two batches were ordered from Mauser (5,000 in 1894 and 7,185 in 1895), but in 1900 production of a slightly modified version started at the Carl Gustav Stads Gevarsfactori at Eskilstuna, Sweden. The design was changed slightly in 1917 with the addition of a bayonet boss beneath the muzzle (Carbine M/1894/17).The Swedish Army also adopted the Mauser system for their infantry, using the same action and magazine as the M1894 carbine, but with a longer barrel which was fielded as the Gevar M1896 (Rifle Model 1896.)

Type: Bolt-action rifle
Origin: Mauser, Oberndorf, Germany & Swedish state arsenal
Caliber: 6.5 x 55mm **Barrel length:** see text

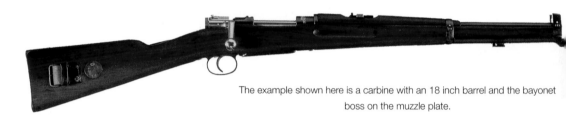

The example shown here is a carbine with an 18 inch barrel and the bayonet boss on the muzzle plate.

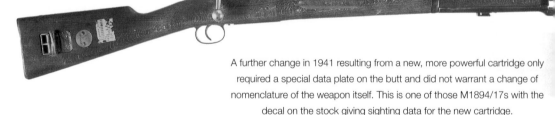

A further change in 1941 resulting from a new, more powerful cartridge only required a special data plate on the butt and did not warrant a change of nomenclature of the weapon itself. This is one of those M1894/17s with the decal on the stock giving sighting data for the new cartridge.

Also in 1941, selected high quality M/1896s were converted to sniper rifles, created by assembling a carefully selected barrel and action, with a new stock and butt, and with the addition of either Swedish or German telescopic sights. The one shown here has the M/44 Swedish AGA 3 x 65.

Mauser K98 Export Models

The Mauser rifle was exported in a wide variety of models, which differed only in caliber and some minor details. Argentina took delivery of an early batch of the Fusil Mauser Argentine Modello 1891 in 7.65 caliber, which was made in Germany by Loewe and DWM, and was accompanied by a shorter carbine version. A new variant was produced for Argentina by DWM, known as the Model 1909, and repeat orders were placed until the outbreak of war in 1939.Chile and Venezuela were also customers of Mauser.Many European armies too used the Mauser, including Croatia in 1941 when that country was an ally of the Germans, and Czechoslovakia before the Germans seized it in 1939.

This gun was supplied to Croatia in 1941 when that country was allied to the Germans.

This example was made at the Brno in Czechoslovakia in the 1920s and was similar to the Kar98 but with Czech improvements.

The Mauser was produced in Hungary during World War II as the G98.

Mauser K98: Nazi Production in Germany

It would be virtually impossible to work out an accurate figure for the production of K98s during the years 1934-45, but it must have been well over ten million. Vast numbers had to be produced to arm the rapidly-expanding German Army, while the newly-formed Luftwaffe had to be equipped right from scratch. The demand was enormous and many factories within Germany that made other goods during peacetime were seconded to arms manufacture. As the Nazis overran other countries, factories in those countries were forced to make arms for the Germans. A good example of this is FN in Belgium who were already making Mausers under license in the 1930s.

Type: Bolt-action, service rifle.
Origin: see text
Caliber: 7.92mm **Barrel length:** 24in

This rifle was one of many issued to the
Luftwaffe (air force) in 1938.

The Erma Werke at Erfurt in Germany began making K98s
such as this one in 1936.

The Austrian factory at Steyr joined the program in 1939 having
then become part of the Third Reich.

The production code of "byf 43" shows that this rifle was made
at the actual Mauser factory at Oberndorf in 1943.

Above: Marked "byf 44" this example
too was made at Oberndorf but in 1944.
By this time of the war, shortages of labor
and materials were starting to reduce the
quality of the guns.

Right: The Reich's Eagle cartouche
on the butt identifies this as a Nazi
production weapon.

This gun is marked "bnz 43" and is thought to have been assembled
at a concentration camp from parts made at the factory in Steyr.

Mauser K98 Sniper Versions

Typical World War II-era sniper rifles such as the K 98 were generally standard-issue rifles (hand-picked for accuracy) with a telescopic sight and cheek-rest fitted, with the bolt turned down (if necessary) to allow operation with the scope affixed. By the end of the war, forces on all sides had specially-trained soldiers equipped with sniper rifles, and they have played an increasingly important role in military operations ever since. The Germans took training for this role very seriously and training films exist to this day showing how thoroughly snipers were prepared for the task.

This Mauser-produced K98 sniper rifle is fitted with the ZF-41/1 sniper scope which is mounted surprisingly far forward and would thus have been at some distance from the firer's eye.

Above: Here we have a special version produced in the late 1930s, chambered for the 5.6 x 61 Von Hofe Super Express cartridge. This weapon, which is number V-70 (Versuch, or trials), may have been produced for pre¬war competition shooting, but would also have been highly suitable for use by a combat sniper.

Below: This scope is marked with SS-proof marks and is a reminder that Himmler's Waffen-SS set itself up in parallel to the army, with its own procurement policies and organisation. Such independence became a serious duplication and waste of resources at a time when the German war effort could afford neither.

Mauser G24 (t)

The Czechoslovak armaments factory at Brno was making the Model 1924, a version of the M1898 which incorporated a number of developments, including shorter butt and improved finish, when the Germans invaded in 1939 and, since it was little different from the K98 already widely used in the Wehrmacht, it was taken into German service as the Gewehr 1924 (t). T being an abbreviation for Tschechoslovakei.

Type: Bolt-action, service rifle.
Origin: Waffen-werke Brunn, German-occupied Czechoslovakia
Caliber: 7.92mm **Barrel length:** 24in

Mauser G33/40 Alpine Carbine

These are two examples of the G33/40, a version of the G33 which had been produced as a carbine for the Czech gendarmerie. It was made at the Brunn (Brno) gun factory between 1940 and 1942 during the German occupation of Czechslovakia and was used to arm the Gibirgsjaeger (the German Army's Alpine mountain troops) and the Luftwaffe's paratroops.

Type: Bolt-action, service rifle.
Origin: Waffen-werke Brunn,
   German-occupied Czechoslovakia
Caliber: 8mm
Barrel length: 18in

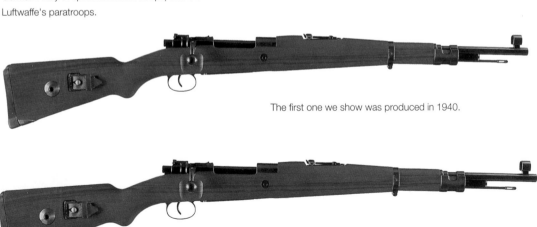

The first one we show was produced in 1940.

This example of the G33/40 was manufactured in 1942.

Mauser Training / Target Rifle

Once the Nazis were in power it was necessary to produce training rifles in large numbers, and lower quality, as with this Mauser-produced .22 rifle, marked "Deutsches Sport Model", which was made to represent the shape, size and weight of the G98. The reference to sport was important to convince the Allies that Germany had no hostile intentions and certainly was not re arming. All their training therefore must appear as pursuing peaceful and wholesome sporting activities. Apart from their service rifles and carbines, Mauser also made a considerable range and number of target and training weapons for the so called "civilian" market.

Type: Bolt-action rifle
Origin: Mauser, Oberndorf, Germany
Caliber: .22
Barrel length: 24in

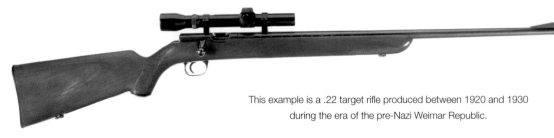

This example is a .22 target rifle produced between 1920 and 1930 during the era of the pre-Nazi Weimar Republic.

This is a Mauser-produced .22 rifle, marked "Deutsches Sport Model", which was made to represent the shape, size and weight of the G98.

Paratroop Rifle

This Japanese paratroop rifle is based on the Type 99 infantry rifle, but reworked so that it could be split into two at the junction of the barrel and receiver, with an interrupted-thread lock to join them. The first prototype was unsuccessful, but the Type 2 (shown here) was developed, using the same principle, but with a new sliding-wedge lock; which was more successful being standardised in 1942.

Type: Bolt-action, magazine-fed paratroop rifle
Origin: Nagoya arsenal
Caliber: 7.7 x 58mm   **Barrel length:** 26in

Pratt & Whitney Semi-Automatic Rifle

This was a prototype built in the 1920s by Pratt & Whitney, under contract to the Nationalist Chinese government of Chiang Kai-Shek.The action is of a straight-pull design similar to that found in the Ross rifle, with a one-piece bolt- carrier/cover and an internal magazine holding either four or five rounds. There is also a muzzle-shroud with two settings, which may function either as a muzzle-brake or as a flash suppressor.

Type: Semi-automatic rifle
Origin: Pratt & Whitney Company, Hartford, Connecticut
Caliber: 4.8mm   **Barrel length:** 26in

Radom WZ .29 Rifle

The Poles examined the Mauser-style short rifles produced by the Czechs -the VZ.24 - and FN - the Modelle 24 – and designed their own equivalent, which was then adopted as the wz.29, seen here with its associated bayonet. This was the weapon equipping all Polish units in 1939, but production ceased when the Germans arrived .The rifle is marked with the Polish shield and Radom stamps.

Type: Bolt-action magazine rifle
Origin: Warsaw, Poland
Caliber: 8mm   **Barrel length:** 24in

Remington Pattern 1914 (British) Mark 1

The P14 had been developed in 1913 because of British concerns about the effectiveness of the new SMLE rifle but hadn't entered production when war broke out.Orders for the P14 were placed in the United States with Remington and Winchester. As it turned out the P14 was less effective than the SMLE, being more susceptible to dirt although extremely accurate, and by the time World War I finished, Remington had delivered over 600,000.

Type: Bolt-action, magazine-fed rifle
Origin: Remington Arms Co., Ilion, New York, and Eddystone, Philadelphia.
Caliber: .303 British   **Barrel length:** 26in

Remington U. S. Rifle Model of 1917

When the United States entered the war on April 6, 1917, the British contracts were terminated by mutual agreement between the two governments, after some 600,000 rifles had been completed. Remington was at that time tooled up for the Enfield Pattern 1914, so rather than switch production to the standard U.S. M1903 rifle, it was decided the easiest solution was to modify the British P14 to take the standard .30-06 U.S. government cartridge. Designated the Model of 1917, the first U.S. government contract for these rifles was signed on July 12, 1917, and between September 1917 and September 1918 one million rifles were completed, a truly astonishing achievement.

Type: Bolt-action, magazine-fed rifle
Origin: Remington Arms Co., Ilion, New York, and Eddystone, Philadelphia.
Caliber: .30-06
Barrel length: 26in

Many surviving rifles like this one ended up in the hands of the British Home Guard in 1940, although as they also had .303 P14s, keeping separate British and U.S. ammunition supplies became a problem.

The rifle shown here is serial number 69,676, and is an early production item.

This one, serial 494,593 was made at almost exactly at the half-way point of the production history. All these rifles are mute remainders of a very great story of American production and determination.

Remington Model of 1934 Military

Remington continued to exploit their experience with the Enfield P14 and in 1933 developed a modified Model of 1917 in 7 x 57mm Mauser caliber. A year later the company was contracted by Honduras to supply 3,000 – now known as the Model of 1934. They used the same receivers as in the Model 30 Express rifle but were fitted for the Springfield-pattern bayonet.

Type: Bolt-action, magazine-fed rifle
Origin: Remington Arms Co., Ilion, New York
Caliber: 7 x 57mm Mauser **Barrel length:** 26in

Remington M1903

As World War Two raged in Europe, the British government once again approached Remington for service rifles, and in mid-1941 issued a contract for the U.S. Model 1903 chambered for the British .303 round. But U.S. national re-armament caused the contract to be canceled as Remington's facilities became essential for home production. Manufacture of the self-loading Garand was only just getting into its stride. After the Pearl Harbor attack and the German declaration of war, Remington began producing the Model 1903 using World War One-vintage equipment that had been used to make the same rifle at Rock Island and Springfield Armories.

Type: Bolt-action, magazine-fed rifle
Origin: Remington Arms Co., Ilion, New York
Caliber: .30-06
Barrel length: 24in

Remington was authorized to produce the sniper variant of the Model 1903. This Model 1903A45 became the U.S. standard sniper rifle throughout the war, and over 28,000 were made, with Weaver scopes.

Rheinmetall Fallschirmgewehr FG42

The FG 42 was another predecessor of the modern assault rifle. It was intended to be able to fire both fully automatic and single shot fire. One problem was that the rifle used the standard 7.92 x 57mm cartridge, which was really too powerful for automatic fire from a light hand-held weapon. Ammunition supply was also an issue, in that the 20-shot detachable box magazine wasn't adequate for sustained fire.

Type: Automatic paratroop rifle
Origin: Rheinmetall-Borsig AC, Germany
Caliber: 7.92 x 57rnm   **Barrel length:** 20in

Rock Island M1903

The Rock Island Arsenal opened in 1862 and is still in business; it made Springfield Model 1903 rifles from 1906 to 1913, and again from 1917 to 1919, completing approximately 400,000 in the process. In the early 1920s all unfinished parts were shipped to the Springfield Arsenal, and some of these were later assembled into complete rifles, still bearing the Rock Island marks. We show two examples below, both made at the Rock Island Arsenal.

Type: Bolt-action, magazine rifle
Origin: Rock Island Arsenal, Rock Island, Missouri
Caliber: .30-60   **Barrel length:** 24in

This M1903 is recorded as being owned by Lieutenant-Commander Leon H. French, U.S.Navy who served in the Marine Corps in the 1930s. The front and rear sights are unique to USMC M1903s.

This is a U.S. Army M1903 and the different sights are apparent.

Ross Rifle

The Ross used an unusual straight-pull bolt design, and at first glance was an extremely good design. Military service soon showed up its shortcomings however. The Ross was unable to cope with dirt, mud and the rigors of combat, and the mechanism continually jammed in use. During World War I many Canadian troops tried to lose their Ross Rifles and scavenge Lee-Enfields from the battlefield instead.

Type: Bolt-action rifle
Origin: Ross Rifle Co., Quebec, Canada
Caliber: .303in   **Barrel length:** 30in

Sako Models M/28-30 and M/1939

Finland obtained its independence from Russia in 1917, but this was followed by a short and bloody civil war, which ended in 1918. The new government then set about building up the armed forces and a defense industry, one outcome of which was the arms company, Sako. Vast stocks of Mosin-Nagant rifles had been captured from the Russians and this weapon formed the basis of Finnish Army issue until after World War Two. The Mosin-Nagant was further developed to meet Finnish needs and conditions. The M/1939 was developed from the earlier M/28-30 by following a list of improvements suggested by both the Army and the Civil Guard.

Type: Bolt-action rifle
Origin: Sako, Riihimaki, Finland
Caliber: 7.62 x 54R
Barrel length: 29in (M/28-30); 28in (M/1939)

The M/28-30 seen here was developed from the M/28, but had a better sight and other minor improvements.

The M/1939 seen here was just entering production when war broke out. This design incorporated further improved sights, a heavier, recontoured and more robust stock, and a revised handguard with the rear barrel-band moved further forwards.

Savage Model 29

The Slide-action Model 29 was introduced in 1929 and remained in production until 1967. Pre-war models had an octagonal barrel and a checkered stock, but these were changed after the war to a round barrel and an undecorated stock. The example shown is a pre-war model with octagonal barrel, smooth slide handle and checkered pistol grip type stock.

Type: Slide-action sporting rifle
Origin: Savage Arms Corporation, Utica, New York
Caliber: .225, .221, .22LR   **Barrel length:** 24in

Sedgley M1903

During the inter-war years Sedgely bought up many surplus M1903 actions and turned them into sporters. However, at the start of World War Two the company used some of the actions lying in their stores and assembled them, with some new production items, to produce an MI903 look-alike for sale to organizations that required a military-looking rifle.

Type: Springfield M1903 rifle
Origin: R.F. Sedgley, Philadelphia, Pennsylvania
Caliber: .30-06   **Barrel length:** 24in

Sedgley Sporter Rifle

Reginald F. Sedgely was a well-known gunsmith who ran his business in Philadelphia from 1910 until his death in 1938. He produced customized sporters based on a variety of actions, including the M1903 Springfield. The one shown here is typical and shows a good quality of workmanship, with a blued barrel and a walnut stock, with checkering.

Type: Springfield action, sporter rifle
Origin: R.F. Sedgley, Philadelphia, Pennsylvania Caliber: .30-06
Barrel length: 24in

Simonov SKS Assault Carbine

The Soviet Army conducted a development program throughout the 1930s with the aim of producing an effective gas-operated, self-loading rifle, and Sergei Simonov was one of the designers who took part. His automatic rifle, the AVS or Model 1936 proved difficult to manufacture and was subject to a variety of problems, particularly jamming, in field use. Simonov used the lessons learned when captured German MP-43s were examined and used to improve the Soviet designs. One outcome was the SKS (also known as SKS-45), which entered full production in 1946, possibly as a safeguard against failure of the more revolutionary Kalshnikov.

Type: Semi-automatic carbine
Origin: State arsenals at Tula and Izhevsk
Caliber: 7.62 x 39.5mm rimmed
Barrel length: 18.0 in

The standard SKS had an integral ten-round magazine,
which was filled either singly or by five-round chargers,
and a rearward-folding integral bayonet.

The SKS was manufactured by Communist-bloc states, such as China
(Type 56), East Germany (Karabiner-S), North Korea (Type 63) and Yugoslavia
(Model 59), as well as by non-Communist Egypt.

This one is a Chinese-produced Simonov-clone, the Type 56. This also has
an integral bayonet, but the blade is much narrower and lighter.

TWO WORLD WARS · **116**

Springfield M1903

In 1894 the U.S. Army began to look at the idea of another rifle, using the Mauser action. It was planned to have a 30 inch barrel for the infantry and a 20 inch barrel for a cavalry carbine, but this was changed to a universal rifle with a 24 inch barrel, firing the .30-03 round. The new rifle, always known as "the Springfield" had a Mauser-type bolt, and a five-round magazine with a cut-off plate. In 1906 the .30-06 round with a lighter bullet with a sharper nose was introduced, having greater muzzle velocity, a lower trajectory, increasing maximum theoretical range to 2,850 yards.

Type: Bolt-action magazine-fed rifle
Origin: National Armory, Springfield, Massachusetts
Caliber: .30-06   **Barrel length:** 24in

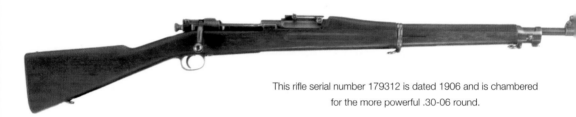

This rifle serial number 179312 is dated 1906 and is chambered for the more powerful .30-06 round.

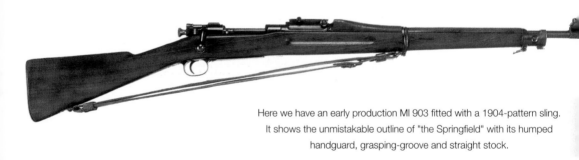

Here we have an early production MI 903 fitted with a 1904-pattern sling. It shows the unmistakable outline of "the Springfield" with its humped handguard, grasping-groove and straight stock.

A similar, early production version, but with a slightly different pattern rear sight.

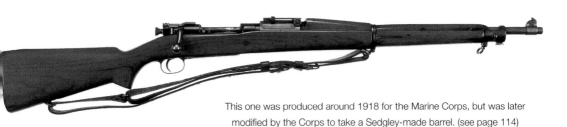

This one was produced around 1918 for the Marine Corps, but was later modified by the Corps to take a Sedgley-made barrel. (see page 114)

Springfield M1903 Mark 1

One of the most important tactical requirements revealed by the U.S. Army's experience in World War One was the need to increase the infantry's firepower, particularly when advancing across "no-man's land". One method of achieving this was the "Pedersen device" which could be inserted, when required, into a modified M1903 to transform the rifle into a semi-automatic, and trials and demonstrations were greeted with great enthusiasm. As a result, the M1903 Mark 1 was developed, which-had minor modifications including an ejection port cut into the left side of the receiver, and small changes to the trigger mechanism and to the cut-off.

Type: Semi-automatic magazine-fed rifle
Origin: National Armory, Springfield, Massachusetts
Caliber: .30-06
Barrel length: 24in

Use in this role required a special round that was fed into the rifle from a 40-round box magazine which stuck out of the top of the rifle, offset slightly to the right.

The example seen here is a Mark 1 conversion, the clearest evidence of which would be the ejection port on the left side.

Springfield M1903 Sniper Rifles

In 1907 experiments began with a telescopic sight developed by the Warner & Swasey company of Cleveland, Ohio, which led to an order for 1,000 sights under the designation "Telescopic Musket Sights, Model of 1908." These 6x prismatic sights were issued on a trials basis in 1910 but soon proved to be unpopular, being clumsy and uncomfortable, and, even worse, their optical performance was poor. They were issued to units in France 1917-18, but the troops did not like them and they were little used. Thus, the U.S. Army came to accept that the prismatic telescopic sight was greatly inferior to straight tube versions.

Type: Bolt-action magazine-fed rifle
Origin: National Armory, Springfield, Massachusetts
Caliber: .30-06
Barrel length: 24in

An improved version of the sight was then designed which was accepted as the "Model of 1913," with 5.2x magnification, which is seen mounted on an MI903 sniper rifle in this example. It was still clumsy.

In World War Two a new sniper version, the M1903A4, was developed. This consisted of the M1903A3 action, with a specially selected barrel with two-groove rifling, and a stock with a special pistol grip.

Springfield M1903 A3

With the outbreak of World War Two there was a requirement for infantry rifles in vast numbers and the MI903 was re-engineered to make it more suitable for mass production in the quantities now required. Sheet-metal stampings were substituted for machined parts wherever feasible, but the most obvious external changes were the deletion of the leaf backsight on top of the barrel.

Type: Bolt-action magazine-fed rifle
Origin: National Armory, Springfield, Massachusetts
Caliber: .30-06   **Barrel length:** 24in

Springfield Special Target Rifles

Several versions of the MI903 were introduced for National Match competition shooting, which consisted of specially selected barrels (which were marked with a star), matched with actions which had been honed to ensure smoothness of operation. There were some minor differences from the normal service rifle; for example, there was no grasping groove, and the butt had an NRA-style pistol grip. Some of these were later reconditioned and reissued for use in lower-level competitions or marksmanship training and were designated "Special Target Rifles."

Type: Bolt-action magazine-fed rifle
Origin: National Armory, Springfield, Massachusetts
Caliber: .30-06   **Barrel length:** 24in

Springfield M1903 With Grenade Launcher

MI903 rifles were used as grenade launchers to give tactical support to platoons/squads to cover the gap between hand-grenades and mortars. This involved the use of the Monarch MI spigot grenade-launching adaptor to be fitted over the muzzle of the rifle, forming an extension to the barrel, as shown in this example. The launcher had a series of rings which served as range indicators, the desired range being set by placing the base of the grenade over the appropriate ring; the further the grenade was placed down the launcher the greater the range. The grenade was launched using a special "ballistite" cartridge.

Type: Bolt-action magazine-fed rifle
Origin: National Armory, Springfield, Massachusetts
Caliber: .30-06   **Barrel length:** 24in + extension

Springfield M1922 Training Rifle

The 1916 National Defense Act authorized the War Department to distribute arms and ammunition to civilian rifle clubs, provided funds for the operation of government rifle ranges, and opened military rifle ranges to civilian shooters.

In 1922 the DCM sponsored the development by Springfield of a .22 caliber weapon, which quickly established itself as the premier .22 rifle of the day. This rifle is an M1922M1 in original condition.

Type: Bolt-action, magazine-fed rifle
Origin: National Armory, Springfield, Massachusetts
Caliber: .22LR   **Barrel length:** 24in

Type 99 Conversion

This rifle started out as a Japanese Arisaka Type 99 infantry rifle, chambered for the 7.7 x 58mm Arisaka cartridge, and produced in Japan from 1939 onwards for the Imperial Japanese Army. It is stamped with the insignia of the Chinese

Nationalist North China Army, which indicates that it must have been captured during the fighting in Manchuria during the Sino-Japanese War between 1939 and 1945 and converted to fire Mauser ammunition.

Type: Bolt-action, magazine-fed rifle
Origin: various arsenals
Caliber: 7.92mm Mauser   **Barrel length:** 26.75in

Tokarev Rifle (SVT)

Known as the Samozaryadnaya i avtomaticheskaya Vintovky sistemy Tokareva (SVT, or semi-automatic and automatic rifle, Tokarev pattern), this was a gas-operated weapon, with locking achieved by the breech-block tail dropping into a

receiver recess. The gas cylinder was above the barrel and a long wooden stock covered about half the barrel with a further vented metal stock in front of that.

Type: Semi-/full-automatic rifle
Origin: State arsenals at Tula and Izhevsk
Caliber: 7.62 x 54mm rimmed **Barrel length:** 26.6in

Walther Gewehr 41 (W)

The Walther brothers began work on a new semi-automatic rifle in the 1930s but their first product, the Gewehr 41 (W), was not a success. It underwent trials in competition with the Mauser Gewehr 41 (M) which the Walther weapon won and was then, with a few modifications, placed in production. Unfortunately, experience in the Russian campaign showed that the muzzle cup became eroded very quickly and the production order was quickly terminated in 1943. The

Gewehr 41(W) is shown here, with its vertically mounted cocking handle and the muzzle cap which deflected some of the gasses back on to an annular piston which drove the working parts to the rear.

Type: Semi-automatic assault rifle
Origin: Carl Walther Waffenfabrik, Zella-Mehlis, Germany
Caliber: 7.92 x 57mm Mauser   **Barrel length:** 22in

A Gewehr 41 (W) from the Berlin-Lubecker
Maschinenfabrik (production code "duv").

This rifle was produced by the Walther factory and
has the production code ac43 showing that it was
the last year of production.

Walther Gewehr G43

 Walther's next weapon the Gewehr 43 was a major success and was placed into production. The disastrous muzzle cup and annular piston were replaced by a more conventional port-and-piston layout, which was a modified version of that

used on the Soviet Tokarev rifle.The new weapon was produced in two versions, Gewehr 43 (Rifle 1943) and its successor, Karabiner 43 (Carbine 43.)

Type: Semi-automatic assault rifle
Origin: Carl Walther Waffenfabrik, Zella-Mehlis,
   Thuringia, Germany
Caliber: 7.92 x 57mm Mauser   **Barrel length:** 23in

Walther K43 Sniper Rifle

There were many small variations introduced on the G/K43 throughout its production cycle. The important consideration is that no changes were made to the rifle design specifically to coincide with the nomenclature change from Gewehr to Karabiner, with the exception of the letter stamped on the side. Careful study of actual weapons will show that many G-marked rifles had features found on K-marked rifles and vice versa. There is therefore no difference in weight or length between the G43 and the K43. Variations in barrel length did exist, but those were the product of machining tolerances, differences between factories, and/or experimental long-barreled rifles.

Type: Semi-automatic sniper rifle
Origin: Carl Walther Waffenfabrik, Zella-Mehlis, Thuringia, Germany
Caliber: 7.92 x 57mm Mauser
Barrel length: 21.5in

Here are three examples of the Sniper version of the K43 which is modified only by addition of the rails on the receiver and the sniper scope. All three examples are fitted with the Voigtlander ZF-4 scope (x 4 magnifications.)

Walther KKW Training Rifle

The Walther factory produced a number of weapons for the Nazi Party training programs. Such weapons, all in .22 caliber, were produced by various weapons manufacturers, under the generic title "Kleinkaliber Wehrsportsgewehr" (small caliber, weapons sports rifle) and there were regular competitions sponsored by the KKW organisation. This weapon, which is in excellent condition, was manufactured pre-war but was still in use in target competitions as late as 1944.

Type: Small caliber, single shot, training and competition rifle
Origin: Carl Walther Waffenfabrik, Zella-Mehlis, Thuringia, Germany
Caliber: .22 **Barrel length:** 26in

Winchester M1917

As the British had found themselves woefully short of rifles in 1914, so, too, did the Americans in 1917 and by happy chance there were three production lines already set up to produce the British Pattern 1914. This rifle and magazine were quickly re-engineered to take the US Army's .30-06 rimless round, the weapon was placed in production as the "Rifle, Caliber .30, Model of 1917."

Type: bolt-action, magazine-fed rifle
Origin: Winchester Repeating Arms Company, New Haven, Connecticut
Caliber: .30-06
Barrel: 25.5in

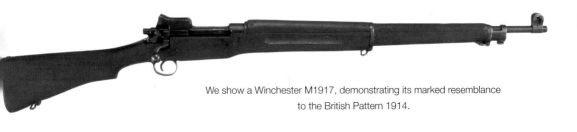

We show a Winchester M1917, demonstrating its marked resemblance to the British Pattern 1914.

This weapon started life as an M1917, but, as happens with some weapons, an owner has modified it. In this case the receiver ears which protected the rearsight have been totally removed by grinding and a new sight installed, and the stock has been completely replaced, leaving the forward half of the barrel and the top of the rear of the barrel totally exposed.

Accuracy International PM

The rifle is based around an extremely rigid aluminum frame, with an attached plastic stock with thumbhole grip and a spring-loaded bipod support. A stainless steel barrel is free-floating above the frame, and the action is a short-throw bolt, which can be operated without the firer having to change their head position.

Type: Bolt-action sniper rifle
Origin: Accuracy International, England
Caliber: 7,62mm **Barrel length:** 25.8in

AR-7 Survival Rifle

In 1959 the legendary Eugene Stoner entered the U.S. Air Force's competition for a very light and compact takedown, survival weapon for downed aircrew; the outcome was the AR-7. One of its most notable attributes was that the entire weapon could be disassembled and stored in the plastic stock and then re-assembled in seconds.

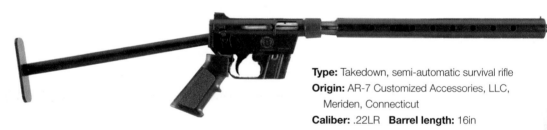

Type: Takedown, semi-automatic survival rifle
Origin: AR-7 Customized Accessories, LLC,
Meriden, Connecticut
Caliber: .22LR **Barrel length:** 16in

Armalite AR-18 Rifle

Intended to be a cheaper alternative to the AR-15 the AR-18 employed a rotating bolt with seven lugs, which lock into the breech end of the barrel, with a short-stroke piston driving the bolt-carrier rearwards.

The AR-18 was of all-steel construction, extensive use being made of pressings for the upper and lower receiver bodies, and for a number of external and internal parts; all furniture was glass-reinforced plastic.

Type: Semi-automatic rifle
Origin: Armalite Inc, Costa Mesa, California
(now at Geneseo, Illinois)
Caliber: .223 **Barrel length:** 20in

This example was made by Sterling in England, and has lugs for a grenade-launcher beneath the barrel, and a mounting for the grenade-launcher sight above the receiver.

Anschütz Target and Sporting Rifles

Members of the Anschutz family have been very active in the gunmaking business in Germany since 1793, mostly producing sporting arms and competition rifles. The company of J.G. Anschutz was established in Suhl in 1856 and remained continuously in business until 1945, when the town was overrun by the advancing Soviet Red Army. The company was re-established at Ulm in 1950, since when it has produced a wide variety of sporting and target rifles, most of them based on the company's own Model 1954 bolt action. A small selection of the company's .22 single-shot rifles are shown on this and the following page.

Type: Bolt –action target rifle
Origin: Anschutz, Ulm, Germany
Caliber: .22
Barrel length: see captions.

This is model 1808 ED chambered for .22LR with a 19.25 inch barrel

This is a model 1710 chambered for .22LR and has a 24 inch barrel.

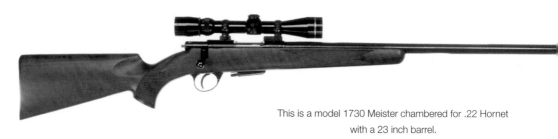

This is a model 1730 Meister chambered for .22 Hornet
with a 23 inch barrel.

This is a model 1720 Meister chambered for .22 Magnum
and has a 23 inch barrel.

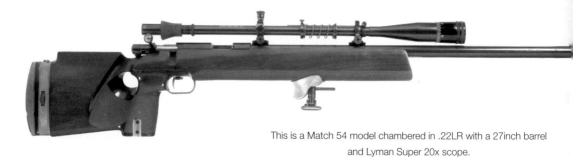

This is a Match 54 model chambered in .22LR with a 27inch barrel
and Lyman Super 20x scope.

Another Match 54 target rifle with an elaborate thumbhole butt
and a micrometer iron sight.

Beretta BM-59

Beretta engineers redesigned the U.S. MI Garand design, the new weapon being accepted by the Italian Army as the BM-59. The top picture shows a BM-59 Mark 1 with a 20 inch barrel, 20-round detachable box magazine, improved trigger group, integral bipod and a so-called "triple compensator." This latter device fitted on the muzzle and served as a combined muzzle-brake, flash suppressor and grenade launcher.

Type: Semi-automatic rifle
Origin: Aram Pietro Beretta SpA, Rome, Italy
Caliber: 7.62mm NATO
Barrel length: see text

This one is a BM-59 Ital Tipo Parachutisti carbine with an 18.5 inch barrel.

Beretta AR-70

This weapon is chambered for the 5.56 x 45mm NATO round, which is fired from a closed bolt; the system is gas-operated, but there is no gas regulator. The trigger group is simple and there are two interchangeable butt-stock configurations, with a high-impact rigid plastic stock with a steel buttplate being used in the assault rifle seen here.

Type: Semi-automatic rifle
Origin: Aram Pietro Beretta SpA, Rome, Italy
Caliber: 5.56mm NATO
Barrel length: 18in

Brenneke Mauser-Action Rifle

The armament company, Wilhelm Brenneke, was established in Leipzig, Germany in 1895 and by 1936 production had reached some 400,000 weapons per year. Like all German armaments firms it was closed down in 1945, but it restarted in West Berlin in 1951. This weapon was produced before World War II and is a Mauser-action, with very high quality steel for the action and barrel, and a walnut stock.

Type: Bolt-action, target rifle
Origin: Wilhelm Brenneke, Leipzig, Germany
Caliber: 7 x 64mm
Barrel length: 27in

Browning BAR Rifle

The BAR appeared in a variety of chamberings, ranging from .243 to .338 Magnum, with either 22 inch or 24 inch barrels, and, as usual, there were different grades of finish.

The weapon seen here is a basic grade 1 finish, chambered for .338 Magnum with a 24 inch barrel.

Type: Gas-operated, semi-automatic rifle
Origin: John Browning and FN, Herstal, Belgium
Caliber: .338 Winchester Magnum **Barrel length:** 24in

Browning BAR Rifle Type 1

The Browning BAR Type I was a gas-operated, semi-automatic sporting rifle, introduced in 1967 in various calibers from .243 up to .338 Magnum, and either a 22 or 24 inch barrel. The BAR Type I was produced in nine standards of finish, from Grade I, the basic, up to Grade V Magnum, the most luxurious, with two sub-grades within grades II, III and

Type: Semi-automatic sporting rifle
Origin: Browning Arms Co., Morgan, Utah
Caliber: see text **Barrel length:** 22in, 24in

Browning BLR

BLR stands for "Browning Lever-action Rifle." Introduced in 1971, this family of weapons was manufactured for one year at FN, Belgium, but production was then switched to B.C. Miroku in Japan, where it has remained ever since. The Model 81 BLR had a 20 inch barrel, a four-round detachable box magazine and a rotary locking bolt.

Type: Lever-action rifle
Origin: John Browning and B.C. Miroku, Kochi, Japan
Caliber: .308 **Barrel length:** see text

Browning High-Power Olympian Grade

The High-Power Bolt-Action Rifle was manufactured from 1959 to 1975, with production taking place at FN, Herstal, Belgium (1959-75) and Sako, Rihimali, Finland (1961-75). It was chambered for a variety of calibers from .22 Remington up to .458 Winchester and featured either a Mauser or a Sako action, with three grades of finish.

Type: Bolt-action, sporting rifle
Origin: John Browning and FN, Herstal, Belgium or Sako, Finland
Caliber: see text
Barrel Length: 24in

This weapons has the basic "Safari" finish and is Sako-made, chambered for .300 Winchester with a 24 inch barrel and 3x-9x Bushnell scope.

Browning Gold Medallion A-Bolt

This series of guns is based on the A-Bolt Hunter, for which a deluxe version, the A-Bolt Medallion was introduced in 1985; this had a highly-polish blue finished barrel and action, and a walnut stock with rosewood ends. The Gold Medallion, introduced in 1988, was an even higher quality weapon, which featured the very top grade of walnut, together with light engraving and gold-inlaid lettering.

Type: Target and sporting rifle
Origin: John Browning and B. C. Miroku, Kochi, Japan
Caliber: .22 LR   **Barrel length:** 22in

Browning Semi-Automatic Rifle

The Browning Semi-Automatic Rifle (which does not appear to have had an abbreviated designation) was manufactured by FN in Belgium from 1956 to 1974 and from 1976 onwards by B.C. Miroku in Japan. This .22 semi-automatic was a blowback- operated self-loader, with a takedown barrel and an eleven-round, tubular magazine inside the butt-stock which is loaded through a port in the right side of the stock. This gun was manufactured as the Remington Model 24 from 1922 to 1935 with the Browning taking over in 1956 and manufactured in Herstal until 1974. Production went to Miroku in Japan from 1976 onward.

Type: Semi-automatic rifle
Origin: John Browning and FN, Herstal, Belgium
   or B.C. Hiroku, Kochi, Japan
Caliber: .22LR   **Barrel length:** 19.25in

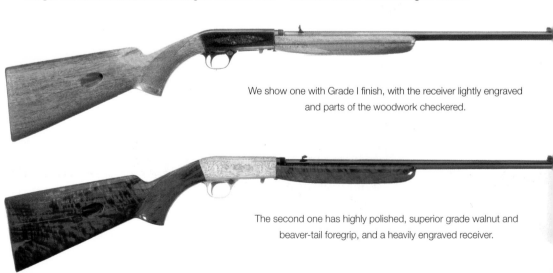

We show one with Grade I finish, with the receiver lightly engraved and parts of the woodwork checkered.

The second one has highly polished, superior grade walnut and beaver-tail foregrip, and a heavily engraved receiver.

Browning Trombone Rifle

The Trombone rifle, as its name suggests, was a slide-action rifle, with a tubular magazine and a hammerless action. It was a very popular line and remained in production at Fabrique National from 1922 to 1974, during which time some 150,000 were produced. They had open sights and featured a takedown design.

Type: Slide-action sporting rifle
Origin: John Browning and Fabrique National, Herstal, Belgium
Caliber: 22   **Barrel length:** 22in

Bushmaster M17S Bullpup

The M17S Bullpup is a lightweight, short-stroke piston, gas-operated, air-cooled, semi-automatic rifle, chambered for the .223 Remington round. It has a 20 inch, hard chrome lined barrel and; ten-round magazine. Overall length is 30 inches and the weapon {without magazine) weighs 8.2 pounds.

Type: Semi-automatic rifle
Origin: Bushmaster Firearms Inc, Windham. Maine
Caliber: .223   **Barrel length:** 21.5in

Bushmaster XM 15 Assault Rifle

This one is a Bushmaster Assault Rifle, based on the company's XM15, but with all unnecessary items deleted and with a tubular, skeleton folding butt replacing the normal fixed type. Like the XM15 it is chambered for 5.56mm but with a 20 inch barrel.

Type: Semi-automatic rifle
Origin: Bushmaster Firearms Inc, Windham, Maine
Caliber: 5.56mm   **Barrel length:** 20in

Bushmaster XM 15-E2S

The Bushmaster XM15-E2S is based on the M16A2 design, and is marketed in a variety of forms for particular purposes, e.g., shooting varmints. There is also a target-shooting version with a long barrel and no carrying handle.

Type: Semi-automatic rifle
Origin: Bushmaster Firearms Inc, Windham, Maine
Caliber: 5.56mm
Barrel length: 24in

Calico Rifle

The Calico company produces a series or futuristic-looking semi¬automatic weapons, first marketed in 1986, Indeed, they are relatively straightforward blow-back weapons, but the exterior is dominated by the large magazine which sits on top of the receiver and holds up to 100 rounds. The Model 100 and Model 100S are both chambered for .22LR and have 17.25in barrels.

Type: Semi-automatic rifle
Origin: Calico, Bakersfield, California
Caliber: see text   **Barrel length:** see text

This Calico Model 900 is chambered for 9mm and has a 16 inch barrel.

Central Arms Co "King Nitro" Rifle

The Central Arms Co was a wholesaler, not a gunsmith, and they bought in their weapons from whatever source offered the best bargain. In this case, "King Nitro" was one of the many trade names used by the Davenport Firearms Co., which was bought by Hopkins & Allen in 1901. Many companies at the time used such names including Hopkins & Allen themselves. The design of this weapon bears a similarity to that of the Savage Model 29.

Type: Slide-action rifle
Origin: Davenport Firearms Co, Providence, Rhode Island (see text)
Caliber: .22   **Barrel length:** 24in

Chinese Type 56 Rifle

The Soviet SKS, entered production in the mid-1940s, and was produced in considerable numbers in several communist bloc countries including Russia, China, East Germany and North Korea The Chinese version was designated Type 56 and was virtually an identical copy of the Soviet original. It had a folding bayonet, wooden stock, ramped rearsight and an integral, charger-loaded ten-round box magazine.

Type: Semi-automatic rifle
Origin: Chinese (PRC) state arsenals
Caliber: 7.62 x 39mm
Barrel length: 21 in

Here is a standard Type 56 showing the high quality manufacture of this communist bloc arm.

We also show a paratrooper's version, which differs rather more from the Soviet original, with plastic bodywork and pistol grip, and a composite stock which folds to the right. It has a more elaborate flash eliminator than the original carbine and does not have a bayonet attachment.

Cobray M10/M11

In the late 1940s gun-designer Gordon Ingram set himself the goal of producing a very small, compact and easy-to-manufacture sub-machine gun, which resulted in a series of weapons, starting with the Ingram Model 6 in 1949. Further work led to the Model 10, which was produced in various types between 1964 and the mid-1980s; approximately 16,000 were manufactured by a number of different companies and sold to the armed forces and police in several countries. The next weapon was the M11, which was similar in design to the M10 but slightly smaller and chambered for the 9 x 17mm Short cartridge.

The first is an M10 carbine, chambered for .45ACP, with an 18 inch barrel with vented metal cooling sleeve and wooden handgrip, together with a fixed wooden butt.

Type: Semi-automatic rifle
Origin: Cobray Industries, S.W.D Inc, Atlanta, Georgia
Caliber: see text
Barrel length: see text

This one is a CM11, chambered for 9mm Short, with a metal cooling sleeve/hand grip and a fixed skeleton butt.

Colt Colteer

The name Colteer was given to an experimental lever-action weapon, the company's first to use such an action since the Colt-Burgess of 1883. The lever-action and the associated rifle seen here were designed in 1962-3, and produced in an experimental batch, but the action proved much too complicated and the whole design was dropped.

Type: Tubular magazine, lever-action rifle
Origin: Colt Armaments Manufacturing Co, Hartford, Connecticut
Caliber: .22LR **Barrel length:** 21.5in

Colt M16 Assault Rifle

In the 1950s the Fairchild Aircraft Corporation formed the new "Armalite" division, headed by Eugene Stoner, to pursue recent advances in aluminum alloy and glass-reinforced plastic (GRP) technology. Stoner, who was an aviation rather than a weapons engineer, designed a new rifle (the AR-15) around the lighter .223 cartridge, which was intended for use against the shorter range targets now specified by the US Army. Making extensive use of light alloys and GRP, the rifle was light, handy and had minimal recoil. The ammunition was also lighter, and an infantryman could carry 280 rounds of .223 compared to 100 rounds of .30.

Type: Semi-automatic rifle
Origin: Colt Armaments Manufacturing Co,
Hartford, Connecticut
Caliber: see text
Barrel length: 20in

This is an early production Colt M16, chambered for the .223 M193 round and with a 21 inch barrel and 20-round magazine.

The M16A2 introduced a new heavier barrel with revised rifling enabling it to take the new NATO SS109 5.46mm round. The fully-automatic capability was also changed to a three-round burst setting.

Colt M16 Sport Variants

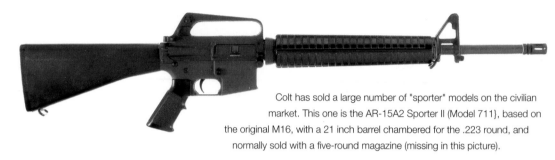

Colt has sold a large number of "sporter" models on the civilian market. This one is the AR-15A2 Sporter II (Model 711}, based on the original M16, with a 21 inch barrel chambered for the .223 round, and normally sold with a five-round magazine (missing in this picture).

The Sporter Match HBAR (Heavy BARrel) has a 20 inch barrel and a TASCO 20x telescopic sight, which is fitted with an extended sunshade.

A Sporter Target Model, with numerous additions for serious target use, including a raised cheek-piece, pistol grip rest and TASCO 3x9 telescopic sight, which is protected by a special rubber coating.

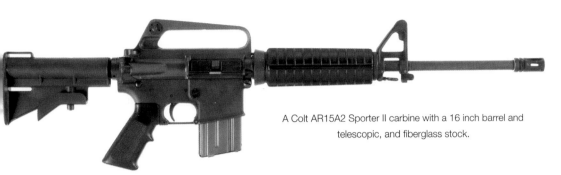

A Colt AR15A2 Sporter II carbine with a 16 inch barrel and telescopic, and fiberglass stock.

Colt-Sauer Rifle

This is a top-of-the-range sporting rifle made in Germany by J.P. Sauer & Son for Colt, who marketed it in the United States. It features an unusual action, with a non-rotating bolt, and a 24 inch barrel. Elegant yet simple, the only decoration on the plain walnut stock is a discreet rosewood fore-end and pistol-grip cap.

Type: Semi-automatic rifle
Origin: Colt U.S. and J,P Sauer & Son ,Germany
Caliber: .25-06, .270 Winchester, .30-06   **Barrel length:** 24in

Cugir AIM Sniper Rifle

Kalashnikov clones were produced in Romania at the government arsenal at Cugir, starting with the AK-47 in 1960. Production then switched to the more advanced ARM, which had a few, very minor Romanian modifications. This sniper version, dated 1997, has an unusual butt and a Romanian-made scope.

Type: Sniper rifle
Origin: Cugir armaments factory, Romania
Caliber: 5.45 x 39mm
Barrel length: 16in

Daewoo K1A1 Carbine

The KI Carbine was the first infantry weapon to be manufactured in the Republic of Korea (South Korea). It was based on the US M16 5.56mm (Armalite) and was produced in the late 1970s .It had a retractable butt and weighed some 6.3 pounds. The K1 is chambered for 5.56mm (.223 Remington) and can fire either M193 or SS109 rounds.

Type: Semi-automatic assault carbine
Origin: Daewoo Industries, Pusan, Republic of Korea
Caliber: 5.56mm (.223 Remington)
Barrel length: 21in

Dakota Arms Model 76

Dakota Arms was formed by Don Allen in 1987, originally to produce a version of the Winchester Model 70, incorporating the Grisel-patented combined bolt-stop/gas-shield/bolt guide, under the designation, Dakota 76. The weapon was produced in two grades, Classic and Safari, and a wide variety of calibers were available ranging from .257 Roberts to .458 Winchester Magnum.

Type: Bolt-action rifle
Origin: Dakota Arms Inc, Sturgis , South Dakota
Caliber: .see text   **Barrel length:** 23in

Dakota Arms Model 97 Long Range Hunter

The Model 97 introduced in 1997 is available in no less than 13 calibers from .250-6 to the company's own .357 Dakota Magnum, with a 24 or 26 inch barrel, depending upon the caliber. The black composition stock is in one piece, complete with a recoil pad. The Model 97 weighs 7.7 pounds and was followed in 1998 by a lightweight version, weighing 6.2-6.5 pounds depending on caliber.

Type: Bolt-action rifle
Origin: Dakota Arms Inc, Sturgis, South Dakota
Caliber: .see text   **Barrel length:** see text

Dakota Arms T-76 Long Bow

The Long Bow has a Dakota long-action receiver combined with a heavy, precision-engineered, stainless steel, barrel with an integral muzzle brake. It has a Kevlar/fiberglass stock with an adjustable cheekpiece and is fitted with a Picatinny rail, which, in this example, carries a very powerful telescopic sight graduated from 50 to 2,000 metres. There is also a full-adjustable bipod.

Type: Bolt-action rifle
Origin: Dakota Arms Inc, Sturgis, South Dakota
Caliber: .338 Lapua **Barrel length:** 28in

Demro XF-7 Wasp/T.A.C. Model 1

Demro (Dean Machine Products) was a small company, based in Manchester, Connecticut, which marketed two very similar weapons. The first was the Wasp, a semi-autornatic weapon with minimal furniture and a folding butt, chambered for .45AC1 and with a 17.8 inch barrel. The second was the T.A.C.-1 semi¬automatic rifle, chambered for the 9mm round, with a similar blow-back action, but with wooden foregrip, pistol grip and fixed butt.

Type: Semi-automatic rifle/carbine
Origin: Demro Inc, Manchester, Connecticut
Caliber: .45ACP or 9mm
Barrel length: 17.8in

This example is the T.A.C.-1 semi-automatic rifle with the wooden furniture.

D-Max SAR

D-Max Corporation of Springfield, North Dakota, run by Darvin Carda, produces a range of weapons, many of them imported from Israel under the Desert Eagle label. This semi¬automatic rifle works on the blow-back principle and the barrel is fitted with a vented cooling shroud. The straight magazine is on the left side of the weapon. The first weapon is chambered for 9mm Parabellum and has a 16.5 inch barrel.

Type: Semi-automatic rifle
Origin: D-Max Corporation, Springfield, North Dakota,
Caliber: 9mm/10mm
Barrel length: see text

The second weapon is chambered for 10mm with a 16 inch barrel.

Dragunov SVD Sniper Rifle

The Snayperskaya Vintovka Dragunova (SVD) appears long and bulky, but, at 9.9 pounds (with scope and empty magazine), it is actually lighter than previous sniper rifles used by the Soviet Army. The weapon entered service with the Soviet Army in 1967. It then became the standard sniper rifle of all Warsaw Pact armies, as well as of many of the USSR's allies.

Type: Semi-automatic sniper rifle
Origin: State arsenal Izhevsk
Caliber: 7.62 x 54mm rimmed
Barrel length: 22in

The example shown here was one of 1,000 imported into the United States in the 1990s and is typical of those built for the Soviet and other armies.

Eagle Arms AR-15 Copy

Eagle Arms is a division of the Armalite Corporation of Geneseo, Illinois and produces a range of AR-15/M16 clones. This weapon is an exact copy of the M16A2 with a heavy stainless steel barrel for competitive shooting and an 800 meter adjustable rear sight; weight is about 9.4 pounds.

Type: Semi-automatic target rifle
Origin: Eagle Arms, Geneseo, Illinois
Caliber: 5.56 x 45mm
Barrel length: 20in

Enfield EM-2

Known as the "Rifle, Automatic, No. 9 Mark 1," or EM-2, it was a gas-operated selective-fire weapon firing from a 20-shot detachable box magazine under the receiver. It also pioneered the so-called "bullpup" configuration, where the chamber, bolt and magazine feed are all behind the trigger group and form part of the butt. It never got beyond the prototype stage.

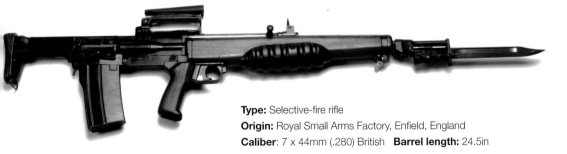

Type: Selective-fire rifle
Origin: Royal Small Arms Factory, Enfield, England
Caliber: 7 x 44mm (.280) British   **Barrel length:** 24.5in

Enfield L1A1 Self-Loading Rifle

The British version of the FN FAL, this entered service in 1954, and served until it began to be replaced by the L85 in the mid-1980s. It is only slightly modified from the FAL, the main changes being the removal of the fully-automatic fire option and the addition of a flash hider at the muzzle.

Type: Semi-automatic rifle
Origin: Royal Small arms Factory, Enfield, England
Caliber: 7.62 x 51mm NATO   **Barrel length:** 21 in

Enfield L85 Individual Weapon

This British design was intended to replace the L1A1, and began to enter service in 1985 .It is made from stampings with a plastic butt plate and ammunition is fed from a 30-round magazine.

Type: Semi-automatic rifle
Origin: Royal Small arms Factory, Enfield, England
Caliber: 5.56 x 45mm NATO   **Barrel length:** 20.4 in

FEG Model AK47

The AK-47 clone seen here is a typical product, but has been given a superior finish and a more elaborate stock with an inbuilt recoil pad to make it attractive to the United States' sporter market.

Type: AK47 clone
Origin: Femaru es Gepygar
   Reszvenutarsasag, Budapest, Hungary.
Caliber: 7.62 x 39mm   **Barrel length:** 17.5in

FN CAL

Based on the Armalite, FN decided to develop a new weapon (effectively a scaled down FAL) intended for the same 5.56mm round. The result was the CAL, seen here but as it was uncertain whether the 5.56mm round would be widely adopted the gun didn't take off.

Type: Experimental semi-automatic rifle
Origin: Fabrique Nationale (FN), Herstal, Belgium
Caliber: 5.56 x 45mm M193   **Barrel length:** 18in

FN F2000

Launched in 2001 the FN F2000is a compact and lightweight (through the extensive use of polymer components) assault rifle following the bullpup layout (see Enfield EM2.) It is chambered for the 5.56mm Nato round.

Type: Selective-fire assault rifle
Origin: Fabrique Nationale (FN),
   Herstal, Belgium
Caliber: 5.56 x 45mm Nato
Barrel length: 15.7in

FN SCAR

The SOF Combat Assault Rifle, or SCAR, is a modular rifle made by FN for the U.S. Special Operations Command (SOCOM) first issued in 2009.This family of rifles consist of two main types- the SCAR-L, for light, chambered in the 5.56x45mm NATO cartridge and the SCAR-H, for heavy, the 7.62x51mm NATO round.

Type: Selective-fire assault rifle
Origin: Fabrique Nationale (FN), Herstal, Belgium
Caliber: see text   **Barrel length:** 13.8in

FN FAL

The FAL (Fusil Automatique Leger, or rifle, automatic, light) was reliable, relatively simple to operate and maintain, and accurate at up to 600 yards. The weapon was originally designed for the 7.92mm cartridge and then adapted for the British .280, finally the FAL was redesigned yet again and, chambered for the 7.62 x 51mm NATO round.

Type: Semi-automatic service rifle
Origin: Fabrique Nationale (FN), Herstal, Belgium
Caliber: 7.62 x 51 mm NATO
Barrel length: 21 in

Fusil D'Assault MAS 5.56mm

Among the features of the FA MAS are the prominent carrying handle (which also houses and protects the sight), left or right-side ejection, a three-round burst option, and a built-in bipod, whose legs fold individually against the receiver when not in use. The weapon seen here is a commercial copy of the French Army FA MAS made by MAS, and is chambered for the .223 Remington round.

Type: Automatic assault rifle
Origin: Manufacture d'Armes de St Etienne, France
Caliber: 5.56 x 45mm   **Barrel length:** 19.2in

Galil ARM

Designed by an Israeli Army officer, Uziel Gal, the Galil 7.62mm assault rifle was the outcome of some twenty years of constant conflict in the Arab-Israeli Wars. Gal based his design on the gas and rotating-bolt system of the Russian AK-47, of which Israel had captured many thousands of examples, and combined these with the firing mechanism of the US MI Garand. The Galil ARM entered service in 1973, chambered for the NATO standard 7.62mm round.

Type: Semi-automatic assault rifle
Origin: Israeli Metal Industries (IMI), Israel
Caliber: 7.62mm
Barrel length: see text

This example is chambered for the .223 Remington round and has an 18 inch barrel, curved magazine and plastic handguard.

This one is chambered for .308 Winchester and has an 18 inch barrel.

This Galil is also in .308 Winchester
but has a 20 inch barrel.

Garand M14

The M14 takes the Garand as its basis, although there are quite a few improvements and changes. The most obvious is the addition of a 20-shot detachable box magazine and much shorter gas tube and fore-end grip, leaving more exposed barrel at the muzzle. It was originally made to fire both semi-automatic single shots and fully-automatic burst fire.

Type: Selective-fire rifle
Origin: National Armory, Springfield
Caliber: 7.62 x 51mrn NATO
Barrel length: 22in

Grendel R-31 Carbine

The R-31 was chambered for the .22 WMR round, it had a 16.75 inch barrel fitted with a muzzle brake, and the 30-round magazine was housed in the pistol grip. The skeleton butt could be extended on two tubes which were housed either side of the receiver.

Type: Semi-automatic carbine
Origin: Grendel Inc, Rockledge, Florida
Caliber: .22 WMR
Barrel length: 16.75in

Grendel 6.5 AR-15 Rifle

AR-15 (for Armalite model 15, often mistaken for Assault Rifle) is the common name for the widely-owned semi-automatic rifle. AR-15 was the commercial name for what became the militarily designated M16, the assault rifle first used by the U.S. in the Vietnam War. This version was manufactured by Alexander Arms for use with their high velocity Grendel cartridge.

Type: Semi-automatic rifle
Origin: Alexander Arms, Radford, Virginia
Caliber: 6.5 Grendel   **Barrel length:** 20in

Gwinn Bushmaster

Mack Gwinn, an SOG member during the Vietnam war, returned to the United States with many ideas on how to improve the AR-15/M16. He set up business in 1972 as Gwinn Firearms, of Bangor, Maine, but after only two years the company became part of Quality Products but is now Bushmaster Firearms Inc. of Windham, Maine.

Type: Semi-automatic rifle
Origin: Gwinn Firearms, Bangor, Maine
Caliber: .223 Remington, 5.56mm   **Barrel length:** 20in

Bushmaster Stainless Varmint Rifle

A development of the original adaptations to the AR series of guns made by Mack Gwinn, the range currently offered by Bushmaster is aimed squarely at the hunting market. The Varmint rifle shown here features a long polished stainless steel barrel, a vented tubular aluminum forend, and mini-risers on the upper receiver to mount a scope.

Type: Semi-automatic rifle
Origin: Bushmaster Firearms, Windham,Maine
Caliber: .223 Remington, 5.56mm   **Barrel length:** 24in

Griffin & Howe Rifles

The New York City firm of Griffin & Howe was established in 1923 by Seymour Griffin, a cabinetmaker by profession, who had been making bolt-action sporting rifles for some years as a sideline, and James V. Howe, the machine shop foreman at the Frankford Arsenal, Philadelphia. The company's clientele has been the rich and famous, and has included such people as Ernest Hemingway, Clark Gable, Gary Cooper and President Dwight D. Eisenhower. The company has

specialized in producing bolt-action rifles to the customer's own specifications, there is no catalog of models, as such and the three weapons shown here are simply indicative of the company's work.

Type: Bolt-action rifle
Origin: Griffin &Howe ,New York
Caliber: see text   **Barrel length:** 24in

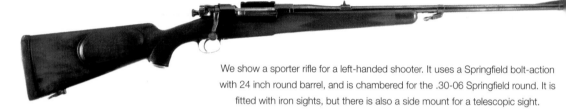

We show a sporter rifle for a left-handed shooter. It uses a Springfield bolt-action with 24 inch round barrel, and is chambered for the .30-06 Springfield round. It is fitted with iron sights, but there is also a side mount for a telescopic sight.

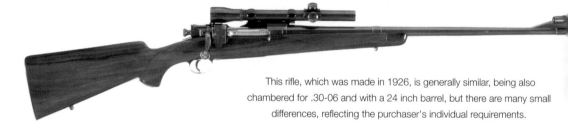

This rifle, which was made in 1926, is generally similar, being also chambered for .30-06 and with a 24 inch barrel, but there are many small differences, reflecting the purchaser's individual requirements.

Another Griffin & Howe, based on the Krag bolt-action and chambered for the .219 Zipper round. The barrel is 24 inches long and the telescopic sight is a Lyman 6x Junior Targetspot.

Harrington & Richardson Rifles

The original Harrington & Richardson company was founded amidst the firearms industry in the Connecticut valley in 1871 continuing in business until 1986. One of the partners Gilbert Harrington was the nephew of Frank Wesson, brother of Daniel B Wesson. The other was William Augustus Richardson. The company was based in Park Avenue, Worcester, Massachusetts from 1894 until it closed in 1986. Both of the original partners died in 1897, the business surviving them by nearly 90 years. During that time they made revolvers and rifles, including a contract to build M1 rifles during the Korean War. The guns shown here are representative of the company's peacetime output.

This is the H&R Model 760 semi-automatic rifle chambered for .22 LR with an 18 inch barrel.

This is the H&R Model 30 bolt-action rifle with a Tasco Golden Antler 3x9 scope on Weaver style mounts with an 18 inch round barrel.

This is an H&R Riesing Model 65 semi-automatic rifle civilian version fitted with a Redfield micrometer rear sight.

Heckler & Koch G3

Following World War Two, some German weapon designers moved to Spain, where they worked on a new rifle for the Spanish Army. This rifle, known as the CETME, used a roller-operated delayed-blowback system and later became the basis for the standard rifle for the (then) newly established West German Army. This weapon, designated Gewehr 3 (G3), became the start-point for every new German rifle design until the mid-1990s. The G3A1 had a folding butt,

while the G3A2 had a free-floating barrel, and the majority of the original G3s were modified to this standard. The G3A3, fielded in 1964, had a new flash suppressor, drum rear sight, and plastic butt.

Type: Semi-automatic rifle
Origin: Heckler & Koch, Oberndorf, Germany
Caliber: 7.62 x 51 mm NATO
Barrel length: 20in

Here is a standard G3 with a fixed butt and free-floating barrel.

This example is a G3 carbine with a short barrel and retracting butt.

Like many other assault rifles the G3 can have a grenade launcher clipped under the barrel.

Heckler & Koch Model 91

The Heckler & Koch Model 91A2, seen here, was developed from the military G3 specifically for the US civil market, with the first examples going on sale in 1974. Externally, the Model 91 is almost identical to the G3, except that it does not have the grenade-launcher ring on the muzzle. Internally, it is chambered for the .308 Winchester cartridge and the magazine carries 20 rounds. It was sold in the USA as a hunting weapon but a number of states have made ownership illegal. The other version is the Model 91A3, which is identical to the Model 91A2 apart from a retracting stock.

Type: Semi-automatic sporting rifle
Origin: Heckler & Koch, Oberndorf, Germany
Caliber: .308 Winchester   **Barrel length:** 17.7in

The Model 93 is similar to the Model 91 but chambered for the .223 round, while the Model 94 is a slightly smaller weapon chambered for 9mm Parabellum.

Both the Model 93 and 94 have 16.4 inch barrels, and in each model there are two versions available: A2 with fixed butt and A3 with retractable butt.

A standard Model 91 with a fixed butt and a 16.4 inch barrel.

Heckler & Koch Model SL7

Originally developed for the Columbian police this weapon was then modified and placed on the civil market as the SL6 in .223 caliber and SL7 in .308 caliber. Although they had a traditional wooden stock and handguard, and looked quite unlike the G3, the SL-6 and SL-7 did, in fact, have the same action.

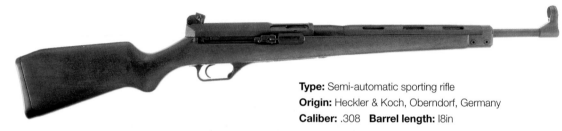

Type: Semi-automatic sporting rifle
Origin: Heckler & Koch, Oberndorf, Germany
Caliber: .308   **Barrel length:** l8in

Heckler & Koch Model SR9 Sporting Rifle

The SR9 is a linear successor to the HK91 but has several important modifications. One is that it has the company's new MSG90 buffer system, which ensures that the SR9 rifle has one of the lowest recoils of any semi-automatic. It is also equipped with a specially-designed thumbhole stock constructed of Kevlar-reinforced fiberglass.

Type: Semi-automatic sporting rifle
Origin: Heckler & Koch, Oberndorf, Germany
Caliber: 7.62x51   **Barrel length:** 19.7in

J & R Engineering M68 Carbine

The M68 carbine is chambered for the 9mm Parabellum round, with 16 inch barrel and either a hardwood or tubular stock. The muzzle was fitted with a prominent flash suppressor and there were front and rear sights with protective hoods. The 30-round magazine fitted into the pistol grip, metal parts were all fabricated from aircraft-grade aluminum.

Type: Semi-automatic police carbine
Origin: J & R Engineering, El Monte, California
Caliber: 9mm   **Barrel length:** 16in

Kalashnikov AK-47/AK-74 Assault Rifle

As soon as World War Two was finished the Soviet Red Army set out to develop a weapon that was as good as the German MP 44 with the help of captured German engineers. The Soviet designer with responsibility for the project was Mikhail Kalashnikov and the weapon bears his name. Designated the AK-47, it was, in every respect, a fine assault rifle, being well-designed, reliable, light, simple to use and to maintain - and cheap. It is also easy to fire with reasonable accuracy out to the ranges necessary in modern warfare, about 300 yards. All known variants carry a 30-round box magazine.

Type: Semi-automatic assault rifle
Origin: Soviet state arsenals
Caliber: AK-47 - 7.62 x 39mm;
    AK-74 - 5.45 x 39.5mm
Barrel length: AK-47 - 16.3in; AK-74 -15.75in

An AK-47 with fixed wooden butt. This is one of a variety of models made in many communist bloc countries.

The AKS shown here was developed with a folding stock for use by paratroopers, vehicle crews and the like. Here it is with the stock extended.

Here is an AK-74-SU with the butt folded. This was chambered for the Soviet 5.56x39.5mm round.

KDF K-14 Insta-Fire

The KDF K-14 is a Mauser-action sporting rifle, which was made in a variety of calibers, and with either 24 inch or 26 inch barrels. As sold, sights were not fitted, but this example has a Redfield scope base.

Type: Bolt-action, sporting rifle
Origin: KDF Seguin, Texas
Caliber: .25-06   **Barrel length:** 24in

Kel-Tec Sub-9 Rifle

This is one of several semi-automatic rifle designs produced by Florida-based Kel-Tec. This weapon is chambered for 9mm Luger and has a 16.1 inch barrel and operates on the blowback principle. The magazine is in the pistol grip and the weapon folds for storage, the hinge being at the front of the receiver, folded length being 16 inches. It weighs 4.6 pounds.

Type: Semi-automatic rifle
Origin: Kel-Tec CNC
   Industries, Cocoa,
   Florida
Caliber: 9mm Luger
Barrel length: 16.1 in

Kimber Model 82

In 1997 Kimber moved its operations from Oregon to a new facility in New York, where pistols are produced in addition to rifles. The Model 82 was the original design produced in the early 1980s; there were a variety of chamberings (.22, .218 or .25-20) as well as different barrel lengths and finishes.

Type: Bolt-action rifle
Origin: Kimber Manufacturing Company, Oregon & New York
Caliber: .22   **Barrel length:** 21 in

This is the Model 82A Government, one of a batch sold through the Civilian Marksmanship Program (CMP). The 25 inch barrel carries a globe-protected foresight, and there is a micrometer rear sight.

Another Model 82 variation, this time with a 22.4 inch barrel, a Leupold Vari scope and a very simple finish.

Krico Target Rifle

The Kriegskorte company was founded in Stuttgart in about 1950 and subsequently shortened its name to Krico. Its initial business lay in marketing refurbished Mauser-action rifles, but the company started producing more modern weapons to its own designs from 1956 onwards. This is a very straightforward bolt-action .22 target rifle.

Type: Bolt-action target rifle
Origin: Krico (Kriegskorte & Co), Stuttgart, Germany
Caliber: 22
Barrel length: 25in

Lewis Shock Action Semi-Automatic Rifle

Colonel Isaac Newton Lewis, U.S. Army, was the inventor of the Lewis light machine gun which was used with great success by the British during Work War I, both in the trenches and in aircraft. Colonel Lewis also designed the semi-automatic rifle seen here. The weapon worked on "shock action" which Lewis claimed, reduced recoil to negligible proportions.

Type: Semi-automatic, gas-operated rifle
Origin: Colonel Isaac Newton Lewis, US Army
Caliber: .30-06   **Barrel length:** 24in

Ma'adi Automatic Rifle Misr (ARM)

When Egypt came under Soviet influence in the 1950s they produced the AK-47, the standard rifle of all Warsaw Pact armies. The Ma'adi Company For Engineering Industries made Kalashnikov-based weapons at their factory in Cairo. The weapon seen here has the large butt with thumbhole seen on Chinese versions of the AK-47, and a ten-round magazine.

Type: Semi-automatic rifle
Origin: Egyptian state arsenals
Caliber: 7.62 x 39   **Barrel length:** 16in

Magnum Research Mountain Eagle

The Mountain Eagle bolt-action rifle was introduced in 1994 as a limited edition of 1,000 weapons, chambered for .270, .280, .30-06, .300 Winchester, .338 Winchester and 7mm Magnum, and other calibers are available. The stainless steel barrel, made by Krieger of Richfield, Wisconsin, is 24 inches long. The action is by Sako, of Rihimaki in Finland.

Type: Bolt-action, magazine-fed target rifle
Origin: Magnum Research Inc, Minneapolis, Michigan
Caliber: .280 Remington   **Barrel length:** 24in

Mannlicher Schoenauer Sporting Rifle

Sporting rifles employing the Mannlicher action combined with the Schoenauer circular magazine proved increasingly popular throughout the 20th century. They were produced in factories in Austria-Hungary (later, plain Austria) and in Germany, where particularly large numbers were made in the munitions town of Suhl by the C.G. Haenel or V.C Schilling companies. The weapon seen here is a Haenel-made model, based on the Gewehr 88, with "butter-knife" (or "spoon"} bolt handle, double set triggers and magazine floor-plate catch in the trigger-guard. It is chambered for the 9 x 57mm round, has a 24 inch barrel and weighs 6.9 pounds unloaded.

Type: Bolt-action rifle
Origin: German and Austrian gunsmiths
Caliber: see text
Barrel length: see text

This is the standard Grade Haenel model manufactured in Suhl ,Germany between 1925 and 1939.

The second weapon is a Mannlicher-Schoenauer Model 1956 made by Steyr in Austria and imported into the United States by Arms Corporation.

Marlin Model 1936 and 336

The Model 1936 was actually introduced in that year although the designation was not given until 1937. It was a direct development of the Model 1893, with a less angular stock and a barrel-band fitted on the semi-beavertail forearm. The second variation, seen here, had a thicker forearm, short tang and a B-prefixed serial number; it was produced only in the calendar year 1941.

Type: Lever-action, repeater rifle
Origin: Marlin Firearms Company, New Haven, Connecticut
Caliber: .30-30   **Barrel length:** 20in

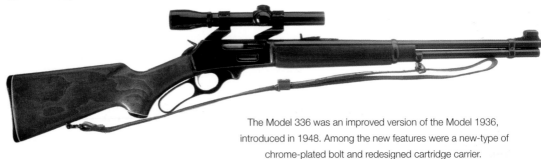

The Model 336 was an improved version of the Model 1936, introduced in 1948. Among the new features were a new-type of chrome-plated bolt and redesigned cartridge carrier.

Marlin Camp 9 Muzzlelite Conversion

Muzzelite has marketed a series of stocks which can be used to convert an existing, conventional weapon into a bullpup type. This results in a much more compact weapon with a strikingly "modern" appearance. In this case, a Marlin Camp 9 Carbine.

Type: Semi-automatic rifle
Origin: Marlin Firearms Company, New Haven, Connecticut
Caliber: 9mm
Barrel length: 16.5in,

Marlin Model 38

The Model 38 Slide-action rifle was introduced in 1920 as a hammerless successor to the Model 32, with a few other minor changes, such as different sights. It remained in production until 1930, but since its production period covered the Depression, not many were actually sold.

Type: Slide-action, repeater rifle
Origin: Marlin Firearms Company, New Haven, Connecticut
Caliber: .225, .221, .22LR **Barrel length:** 24in

Marlin Model 444S

The Model 444 is based on the Model 336, but modified to take the larger and even more powerful .444 Marlin cartridge. When the Model 444 was first marketed in 1965 it had a 24 inch barrel but this was reduced to 22 inches in 1971; there was a singe barrel band and a five-round tubular magazine.

Type: Lever-action, repeater rifle
Origin: Marlin Firearms Company, New Haven, Connecticut
Caliber: .444 Marlin   **Barrel length:** see text

Meriden Model 15 Slide-Action Rifle

The Meriden Firearms Company was in business from 1905 to 1918, making high grade double- and single-barrel shotguns and rifles, many of them with engraving of exceptional quality, although their prices, by contemporary standards, were very reasonable. We show a Model 15 with a 24 inch octagonal barrel with fancy checkering on the walnut forearm and stock, and a folding fore and rear sights.

Type: slide-action rifle
Origin: Meriden Firearms Company, Meriden, Connecticut
Caliber: .225, .221, .22LR   **Barrel length:** 20in

Mossberg Model 144 Target Rifle

From 1930 onwards Mossberg, one of the oldest family-owned firearms companies in the United States, produced a series of low-priced, bolt-action rifles, one of them, being this Model 144LSB. It has a 27.25 inch barrel chambered for the .22LR cartridge and is fitted with a globe front and micrometer rear sight. A good, no-nonsense, no frills design.

Type: Bolt-action, magazine-fed target rifle
Origin: O.F. Mossberg & Sons, North Haven, Connecticut
Caliber: .22 LR   **Barrel length:** 27.25in

Norinco Type 79 Sniper Rifle

The Type 79 has a 4x PSO sniper scope, which is calibrated for ranges out to 1,300m. The Soviet Army developed sniping to a very high level against the Germans during World War Two and this Russian design incorporated all the lessons of that conflict. The Type 79 weighs 9.9 pounds with its sight and empty magazine.

Type: Semi-automatic sniper rifle
Origin: NORINCO, China
Caliber: 7.62 x 54mm R   **Barrel length:** 24in

Norinco Model 305

The US Garand Rifle M14 was a development of the famous MI, converted to the newly-standardized 7.62mm NATO round and with a box magazine. It was produced in very large numbers, so why NORINCO should have chosen to produce a carbon copy is not at all clear-the weapon is clearly marked "Made in Rep. of China."

Type: Semi-automatic sniper rifle
Origin: NORINCO, China
Caliber: 7.62 x 51mm NATO   **Barrel length:** 24in

Norinco Model 86 Bullpup

The Type 86 was an attempt by NORINCO designers to adapt the Kalshnikov AK-47 action to a bullpup design. It is of all-metal construction, with an AK-47 bayonet, vertically-mounted, forward-folding handgrip, sight in the fixed carrying handle, and a 30-round magazine. The example shown here has a fixed bayonet, but no magazine.

Norinco MAK-90

In the early 1990s NORINCO's U.S.-based subsidiary started to import a series of Chinese-produced weapons based on the Soviet AK-47, under the generic title "MAK-90." All are chambered for the Russian 7.62 x 39mm round. Shown here are various different types, some of which vary greatly from the Soviet original.

Type: Semi-automatic assault rifle
Origin: NORINCO, China
Caliber: 7.62 x 39mm
Barrel length: 24in

Shown here is the standard model which is virtually identical to the Soviet original.

Next, we have the standard Kalashnikov action and barrel, but with the stock and handguard made of fiber. The butt is also of an unusual skeleton shape similar to that fitted to the Type 79 sniper rifle.

Our third example has a wooden stock and handgrip, but the stock is of an unusual shape with a built-in pistol-grip, which is reported by those who have used it to be particularly comfortable.

Remington Autoloading Repeating Rifle

This rifle, eventually known as the Model 8, is recoil operated. The recoil force from the cartridge pushed the barrel and breech backwards against a powerful spring, the barrel moving inside a fixed metal sleeve. The breechblock separates; throwing the empty case out of the ejection port, then a new round is picked up from the magazine and forced into the breech as both barrel and block return forward into the firing position. Five rounds are held in the fixed box magazine, and can be reloaded either singly or using a five-shot clip.

Type: Semi-automatic rifle
Origin: Remington Arms Co., Ilion, New York
Caliber: .25, 30, .32 and .35 REM centerfire
Barrel length: 22in

The standard Model 8 rifle shown here has a telescopic sight fitted. A total of 69,514 of these rifles were made.

In 1937 Remington offered the Model 81 "Woodmaster," an improved Model 8.

Remington Model 12 Slide-Action Rifle

Closely resembling a slide action shotgun, the Model 12 used a similar under-barrel tubular magazine to hold the cartridges. It became one of the best selling sporting rifles ever, with over 831,000 made in a 27-year period from 1909 to 1936.

While all Model 12s fired .22 rounds, they came chambered for a range of cartridges, with the magazine capacity varying from 10 to 15 with the size of the cartridge.

Type: Slide action repeating rifle
Origin: Remington Arms Co., Ilion, New York
Caliber: .225, .221, .22LR, .22 Remington   **Barrel length:** 22in

The Model 12B Gallery special came with a 24in barrel and extended magazine for 25 .22 Short cartridges.

This Model 12 has a factory-engraved receiver and rounded understock grip.

Remington Model 14 Slide-Action Rifle

Another designer who worked with Remington was John D. Pedersen, who in 1907 designed the Remington Model 12 slide-action .22 rifle, (see above.) The Model 14 was introduced by Pedersen in 1912. In essence it was a Model 12 modified to fire more powerful ammunition, and over 125,000 were sold by the time it was withdrawn in 1935. There were both standard versions with the 22in barrel and "carbine" models with a shorter 18in one.

Type: Slide action repeating rifle and carbine
Origin: Remington Arms Co., Ilion, New York
Caliber: Remington .25, .30, .32 and .35
Barrel Length: 18in and 22in

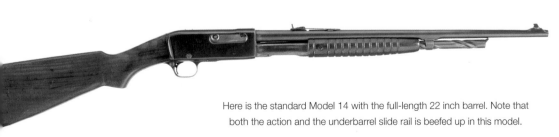

Here is the standard Model 14 with the full-length 22 inch barrel. Note that both the action and the underbarrel slide rail is beefed up in this model.

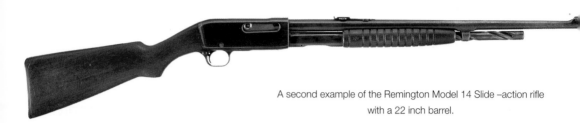

A second example of the Remington Model 14 Slide –action rifle
with a 22 inch barrel.

Remington Model 30 Express

Once World War One had ended, Remington had many parts left over from the Model 1917 Enfield rifles they had been making in such huge quantities. So in 1922 they announced the Model 30, a civilianized hunting version firing the same .30-06 cartridge. It turned out to be too heavy and expensive to be really popular, so by 1926 Remington switched to this lighter, shorter, improved version.

Type: Bolt-action, magazine-fed rifle
Origin: Remington Arms Co., Ilion, New York
Caliber: .30-06   **Barrel length:** 22in

Remington Model 24 Autoloader

Remington began selling the Model 24 in April 1922. The loading slot can be seen in the stock, just behind the semi pistol grip, which fed into a magazine holding up to 15 cartridges. The first model had a 19 inch barrel and only fired .22 S, but later variants were chambered for .22 LR and had 21 inch barrels. The Model 24 remained on sale until 1935.

Type: Semi-automatic, magazine-fed rifle
Origin: Remington Arms Co., Ilion, New York
Caliber: .22 Short, .22 Long Rifle
Barrel length: 19in and 21 in

Remington Model 34

The Remington Model 34 was first delivered in 1932. This neat bolt-action target rifle held between 22 Short, 17 Long or 15 Long Rifle rimfire rounds in its under-barrel tubular magazine. Later variants like the Model 34 N.R.A. had higher- quality Lyman adjustable rearsights, and Partridge type front sights. The whole series sold a respectable 169,922 through until 1936.The rifle weighs just 5lbs 4oz.

Type: Bolt-action tubular magazine-fed rifle
Origin: Remington Arms Co., Ilion, New York
Caliber: .22 Short, .22 Long Rifle   **Barrel length:** 24in

Remington Model 141 Gamemaster

This 1935 replacement for the Model 14 had minor improvements over the earlier gun, including a slightly longer barrel -24 inches in the rifle version, reshaped semi-beavertail fore-end and restyled stock with shotgun-style steel buttplate. The carbine model had an 18 inch barrel and only fired .30 and .32 ammunition. The Model 141 was sold until 1950, and 76, 812 were delivered.

Type: Slide-action repeating rifle and carbine
Origin: Remington Arms Co., Ilion, New York
Caliber: Remington .30, .32, and .35   **Barrel length:** 18in and 24in

Remington Model 241 Speedmaster

The Model 241 was a slightly larger, heavier upgrade of the Browning-designed Model 24. Higher-quality interior parts, an improved breech locking device and redesigned stock all made for a popular and effective package. Initial variants fired .22 Short (capacity 15 cartridges) and .22 Long Rifle (10 cartridges). Routledge proprietary smooth bore barrels were introduced in the late 1930s, although only for special orders.

Type: Bolt-action, tubular, magazine-fed rifle
Origin: Remington Arms Co., Ilion, New York
Caliber: .22 short, .22 long rifle   **Barrel length:** 24in

Remington Model 121 Fieldmaster

A 1936 development of the Model 12/Model 14 series, the Model 121 had a redesigned stock with larger pistol grip, a checkered steel butt plate, remodeled and grooved fore-end, improved recoil mechanism, 24in barrel, Model 34-style sights and higher-capacity magazine tube (14 LR, 16 L or 20 S). A later variant the 121 SB was a smooth bore (non-rifled barrel) and a magazine holding 14 Long Rifle shot cartridges.

Type: Slide-action repeating rifle
Origin: Remington Arms Co., Ilion, New York
Caliber: .22 S, .22 L, .22 LR, .22 Remington   **Barrel length:** 24in

Remington 500 Series

The first 500 series rifle was the Model 510 "Targetmaster," delivered from March 1939 as a single shot, bolt-action .22 rifle firing .225, .22L and .22LR. Later models were also bored for .22 Remington and some had 26in smoothbore barrels. Various designs of sight were used, and a scoped example is shown here.

Type: Bolt-action rifle
Origin: Remington Arms Co., Ilion, New York
Caliber: .22 S, .22 L, .22 LR, .22 Remington   **Barrel length:** 24in

Remington Model 513T Matchmaster

The 500 series was further developed to produce this target rifle. Bolt-action, as were most of the 500s, it featured a heavy 27-inch semi-floating barrel, revised stock, adjustable sling swivels, 6-shot detachable box magazine and a Retfield micrometer sight. From 1939 to 1968, over 123,000 of this successful target shooter were produced.

Type: Bolt-action target rifle
Origin: Remington Arms Co., Ilion, New York
Caliber: .225, .221, .22LR, .22 Remington   **Barrel length:** 24in

Remington Model 550 Autoloader

This was the first 500 series Remington made as a semi-automatic autoloader. Chambered for .22 ammunition, it used the blowback method, where the recoil force of the cartridge was sufficient to simply move the unlocked breechblock to the rear, eject the case and reload the next round. Various types of .22 cartridge can be used interchangeably without adjustment, and the tubular magazine could hold up to 22 Short cartridges.

Type: Semi-automatic sporting rifle
Origin: Remington Arms Co., Ilion, New York
Caliber: .22S, .22L , .22LR   **Barrel length:** 24in

Remington Model 720 Navy Trophy

A modernized replacement for the Model 30 Express, production was scheduled to begin in 1941. However, only a few thousand examples were made before war intervened, causing Remington to switch to military production.

Type: Bolt-action, hunting rifle
Origin: Remington Arms Co., Ilion, New York
Caliber: .30-06
Barrel length: 22 and 24in

Remington Model 721

The Model 721 had a long action (and long receiver), and went on sale in March 1948 in .270 Win, .30-06 and for hunters of larger game, a version with a 26 inch barrel chambered for .300 H 6c H Magnum caliber. A shrouded bolt head and ring extractor made the mechanism extremely strong, reliable and safe. In 1960 they added a .280 Remington caliber.

Type: Bolt-action, single shot rifle
Origin: Remington Arms Co., Ilion, New York
Caliber: .30-06   **Barrel length:** 24in

Remington Model 722

The Model 722 was offered simultaneously, had a shorter receiver and action, and was a little lighter than its stablemate. The standard barrel remained at 24 inches, and the rifle was initially chambered for .257 Roberts and .300 Savage. Other calibers were introduced during the life of the rifle, included .222 Remington in 1950.

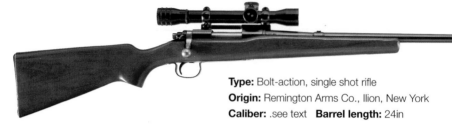

Type: Bolt-action, single shot rifle
Origin: Remington Arms Co., Ilion, New York
Caliber: .see text   **Barrel length:** 24in

Remington Model 514A

Announced in 1948, this light bolt-action rifle was a further development of the 500 series, firing .22 ammunition from a 24 inch barrel. A Model 514BC "Boys Carbine" was produced in 1961, with a 20 inch barrel and shorter stock.

Type: Bolt-action, single shot rifle
Origin: Remington Arms Co., Ilion, New York
Caliber: .22
Barrel length: 24in

Remington Model 760 Gamemaster

In 1952 Remington took their Model 12/14/141 concept and beefed it up to fire the heavier .30-06 cartridge. Other chamberings followed. The later Model 760 BDL had a 22 inch barrel and 4-shot detachable box magazine. The company had identified a strong market for such a powerful repeater, and 1,034,462 were sold through to 1980, when it was replaced by the Model 7600.

Type: Slide-action magazine rifle
Origin: Remington Arms Co., Ilion, New York
Caliber: .30-06   **Barrel length:** 24in

Remington Model 572 Fieldmaster

Introduced in 1954, the Model 572 .22 rifle was intended to replace the Model 121. The tubular magazine held 20 Short, 17 Long or 15 Long Rifle rimfire cartridges. A smoothbore variant was introduced in 1962 and a lightweight variant in 1957. The Standard version is still made at the time of writing.

Type: Slide-action, magazine rifle
Origin: Remington Arms Co., Ilion, New York
Caliber: .22 S, .22L, .22LR
Barrel Length: 24in

Remington Model 40X Rangemaster

The bolt and action of the Remington Model 721 formed the basis of this highly-accurate precision target rifle. The receiver was made to be extremely rigid; the trigger was adjustable, while the barrel rested in large cylindrical bedding surface.

Type: Bolt-action, single shot target rifle
Origin: Remington Arms Co., Ilion, New York
Caliber: .308 Win
Barrel length: 24in

Remington Model 725

The Model 725 was intended to compete with Winchester's Model 70. The new rifle had an internal magazine holding four shots, and was designed with adjustable foresights and rearsights, or could be fitted with a range of scopes. It was initially offered in .270 Win, .280 Remington and .30-06.

Type: Bolt-action, magazine hunting rifle
Origin: Remington Arms Co., Ilion, New York
Caliber: see text   **Barrel length:** 22in and 24 in

Remington Nylon 66

Gun users are often thought of as a conservative group, and new technological developments can take time to gain general acceptance. So in December 1959 this .22 caliber autoloader built on a DuPont Zytel nylon frame was seen as a startling departure. A one-piece nylon stock and receiver mounted a 19 inch barrel, steel bolt and a tubular butt magazine holding up to 14 Long Rifle cartridges. The receiver also had metal cover plates, and the whole package was remarkably light, at just over 4 pounds. Variants included green, black and brown stocks, scoped rifles, and presentation weapons with engraved receivers and chrome plating.

Type: Self-loading magazine rifle
Origin: Remington Arms Co., Ilion, New York
Caliber: .22 LR   **Barrel length:** 19in

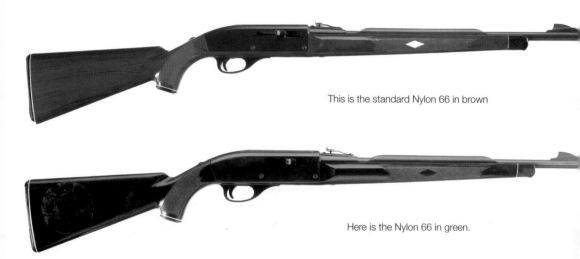

This is the standard Nylon 66 in brown

Here is the Nylon 66 in green.

Remington Model 742 Woodsmaster

This autoloader is unusual in that it used gas operation, a method more commonly seen on military rifles. Based on the Model 760, it used a rotary breech block and working parts coated with Teflon. Ammunition was held in a 4-shot detachable box magazine, and the initial offerings were chambered for .280 Remington, .30-06 and .308 Win. In 1963 Remington introduced a 6mm cartridge, then .243 Win in 1968.

Type: Self-loading magazine rifle
Origin: Remington Arms Co., Ilion, New York
Caliber: see text   **Barrel length:** 22in

Remington Model 700 Series

Based on an improved Model 721/722 the Model 700 was introduced in 1962 with a fixed magazine and 24in barrel. A significant redesign was launched in 1969, where the rear bolt shroud was extended. Since then a bewildering range of models has been produced, chambered for every important high-powered cartridge and with differing finishes, stock designs, sights and barrel lengths. Magazines were either fixed or detachable boxes. Police variants were made with Kevlar stocks, while the Model 700 also formed the basis of the Marine Corps M40 sniper rifle, some 1,000 of which saw service in Vietnam.

Type: Bolt-action, magazine rifle
Origin: Remington Arms Co., Ilion, New York
Caliber: various
Barrel length: 22in, 24in and 26in

This is a BDL, or B Deluxe Grade, one of the standard Model 700 configurations.

Known as the Varmint, this one has a laminated stock and a heavy 26 inch barrel.

This Model 700 BDL has a green synthetic stock and a satin finish to the metalwork.

Remington Model 700 Muzzleloader

There is a thriving enthusiast community for black powder shooting, although this is more common with reproduction or genuine antique firearms. Remington produced this unusual series in 1966, based on the Model 700 mechanism, but with a steel plug and percussion nipple blocking the breech, and a cylindrical hammer within the breech block instead of a firing pin. The stocks are synthetic, and come in green, grey, camouflage and black colors.

Type: Muzzleloading black powder rifle
Origin: Remington Arms Co., Ilion, New York
Caliber: .50 **Barrel length:** 22in

Here are two muzzleloaders with green synthetic stocks, one with
bright metalwork and one with blued metalwork.

Remington Model 788

This bolt-action weapon had an extremely fast and smooth action. Ammunition was fed from a 4-shot detachable box magazine, and rifles were usually sold fitted with 4 x scopes. When production ended in December 1983, over 564,000 had been sold.

Type: Bolt-action magazine rifle
Origin: Remington Arms Co., Ilion, New York
Caliber: .222, .243 Win, .308 Win, .223
Remington, .22-250, **Barrel length:** 24in

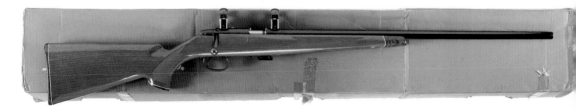

Remington Model 600 Carbine

This 1964 hunting rifle may have been relatively small and light, but it turned out to be an effective weapon with plenty of stopping power. Bolt-action, it fed from a 4-shot fixed box magazine and weighed only 5lb 8oz. We show here the Model 600 Magnum Carbine, introduced in 1965.

Type: Bolt-action magazine rifle
Origin: Remington Arms Co., Ilion, New York
Caliber: .350 Magnum
Barrel length: 18in

Remington Model 541-S Custom

A smooth bolt-action loaded ammunition from a 5-shot box magazine, and the standard of finish was high, with a one-piece walnut stock with checkering at the fore-end and grip and a scroll-engraved receiver.

Type: Bolt-action magazine rifle
Origin: Remington Arms Co., Ilion, New York
Caliber: .22
Barrel length: 24in

Remington Model 7600

Based on the earlier Model 6, this slide-action rifle was introduced in 1981. The Model 7600 was initially offered with a 22 inch barrel and a finely decorated stock and fore-end with patterned checkering.

Type: Slide-action magazine rifle
Origin: Remington Arms Co., Ilion, New York
Caliber: .30-06
Barrel length: 22in

Ruger No.1 Rifle

The Ruger No. 1 single-shot rifle has been available for many years in a various forms (Sporter, Standard, Tropical, Varminter, etc) and in some thirty different calibers; barrel lengths also vary according to the caliber from 20 thru' 22 and 24 to a maximum of 26 inches. Some are offered with open iron sights, others have no sights but are fitted with mounts for scopes.

The weapons shown here are all Number 1-Bs with 26 inch barrels, but are chambered for different calibers and have varying sighting arrangements.

Type: Single-shot rifle
Origin: Sturm, Ruger & Co, Southport, Connecticut
Caliber: see text   **Barrel length:** see text

This one is chambered for the .243 Winchester round and mounts a Weaver Classic 400 scope.

Shown here is one chambered for the .300 Winchester Magnum round and is equipped with a Leupold Vari-XII 2x7 scope.

This rifle is chambered for .270 Winchester, has both iron sights and a Bausch & Lomb scope on a Ruger mount.

Ruger Mini 14 Carbine

The Mini 14 was introduced in 1975 as a paramilitary-style semi¬automatic carbine. It had an 18.5 inch barrel and was chambered for the .223 Remington round, and used a gas-operated action. It was originally sold with five, ten or twenty round magazines, but the two larger magazines are now available to law-enforcement agencies only.

Type: Semi-automatic carbine
Origin: Sturm, Ruger & Co, Southport, Connecticut
Caliber: .223 Remington
Barrel length: 18.5in

Shown here is the standard version with the 18 inch barrel chambered for the .223 round.

This is more recent 7.62x39mm version with a 20 inch barrel and flash suppressor.

This is the alloy stocked version with folding butt, pistol grip, finned action, and ribbed forend.

Ruger Carbine

Designed to fulfil the roles of sporting, personal defense and law enforcement this compact carbine weighs in at only 6.38 pounds. Available in 9mm or .40 S&W calibers, the magazine holds 15 and 10 rounds respectively. The gun has a high impact synthetic stock with rubber recoil pad, a rugged steel receiver and chrome molybdenum barrel.

Type: Semi-Automatic Carbine
Origin: Sturm, Ruger & Co, Southport, Connecticut
Caliber: 9mm   **Barrel length:** 16.38in

Ruger Model 10/22 Rifle

The Model 10/22 appeared in 1964 and has since established an excellent reputation for accuracy and dependability. All are chambered for .22LR or .22 Magnum and are fitted with a 10 round detachable magazine and a variety of barrels and finishes. The model shown here is the Laminated Stock Sporter with a Bushnell 4x12 scope.

Type: Autoloading Rifle
Origin: Sturm, Ruger & Co, Southport, Connecticut
Caliber: see text   **Barrel length:** 20.5in

Ruger All-Weather Mini Thirty

The Ruger Mini Thirty in 7.62x39mm centerfire caliber is a good choice for small and medium sized game. A neat carbine style gun weighing in at 7 pounds, it has a synthetic stock, protected front blade sights and adjustable Ghost Ring rear sights. It also has built in scope mounts from the factory. The example shown is in matte stainless finish.

Type: Autoloading Rifle
Origin: Sturm, Ruger & Co, Southport, Connecticut
Caliber: see text   **Barrel length:** 18.5in

Ruger Model 77 Rifle

The Model 77 bolt-action rifle has been marketed since 1968 as a hunting rifle combining good quality with a reasonable price, and was in production in many versions until 1991. A five-round magazine was standard on all Model 77s

Type: Bolt-action rifle
Origin: Sturm, Ruger & Co, Southport, Connecticut
Caliber: .22
Barrel length: 22in

Ruger Model 96

Ruger also offer this modern take on a traditional lever-action rifle which according to the manufacturer offers quick follow-up shots with just a flick of the wrist. The action is enclosed to avoid grit or water affecting reloading. It is available in .17HMR,.22WMR and .44 Magnum.The 96/44 Magnum model shown features a blued barrel band, solid steel receiver ,integral scope mounts and free Ruger scope rings.

Type: Lever-Action Rifle
Origin: Sturm, Ruger & Co, Southport, Connecticut
Caliber: see text **Barrel length:** 18.5in

Ruger Ranch Rifle

The Ruger Ranch Rifle is the ideal gun to have to hand on the farm or ranch. Its handy compact form (just over 37 inches) and light weight (6.75 pounds) make it easy to stow in the pickup and just as easy to bring into action. Chambered for .223 Remington rounds, the gun has a matte stainless and blued finish, and a traditional hardwood stock.

Type: Autoloading Rifle
Origin: Sturm, Ruger & Co, Southport, Connecticut
Caliber: see text **Barrel length:** 18.5in

Sako 75 Finnlight

This latest state-of-the-art rifle from Finnish rifle producer Sako has an synthetic stock, injection molded in two parts - the pistol grip and forend is made of softer material to give a more tactile grip and to absorb recoil. The free floating barrel is cold-forged stainless steel. The gun comes in .243 Win, .260 Rem, 7mm-08 Rem and .30 Win as well as various Magnum rounds.

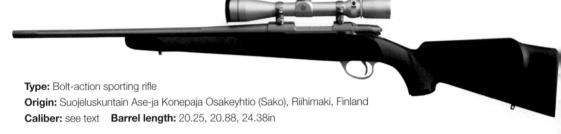

Type: Bolt-action sporting rifle
Origin: Suojeluskuntain Ase-ja Konepaja Osakeyhtio (Sako), Riihimaki, Finland
Caliber: see text   **Barrel length:** 20.25, 20.88, 24.38in

Sako Quad Hunter

This bolt action hunting rifle is designed to look and feel like a traditional hunting rifle but has a lot of the latest technology such as color coded magazines and barrels. The customer can change barrels, choosing between .22LR (coded green), 17 Mach 2 (coded blue),17 HMR (coded orange), and 22 WMR coded yellow). There is a standard 5-round short magazine and an optional 10 round long version.

Type: Bolt-action sporting rifle
Origin: Suojeluskuntain Ase-ja Konepaja Osakeyhtio (Sako), Riihimaki, Finland
Caliber: see text   **Barrel length:** 22in

Sako Sporter

Established in 1921, Sako has a varied and eventful history. First created to build and service firearms for the Civil Guard in Finland, the company played a key role in Finland's struggle for survival during World War II. Later the company grew through focusing on production excellence, and by providing innovative solutions to shooters' emerging needs. For decades Sako has developed military, target and hunting rifles, as well as cartridges. By integrating its knowledge of both the rifle and cartridge production, Sako has produced a successful range of sporting rifles, one of the earliest post-war ranges being the "Sporter" which appeared in numerous variations, many of the names being prefixed "Finn."

Type: Bolt-action sporting rifle
Origin: Suojeluskuntain Ase-ja Konepaja Osakeyhtio (Sako), Riihimaki, Finland
Caliber: see text
Barrel length: various

Among these was the Finnbear seen here in .270 caliber and with 25 inch barrel, and with a Weaver K series scope on Weaver mounts.

Another in the range, the Forester, has a shorter action and is chambered for .243 caliber, with a 23.5 inch barrel.

Here is a custom version of the Sporter based on the Model 70 in .22-250 caliber with a 24 inch barrel and fancy grain walnut stock.

Sako TRG Sniper Rifle

The TRG-22 is designed to fire .308 Winchester ammunition, while the TRG-42 uses the more powerful .300 Winchester Magnum and .338 Lapua Magnum ammunition and has a longer barrel. They are available with olive drab green (seen here) desert tan or black stocks, and are also available with a folding stock. Muzzle brakes are fitted to reduce recoil and flash, and a Zeiss or Schmidt & Bender PM II scope.

Type: Bolt-action sniper rifle
Origin: Sako, Riihimaki, Finland
Caliber: see text
Barrel length: 20 and 26in

Savage Model 19 N.R.A.

This bolt-action rifle was designed specially for NRA competition shooting. The barrel was 25.25 inches long, the magazine was detachable and the stock was extended almost to the muzzle in the style of a military rifle. It was fitted with a blade foresight and an adjustable rear sight.

Type: Bolt-action competition rifle
Origin: Savage Arms Corporation, Utica, New York
Caliber: .22   **Barrel length:** 25.25in

Savage Anschütz Model 164

In the 1960s and '70s Savage imported and re-badged the Anschutz Model 164 from Germany. This fired .22 LR ammunition from a five-round removable magazine. This weapon, while not expensive, had a good reputation for accuracy, even with cheap ammunition. The example seen here mounts a Bushnell 4x telescopic sight, but also has a folding-leaf rearsight and a hooded ramp foresight.

Type: Bolt-action sporting rifle
Origin: Savage Arms Corporation, Utica, New York
Caliber: .22 LR   **Barrel length:** 24in

Savage Model 110CL

The Model 110 was introduced in 1958 and is still in production today. It is a bolt-action weapon with either integral or detachable four-round magazines. It is produced in a variety of calibers and barrel lengths between 20 and 26 inches. The gun shown was one of a batch of ten, made in 1986, for a "top-of-the range" special issue.

Type: Bolt-action sporting rifle
Origin: Savage Arms Corporation, Utica, New York
Caliber: 30-06   **Barrel length:** see text

Savage Model 116FSS

This is the Model 116FSS, which has a top-loading action with a round, 22 inch stainless steel barrel. It is one of the models in the series where a muzzle brake is not an option.

Seven calibers are available; this one is chambered for .270 Winchester. It is fitted with a Bushnell Sportview 3x 9 scope with a stainless steel tube.

Type: Bolt-action sporting rifle
Origin: Savage Arms Corporation, Utica, New York
Caliber: .270 Win   **Barrel length:** 22in

Savage Model 10FCM Scout

The Model 10FCM is chambered for the .308 Winchester round and has a 20 inch round barrel. It is fitted with a ramp foresight and a Williams adjustable peep sight and a B-Square rail for a telescopic sight, on the barrel. It is fitted with a four-round detachable magazine.

Type: Bolt-action sporting rifle
Origin: Savage Arms Corporation, Utica, New York
Caliber: .308 Win   **Barrel length:** 20in

Sauer Model 98

This Model 98 is a fine example of long established Sauer's post-war products. It is chambered for the 9 x 57mm round and is fitted with a Voigtlander scope.

Type: Bolt-action target rifle
Origin:]. P. Sauer & Sohn, Eckernforde, Germany
Caliber: 9mm   **Barrel length:** 24in

Sauer Model 200 Supreme

This very high quality sporting rifle was produced in a variety of calibers and barrel lengths; this weapon is chambered for .30-06 and has a 23.7 inch barrel. It is fitted with a five-round magazine, and has iron sights (ramped foresight; adjustable leaf rear sight) and a spoon-shaped bolt handle.

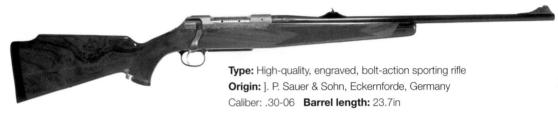

Type: High-quality, engraved, bolt-action sporting rifle
Origin:]. P. Sauer & Sohn, Eckernforde, Germany
Caliber: .30-06 **Barrel length:** 23.7in

Sears & Roebuck Ranger

The Sears & Roebuck mail-order catalog could provide customers with almost anything including firearms. The catalog company bought in models from well-known firearms manufacturers and sold them under their own label at bargain prices. This weapon, # 102.35 in the relevant Sears catalog, was in reality the Savage Model 29.

Type: Sporter rifle
Origin: Sears & Roebuck & Co.
Caliber: .225, .221, -22LR **Barrel length:** 24in

Smith & Wesson Light Rifle

The experimental "Light Rifle" was designed to compete with the MI carbine. The design was that the empty cartridge cases were ejected downwards through a slot between the magazine and the trigger group; which was extremely dangerous for any unfortunate who tried to fire the weapon.

Type: Semi-automatic military carbine.
Origin: Smith & Wesson, Springfield, Massachusetts.
Caliber: 9mm
Barrel length: 10in

Smith & Wesson Model 1500

The Model 1500 was made in Japan and chambered for .243 Winchester, .270 Winchester, .30-06 Springfield, or 7mm Remington Magnum, and there were two grades of finish: standard or deluxe. Standard grade guns had a plain wood stock and a straight comb, while the deluxe model (seen here) had a jeweled bolt and a stock of select wood with checkering.

Type: Bolt-action, magazine-fed sporting rifle
Origin: Howa Machinery, Ltd., Aichi-Ken, Japan
Caliber: .270 Winchester **Barrel length:** 22in

Squires Bingham (Armscor) M1600R

The M1600R is a semi-automatic carbine, chambered for the .22 LR round, with a 19 inch barrel. It has either ten or fifteen round magazines and is fitted with a post foresight, peep rearsight, hooded barrel, flash suppressor, and a retractable butt. The grip is made of grey plastic.

Type: Semi-automatic carbine
Origin: Armscor, Parang, Marikina, Philippines
Caliber: .22 LR
Barrel length: 19in

Standard Semi-Automatic Rifle

The Model G, seen here, looks like a slide-operated weapon, but was, in fact, a gas-operated semi-automatic, which, very unusually, could also be operated manually by releasing a catch which disconnected the gas system and then using the hand-grip which was wrapped around the gas-piston.

Type: Semi-automatic rifle (manual reversion)
Origin: Standard Arms Company, Wilmington, Delaware
Caliber: .30 **Barrel length:** 22.5in

Steyr Aug

The AUG (Armee Universal Gewehr, or army universal rifle) is actually a family of weapons built around the same bullpup frame and plastic stock. Variants can be quickly assembled by replacing components, and the family includes a 5.56mm light machine gun, a 9mm sub-machine gun and a 9mm semi-automatic carbine.

Type: Automatic assault rifle
Origin: Steyr-Mannlicher, Steyr, Austria
Caliber: 5.56mm
Barrel length: 20in

Steyr-Mannlicher Sporter Model SL

The Sporter series all have a five-round rotary magazine and are available in a wide variety of calibers. They are produced in four different action lengths (S Magnum; M - medium; L - light; and SL - super light) and with either single- or double-set triggers. The model shown here is a Sporter SL, made in 1973, with 23 inch barrel and chambered for the .223 Remington cartridge.

Type: Bolt-action sporting rifle
Origin: Steyr-Mannlicher, Steyr, Austria
Caliber: .223 Remington   **Barrel length:** 23in

Steyr-Mannlicher Luxus

The Steyr Luxus range of sporting rifles covers a wide range of calibers, but this weapon is chambered for the 6 x 62mm Freres cartridge. This recently-introduced round is manufactured by M.E.N. of Germany and is equivalent in performance to the North American 6mm-06 Wildcat, combining flat trajectory, good killing power and moderate recoil.

Type: Bolt-action sporting rifle
Origin: Steyr-Mannlicher, Steyr, Austria
Caliber: 6 x 62 Freres   **Barrel length:** 26in

Steyr Model 96 SBS

The Steyr SBS (Safe Bolt System) is produced in a wide variety of calibers: .243 Win, 25-06, .270 Win, 6.5x55, 7x64, 7mm/08, .308 Win, .30-06, 7mm Remington Magnum, .300 Winchester Magnum, 8x57JS and 9.3x62. The example shown here is in .25-06 caliber, finished in blue matte and without the scope which would normally be fitted.

Type: Bolt-action sporting rifle
Origin: Steyr-Mannlicher, Steyr, Austria
Caliber: see text   **Barrel length:** 24in

Universal Firearms Model 3000 Enforcer Carbine

The Model 3000 Enforcer is a redesign, which uses the MI action, but with an 11 inch barrel, a vented barrel cover, extended forearm and pistol grip, and without a stock-butt. It packs a lot of firepower in a very small envelope.

Type: MI-based carbine
Origin: Universal Firearms, Jacksonville, Arkansas
Caliber: .30
Barrel Length: 11 in

Valmet M1962 Assault Rifle

The M1962 is a version of the Kalashnikov AK-47 made in Finland. One of the changes to the original Kalashnikov design was that the back sight was moved from the forward end of the receiver cover to the rear end, thus considerably extending the sight-base and improving accuracy. The Finnish version also had a folding butt.

Type: Semi-automatic rifle
Origin: Valmet, Uusikaupunki, Finland
Caliber: 7.62 x 39mm Soviet
Barrel length: 16.5in

Valmet M1978 Assault Rifle

Among the Kalashnikov models made by Valmet was the M1978 which was chambered for the Soviet 7.62 x 39mm round, but had a 23 inch barrel. The weapon seen here differs from the usual M1978 made by Valmet in that it is chambered for 5.56mm, lacks a carrying handle and the rear sight is on the end of the receiver.

Type: Semi-automatic rifle
Origin: Valmet, Uusikaupunki, Finland
Caliber: 5.56mm (usually 7.62 x 39mm) **Barrel length:** 23in

Valmet M1982 Bullpup Assault Rifle

The Valmet M1982 was one of many assault rifles to appear in the late 20th century which employed the "bullpup configuration" in which the magazine is placed behind the trigger/pistol grip. The basic action was the same as in the Kalashnikov, but rearranged to suit the new configuration, and contained in a shockproof plastic polymer housing. Overall length was 28 inches and the box magazine carried 30 rounds.

Type: Semi-automatic rifle,
 bullpup configuration
Origin: Valmet, Uusikaupunki,
 Finland
Caliber: 5.56 x 45mm NATO
Barrel length: 16.5in

Walther Model KK

The Walther company has a long tradition of highly accurate, specialised .22 caliber target rifles, and following World War Two it has produced a series of weapons under the generic name Model KK (Klein Kaliber, small caliber). The example seen here is one such, fitted with a thumbhole stock and micrometer adjustable rear sight.

Type: Bolt-action, single-shot target rifle
Origin: Carl Walther, Ulm/Donau, Germany
Caliber: .22 **Barrel length:** 22in

Weatherby Mark V Rifles

Roy Weatherby founded his company in Atascadero, California in 1945 to produce top quality, high velocity rifles, mainly firing cartridges also made to his own design, although other calibers are also catered for. His rifles were originally produced in the former West Germany and a few in Italy, but all production recently moved to Japan, although without any loss in quality or craftsmanship. The Mark V is a bolt-action rifle with a Mauser action that has been produced in a large number of versions, covering many calibers and barrel lengths. This entry is designed to illustrate the wide variety of custom finishes available.

Type: Bolt-action, single-shot hunting rifle
Origin: Weatherby, Atascadero, California
Caliber: see text
Barrel length: see text

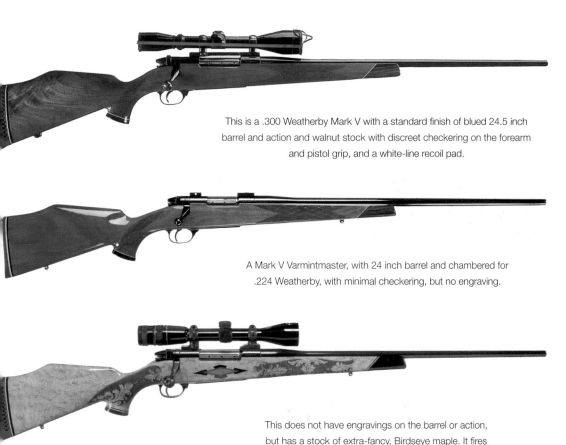

This is a .300 Weatherby Mark V with a standard finish of blued 24.5 inch barrel and action and walnut stock with discreet checkering on the forearm and pistol grip, and a white-line recoil pad.

A Mark V Varmintmaster, with 24 inch barrel and chambered for .224 Weatherby, with minimal checkering, but no engraving.

This does not have engravings on the barrel or action, but has a stock of extra-fancy, Birdseye maple. It fires .240 Weatherby through a 24 inch barrel.

Weatherby Crown Custom

This bolt-action Crown Custom model is fitted with a Weatherby Premier 3x-9x telescopic sight. It has a damascened bolt, rosewood cap to the pistol grip and to the forearm tip. Note the engraving on the barrel, receiver and floor plate, on the intricacy of the carving on the forearm and butt, and the contrasting wood inlay.

Type: Bolt-action, single-shot hunting rifle
Origin: Weatherby, Atascadero, California
Caliber: .224 Weatherby   **Barrel length:** 24in

Weatherby Mark XXII

The Type XXII was a semi-automatic .22 caliber weapon with a 24 inch barrel, which was originally produced in an Italian factory, and later in Japan. It was available in two versions: one, seen here, had a detachable box magazine, the other a tubular magazine. The gun had good quality walnut furniture and blued barrel and action.

Type: Semi-automatic rifle
Origin: Weatherby, Atascadero, California
Caliber: .22 LR   **Barrel Length:** 24in

Weaver Nighthawk Carbine

The Nighthawk semi-automatic carbine was designed in 1983 and made use of a telescoping wire stock together with a contoured wooden foregrip to assist in accurate shooting. It employed a simple blowback system.

Type: Semi-automatic carbine
Origin: Roy Weaver Arms, Escondido, California
Caliber: 9mm Parabellum
Barrel length: 16.5in

Winchester Model 52

The Model 52 target rifle was in production from 1920 to 1980 in eight successive and improved variants, as shown below. There was also a Model 52 Sporter which was in production from 1934 to 1958, which went through a similar series of improvements, with similar letter suffixes, (Sporter A, Sporter B, etc).

Type: Bolt-action rifle
Origin: Winchester Repeating Arms Company, New Haven, Connecticut
Caliber: .22
Barrel length: 28in

This is a Model 52 Target made in the early 1930s. It has a globe style foresight and a Marble-Goss rear sight.

A very late production Model 52 Target B, fitted with a Unertl 10x scope and a military style sling.

Only a very few Model 52 International Match rifles were produced and this is the prototype. It has a laminated maple and walnut stock, a very large pistol grip and cheekpiece, with an adjustable butt. There is also a full-length channel under the forearm for an adjustable aluminum fingerstop. The rear sight is a Redfield Palma model and the foresight an International Match from the same company.

Winchester Model 53

The Model 53 was an updated version of the Model 1892, which was available in just one version, the Sporting Rifle, although the purchaser was still offered a number of options.

It was available as either solid-frame or takedown, and the available calibers were .25-20, .32-20 and .44-40. There was also a choice of butt styles.

Type: Lever-action, repeater rifle
Origin: Winchester Repeating Arms Company, New Haven, Connecticut
Caliber: see text   **Barrel length:** 22in

Winchester Model 54

The Model 54 was a high-quality rifle with bolt-action and a fixed magazine, firing heavy, high velocity ammunition, including .22 Hornet, .220 Swift, .257 Roberts, .250-3000, .270, .30-06 Government, .30-30, and 7mm, 7.65mm, and

9mm. There were six rifle variants and one carbine. Rifle variants and barrel lengths were: Standard (20in, 24in or 36in); Sniper (26in); NRA (24in); Super Grade (24in); Target (24in) and National Match (24in).

Type: Bolt-action, non-detachable magazine-fed rifle
Origin: Winchester Repeating Arms Company, New Haven, Connecticut
Caliber: see text   **Barrel length:** see text

Winchester Model 61

The Model 61 was a takedown, hammerless weapon with a 24 inch round or octagonal barrel and the sales figure of 342,000 attests to its popularity. It was chambered for .22 Short, .22 Long, .22 LR only, or all three, or.22 Winchester

Magnum only. The example shown is a late production (1960) rifle with a longer slide and Redfield sight mounted on the receiver.

Type: Slide-action, magazine-fed rifle
Origin: Winchester Repeating Arms Company, New Haven, Connecticut
Caliber: .22   **Barrel length:** 24in

Winchester Model 62

The Model 62 replaced the Models 1890 and 1906 in the Winchester product line in 1932. A takedown, slide-action rifle, it had a 23 inch round barrel and the three most widely available .22 rounds - Short, Long and LR - were interchangeable. There was also a shooting gallery version, chambered for .22 Short only. The weapon shown here, which was made in 1934, is in excellent condition.

Type: Slide-action, magazine-fed rifle
Origin: Winchester Repeating Arms Company, New Haven, Connecticut
Caliber: .22   **Barrel length:** 26in

Winchester Model 67

The Model 67, introduced in 1934, was an improved and updated version of the Model 60 bolt-action rifle in .22Short, .22 Long and .22 LR and there were four variants. The Sporting Rifle had a 27 inch barrel, but there was also a Smoothbore version with a 27 inch barrel, chambered for .22 long or LR shot.

Type: Bolt-action, magazine-fed rifle
Origin: Winchester Repeating Arms Company, New Haven, Connecticut
Caliber: .22   **Barrel length:** 27in

Winchester Model 69

The Model 69 was a bolt-action rifle, introduced in 1935, designed to meet the need for a hunting and target rifle in .22 caliber, which would combine good quality with a reasonable price. The design was generally plain and business-like, with a simple walnut stock and a 24 inch barrel without tappings for iron sights.

Type: Bolt-action, magazine-fed rifle
Origin: Winchester Repeating Arms Company, New Haven, Connecticut
Caliber: .22   **Barrel length:** 24in

Winchester Model 70

The Winchester Model 70, manufactured between 1936 and 1963, is widely and justifiably known as "the Rifleman's Rifle." It started life as a replacement for the Model 54, incorporating a host of minor improvements, and there were a variations in at least eighteen calibers ranging from .22 Hornet to .458 Winchester Magnum during its 27 year production run. In 1964 Winchester introduced a new Model 70, which introduced many changes which aficionados of the old Model 70 found very hard to accept. The "pre-1964 Model 70" has a special place in the heart of most serious shooters and it is that weapon that is covered here.

Type: Bolt-action, magazine-fed rifle
Origin: Winchester Repeating Arms Company, New Haven, Connecticut
Caliber: see text **Barrel length:** see text

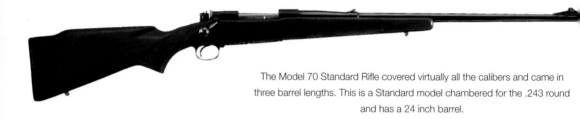

The Model 70 Standard Rifle covered virtually all the calibers and came in three barrel lengths. This is a Standard model chambered for the .243 round and has a 24 inch barrel.

In comparison, this rifle is a Standard model, but with Super Grade finish; it has a 24 inch .270 Winchester caliber barrel and mounts a Kollmorgen 2-3/4x telescopic sight on a Redfield mounts.

A scoped rifle, chambered for the US Government .30-06 round and with a 26 inch barrel. It has a Weaver K scope, but retains its iron sights.

Winchester Model 70 Featherweight

Offered as a lightweight hunter's rifle, the Model 70 Featherweight had a 22 inch barrel and was fitted with an aluminum floorplate, trigger guard and butt-plate to reduce its overall weight, the latter being replaced by a plastic plate in later models. The original Model 70 Featherweight came in a variety of calibers including .243,.264,.270,.308,.30-06,.358 between the years of 1952 and 1963 when the revised (and not immediately popular) version replaced it.

There was a Featherweight "Super Grade," so called because of the super grade stock that it was fitted with.

Type: Bolt-action, magazine-fed rifle
Origin: Winchester Repeating Arms Company, New Haven, Connecticut
Caliber: see text
Barrel length: 22in

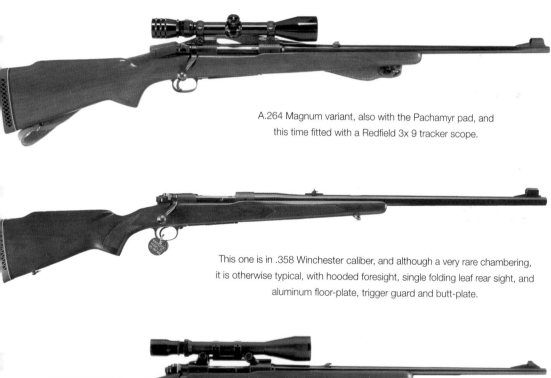

A.264 Magnum variant, also with the Pachamyr pad, and this time fitted with a Redfield 3x 9 tracker scope.

This one is in .358 Winchester caliber, and although a very rare chambering, it is otherwise typical, with hooded foresight, single folding leaf rear sight, and aluminum floor-plate, trigger guard and butt-plate.

Chambered for the .243 Winchester round, this one is fitted with the Bausch & Lomb Balart 8x scope and has the Winchester aluminum butt-plate.

Winchester Model 70 Specials

As with all of their successful models, Winchester's policy of giving the customer as many different options as possible more than prevailed with the Model 70 series. Produced in a era when many Americans were experiencing the financial boom of the post war years and for the first time for many had disposable income to spend on lifestyle luxuries like hunting rifles and ever more sophisticated hunting travel plans, including Safaris in Africa. The range of guns reflected these expectations with names like African, Alaskan and Westerner.

Type: Bolt-action, magazine-fed rifle
Origin: Winchester Repeating Arms Company,
New Haven, Connecticut
Caliber: see text
Barrel length: see text

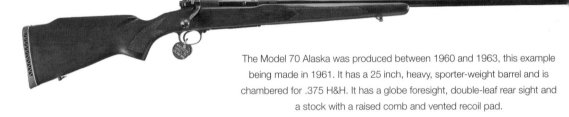

The Model 70 Alaska was produced between 1960 and 1963, this example being made in 1961. It has a 25 inch, heavy, sporter-weight barrel and is chambered for .375 H&H. It has a globe foresight, double-leaf rear sight and a stock with a raised comb and vented recoil pad.

A Model 70 African, this was made in 1956 and is reputed to be either the first or second of this type ever made. It has a .458 caliber 25 inch barrel, with "super-grade" checkering on forearm and pistol grip. The rear sight is mounted atop an unusual platform.

Made in 1953 and another African model, but in the standard grade, without any checkering. The metal rear sight has been removed and replaced by a Zeiss-Diavari-C 1.5-.5x 18 telescopic sight.

Another pre-1964 Model 70 African, made in the Custom Shop, chambered for the .375 H&H Magnum, and with a green composition stock.

This one is a Bull-Barrel, long-range target rifle, chambered for the .300 Magnum round and with a heavyweight 28 inch barrel; it was made in 1948.

Winchester Model 70 Customized

These two examples, both Model 70s, show different approaches to decoration. This first is unusual in that the stock, while of very good quality walnut, has only the most discreet checkering on the pistol grip and a rosewood forearm cap; there is none of the flamboyant carving as on the second example. Instead, the decoration is concentrated on the metal work with elaborate scrolling on the receiver and floor plate.

Type: Bolt-action, magazine-fed rifle
Origin: Winchester Repeating Arms Company, New Haven, Connecticut
Caliber: .243 Win   **Barrel length:** 28in

Here, on the other hand, the attention has been paid to the stock which is made of triple-X fancy English walnut, with an ebony forearm cap. The forearm and pistol grip are embellished with an unusual basket-weave carving and an African "bush" scene.

Winchester Model 70 Rarities

The Model 70 was made in such numbers and in so many varieties that it is inevitable that there should be some rarities, even some "one-offs" - and a tiny selection is shown here.

Type: Bolt-action, magazine-fed rifle
Origin: Winchester Repeating Arms Company, New Haven
Caliber: .243 Win   **Barrel length:** 28in

This one is unusual because only 2,500 Model 70s were made in the .250-3000 Savage caliber.

A Model 70 in .35 Remington caliber, made in 1946. This is another rarity which was made in only slightly larger numbers than the .300 Savage weapons.

This was an experimental model with a 28 inch barrel, chambered for the .305WCF round. It was a single-shot weapon, with a solid bottom to the receiver and no magazine parts under the floor.

Winchester Model 71

The Model 71 replaced the Model 1886 in 1935 and was, in effect, the Model 1886 updated and strengthened to take the more powerful .348 cartridge. There were two variants, Rifle {24 inch barrel) and Carbine (20 inch barrel), each with two grades, Standard and De Luxe. A total of about 47,000 were manufactured between 1935 and 1957.

Type: Lever-action, repeater rifle
Origin: Winchester Repeating Arms Company, New Haven, Connecticut
Caliber: .348   **Barrel length:** 24in and 20in

Winchester Model 72

The Model 72 was another entry in the huge .22 market, being introduced in 1938 and remaining in production until 1959, during which time some 161,000 rifles were manufactured. It was a bolt-action, single-shot rifle, with a tubular, under-barrel magazine. Most were sold with open or peep sights, although some of the earlier sales had simple telescopic sights.

Type: Bolt-action rifle
Origin: Winchester Repeating Arms Company, New Haven, Connecticut
Caliber: .22   **Barrel length:** 25in

Winchester Model 74

This semi-automatic rifle had a 24 inch barrel and was chambered for the .22 Short and .22 LR, the rounds being held in a tubular magazine in the buttstock. There were two variants, one a Sporting Model, the second a Gallery Special, which was chambered for .22 Short only.

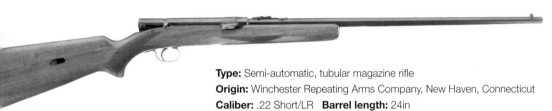

Type: Semi-automatic, tubular magazine rifle
Origin: Winchester Repeating Arms Company, New Haven, Connecticut
Caliber: .22 Short/LR   **Barrel length:** 24in

Winchester Model 75

The Model 75 was a .22 bolt-action rifle which was available as a Sporting Rifle with a 24 inch round barrel and walnut stock and a Target Rifle had a 28 inch barrel.

Type: Bolt-action rifle
Origin: Winchester Repeating Arms Company, New Haven,
Caliber: .22   **Barrel length:** see text

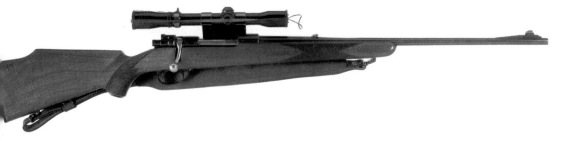

Winchester Model 77

The Model 77 was manufactured from 1955 to 1963, a relatively short production run, but during which some 217,000 were sold. It was a blowback rifle with a 22 inch barrel, and was chambered for the .22LR only, the rounds being fed from either a detachable box magazine or from an under-barrel tubular magazine.

Type: Semi-automatic rifle
Origin: Winchester Repeating Arms Company,
New Haven, Connecticut
Caliber: .22   **Barrel length:** 22in

Winchester Model 88

The Model 88 was introduced in 1955 to mark the Winchester company's one-hundredth anniversary and is often known as the "Centennial Model." There were two variants, the Rifle, with a 22 inch barrel, introduced in 1955 and the Carbine, with a 19 inch barrel, in 1968, production of both ending in 1968 after some 283,000 had been produced. Both Rifle and Carbine had a short-stroke lever action.

Type: Lever-action rifle
Origin: Winchester Repeating Arms Company, New Haven, Connecticut
Caliber: see text   **Barrel length:** 25in

Winchester Model 94

The new Model 94 entered production in 1964 as an updated Model 1894. The design features a short-stroke lever action with 20 or 24 inch barrels, chambered for .30-30, 7-30 or .44 Magnum cartridges, and a tubular magazine accommodating six or seven rounds, depending on the barrel length. There have been minor changes over the years; for example, .480 Ruger caliber was added in 2003.

Type: Lever-action rifle
Origin: Winchester Repeating Arms Company, New Haven, Connectic
Caliber: see text   **Barrel length:** 20 or 24in

There were two spectacular special issues by the Custom Shop in support of the Hunting and Shooting Sports Heritage Fund, both with 26 inch part octagonal barrels chambered for .38-55. In the "One-of-a-Thousand" issue the action was engraved with gold wire borders and gold inlaid vignettes on either side, with the stock in very high quality walnut stock with checkered pistol grip and forearm.

Winchester Model 9422

The Model 9422, introduced in 1971, has the appearance of a Model 94 but in the ever-popular .22 caliber, with a 20.5 inch barrel chambered for .22 and .22 Magnum rimfire. It is fitted with a tubular, under-barrel magazine, which houses various numbers of rounds depending on the caliber: .22 Short (21); .22 Long (17); .22 LR (15); and .22 Magnum (11).

Type: Lever-action rifle
Origin: Winchester Repeating Arms Company, New Haven, Connecticut
Caliber: .22   **Barrel length:** 20.5in

Akah Drilling

Akah is a large (and existing) German sports goods chain, the name being the German phonetic abbreviation for Albrecht Kind (AK = Albrecht and child). Like United States hardware chains and mail order houses, Akah buys in goods such as shotguns from established manufacturers and then sells them under its own name. This drilling has two 16 gauge shotgun barrels and one 8mm rifle barrel.

Type: Shotgun/rifle
Origin: Akah, Germany
Caliber: 16 gauge/8mm   **Barrel length:** 25.5in

Antonio Zoli Ritmo Single-Barrel Trap Shotgun

Antonio Zoli of Brescia makes a range of shotguns, amongst which is this Ritmo trap gun, with an unusually configured vented rib, designed to maximize the heat dissipation from the barrel. The gun has a checkered pistol grip style walnut stock with a recoil pad on the butt.

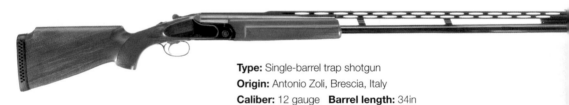

Type: Single-barrel trap shotgun
Origin: Antonio Zoli, Brescia, Italy
Caliber: 12 gauge   **Barrel length:** 34in

Antonio Zoli Combinato Safari De Luxe Shotgun/Rifle

The Combinato (combination), shown here combines a rifle barrel in 7mm caliber and a shotgun in 12 gauge in an over-and-under configuration, but is also made with barrels in .222 caliber and 20 gauge. The Combinato has box-lock action, double triggers, a folding-leaf rear sight and a 2.75 inch chamber with screw-in choke system.

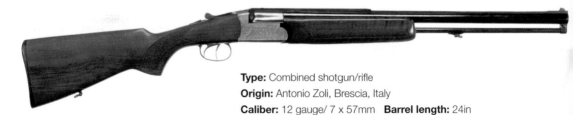

Type: Combined shotgun/rifle
Origin: Antonio Zoli, Brescia, Italy
Caliber: 12 gauge/ 7 x 57mm   **Barrel length:** 24in

Angelo Zoli Over-and-Under Shotgun

This over-and-under shotgun was made by Italian gunsmith Angelo Zoli (not to be confused with Antonio Zoli, also of Brescia, Italy). This shotgun has an extra full ventilated rib above the top barrel and vents in the spine between the upper and lower barrels. The gun is very well finished with engraved side plates and a Monte Carlo stock with a white line butt recoil pad.

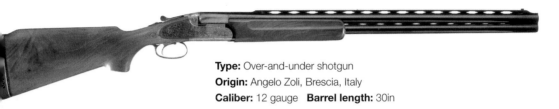

Type: Over-and-under shotgun
Origin: Angelo Zoli, Brescia, Italy
Caliber: 12 gauge   **Barrel length:** 30in

American Arms Brittany Double-Barrel Shotgun

The traditionally designed Brittany model entered production in 1989 and was a double-barrel, boxlock shotgun in either 12 gauge with a 27 inch barrel or 20 gauge with a 25 inch barrel. It had automatic ejectors and a single selective trigger. The action was engraved and the walnut stock was checkered.

Type: Double-barrel shotgun
Origin: American Arms, Inc., North Kansas City, Missouri
Caliber: 12/20 gauge
Barrel length: 25, 27in

American Arms Model Silver II Over-and-Under Shotgun

The American Arms company has some manufacturing capability in the United States but the majority of their products are imported from Europe, including the shotguns from Spain where there is a tradition in the manufacture of fine shotguns. This small bore over-and-under shotgun, the Silver II, has two superposed 26 inch vent-ribbed barrels, engraving on the action and a walnut stock.

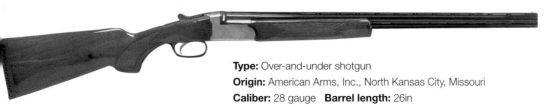

Type: Over-and-under shotgun
Origin: American Arms, Inc., North Kansas City, Missouri
Caliber: 28 gauge   **Barrel length:** 26in

Aubrey Double-Barrel Shotgun

Albert J. Aubrey had a gunmaking business at Meriden, Connecticut and much of his output was sold through Sears, Roebuck of Chicago, Illinois. This double-barrel, side-by-side shotgun is a typical traditional looking product, with 32 inch barrels, sidelock action, extractors, double triggers and tang safety.

Type: Double-barrel shotgun
Origin: A.J. Aubrey, Meriden, Connecticut
Caliber: 12 gauge   **Barrel length:** 32in

Baker Trap Gun Elite Grade

Absorbed into Stevens Arms in 1933, the Baker range ceased to be produced in about 1923. The Baker Trap Gun was produced in two finishes, of which the one shown here was the higher, Elite Grade. It has a vent-ribbed 32 inch barrel, with two ivory beads and full choke, and a floral engraved action, with bird dog and duck scenes. The extra fancy pistol grip has extensive fleur-de-lis checkering.

Type: Single-barrel trap shotgun
Origin: Baker Gun & Forging Co., Batavia, New York
Caliber: 12 gauge
Barrel length: 32in

Belknap Shotgun

The Belknap Hardware company bought their firearms from professional manufacturers such as Savage, and Stevens. The Belknap weapons, like their other hardware, were known for their combination of ruggedness, serviceability and reasonable prices. This slide-action shotgun, the Belknap Model B64, is a typical product, being simple, easy-to-use, but thoroughly effective. It is a 12 gauge gun with a 28 inch barrel.

Type: Slide-action shotgun
Origin: Belknap Hardware Co., Louisville, Kentucky
Caliber: 12 gauge   **Barrel length:** 28in

Beretta AL 390 Silver Mallard

Beretta's AL 390 series of semi-automatic shotguns are produced in a variety of models including the Silver Mallard, shown here. This is in keeping with the company's policy of naming guns after game birds. This is a 12 gauge gun with a 28 inch vent-rib barrel and a three-round tubular magazine. It has a 2.75 and 3 inch chamber and a screw-in variable choke system.

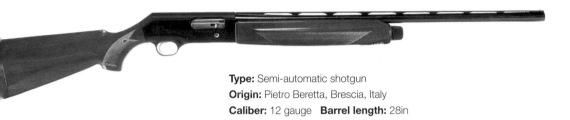

Type: Semi-automatic shotgun
Origin: Pietro Beretta, Brescia, Italy
Caliber: 12 gauge   **Barrel length:** 28in

Beretta BL Series Over-and-Under Shotgun

Beretta's BL shotguns are in either 12 or 20 gauge with 26, 28 or 30 inch vent-ribbed barrels, or, in the case of the BL-2 only, in 18 inch unribbed. They have boxlock actions (sidelock in BL-6), either manual extraction or automatic ejection, and are fitted with either single or double triggers. The series was in production from 1968 to 1973 and some eleven variants were offered.

Type: Over-and-under shotgun
Origin: Pietro Beretta, Brescia, Italy
Caliber: 12 gauge
Barrel length: 28in

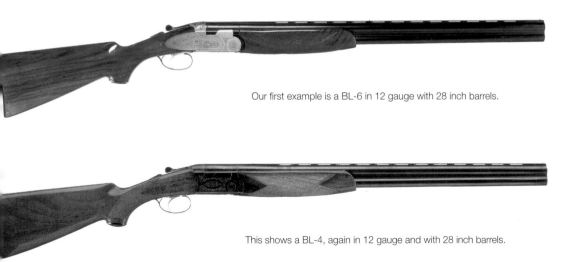

Our first example is a BL-6 in 12 gauge with 28 inch barrels.

This shows a BL-4, again in 12 gauge and with 28 inch barrels.

Here we show a BL-2 "Stakeout," also in 12 gauge, but with much shorter 18 inch barrels. As the name suggests this is for martial use rather then sporting.

Beretta Model S682 X

The Beretta 682 series high-quality over-and-under shotguns are made in Italy in four calibers and various barrel lengths. All are fitted with a single trigger and automatic ejectors, and the barrels have a vented-rib. As part of the quality image the stock and forearm are made from high-grade walnut with checkering, and the frame is engraved. The model shown here is the S682X, which has a very prominent vented-rib barrel, 32 inches in length with Briley-type chokes. The Monte Carlo stock has an adjustable butt and a leather-covered adjustable butt.

Type: Over-and-under shotgun
Origin: Pietro Beretta, Brescia, Italy
Caliber: 12 gauge   **Barrel length:** 32in

Bernardelli Gamecock Double-Barrel Shotgun

The Bernardelli Gamecock double-barrel shotgun is produced with 25.75 or 27.5 inch barrels in 12, 16, 20, or 28 gauge, with a variety of chokes. Extractors were standard but ejectors could be installed, if requested. The example seen here has 28 inch barrels with modified and improved chokes and 3 inch chambers. It has a walnut stock with a straight grip in what is known as "the English style."

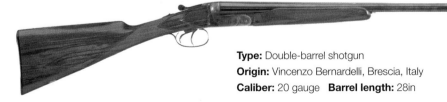

Type: Double-barrel shotgun
Origin: Vincenzo Bernardelli, Brescia, Italy
Caliber: 20 gauge   **Barrel length:** 28in

Collath Side-by-Side Shotgun/Rifle

This weapon has two barrels, a 9mm rifle and 18 gauge shotgun, a combination normally known as a "cape gun." It has underlever action, which is covered in deep-relief engravings depicting fox and duck on the left, rabbit and partridge on the right, with a stag's head, roebuck and capercaillie on the tang. There is also a prominent butterfly-wing safety on the tang.

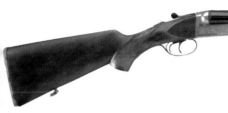

Type: Shotgun/rifle
Origin: W. Collath & Sohne, Frankfurt a. O, Germany
Caliber: 18 gauge/9mm
Barrel length: 27.5in

Cosmi Standard

Cosmi is a small Italian gunmaker, whose weapons are imported into the United States by Autumn Sales, Inc, of Fort Worth, Texas. Cosmi's main current product is the Standard Model semi-automatic shotgun, which is available in either 12 or 20 gauge. It is of very unusual design, in that it is a top-break weapon, but up to eight cartridges are then loaded through the open action back into the buttstock.

Type: Semi-automatic shotgun
Origin: A & F Cosmi, Torrette, Italy
Caliber: 20 gauge   **Barrel length:** 25in

Classic Double Model 201 Double-Barrel Shotgun

Classic Double is a Japanese company, whose shotguns were imported into the United States until 1987 by Winchester. The example seen here is the Classic Model 201, which became the Winchester Model 101. It is a double-barrel, side-by-side boxlock shotgun in either 12 or 20 gauge, but with a barrel length of 26 inches only. The barrels have vented ribs and screw-in chokes, and there is a single selective trigger.

Type: Double-barrel shotgun
Origin: Classic Double, Togichi City, Japan
Caliber: 12 gauge   **Barrel length:** 26in

Browning Model Auto-5

The Auto-5 recoil-operated, semi-automatic shotgun was designed by John Browning and has been produced in great numbers in Belgium, Japan and the United States, but always under the Browning label. It was made by Fabrique Nationale in Belgium from 1903 to 1939, then by Remington in the United States on Browning's behalf from 1940 to 1942. Production returned to Belgium again in 1952 and remained with FN until 1976, by which time FN's total production since 1903 had totalled 2,750,000.

Production then switched to B.C. Miroku in Japan, where it continued until 1999, when production ended with a "final tribute" series of one thousand.

Type: Semi-automatic shotgun
Origin: Browning (Fabrique Nationale, Herstal, Belgium).
Caliber: 12 gauge
Barrel length: see text

This one is a Belgian-made Auto-5 with a 26 inch solid-ribbed barrel and fancy checkering on the walnut forearm and stock.

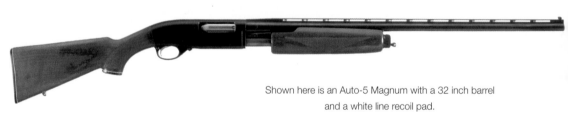

Shown here is an Auto-5 Magnum with a 32 inch barrel and a white line recoil pad.

This Auto-5 "Sweet Sixteen" 16 gauge shotgun, with a 28 inch barrel, modified choke, 2.75 inch chamber and walnut stock with a round-knob pistol grip.

Browning Superposed Diana Grade 3 Shotgun

This Browning Superposed shotgun has the Diana Grade Three finish with engravings by Felix Funcken. The engravings feature pheasants on the left and ducks on the right with quails on the bottom and rabbits on the trigger guard. Most sporting shotguns feature game birds and animals by tradition. The walnut stock is fitted with a Pachmayr white line recoil pad. It is a 12 gauge gun with 30 inch barrels.

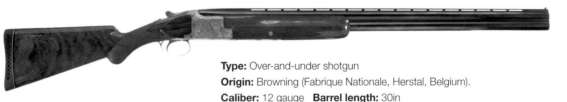

Type: Over-and-under shotgun
Origin: Browning (Fabrique Nationale, Herstal, Belgium).
Caliber: 12 gauge   **Barrel length:** 30in

Browning Liege Over-and-Under Skeet Shotgun

The Browning Liege 12 gauge over-and-under was manufactured by FN, Herstal from 1973 to 1975, and was made in only three barrel lengths - 26.5, 28 and 30 inches - all with vented ribs and a variety of chokes. It had a boxlock action and blued finish with checkered walnut stock. Shown here is the Grand De Luxe version with a Broadway vented rib and skeet chokes.

Type: Over-and-under (superposed) skeet shotgun
Origin: Browning (Fabrique Nationale, Herstal, Belgium).
Caliber: 12 gauge   **Barrel length:** 27.5in

Browning Lightning

The Browning Superposed shotgun, , was introduced in 1930, and remained in production at Fabrique Nationale in Belgium, until the war disrupted manufacture, returning to production in 1947 until 1976.There were four grades of finish: Grade I, Pigeon, Diana, and Midas. Only 12 Gauge was offered initially with 20, 28,and .410 gauge being added as production continued. The gun shown here was built in 1966 and has a 26.5 inch vent-rib barrel, some engraving and a gold-washed trigger.

Type: Over-and-under shotgun
Origin: Browning (Fabrique Nationale,Herstal, Belgium).
Caliber: see text   **Barrel length:** see text

Double Automatic Shotgun

The "Double Automatic" derives its name from the fact that its tubular magazine holds just two rounds, giving it no more firepower than a double-barreled or over-and-under shotgun, but perhaps with a slight saving in weight. The example shown here has a 30 inch barrel, but lengths of 26 and 28 inches were also available.

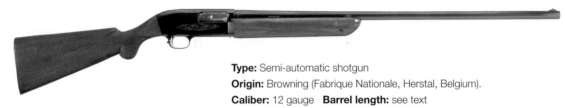

Type: Semi-automatic shotgun
Origin: Browning (Fabrique Nationale, Herstal, Belgium).
Caliber: 12 gauge   **Barrel length:** see text

Browning Waterfowl Series

Each of the series was named for and depicted a particular bird in the engraved vignettes. First was the "Mallard" issued in 1981 All were in 12 gauge, with 28 inch vent-ribbed, blue/satin grey, barrels, French grey action and black walnut stock with round knob stock. The action, trigger and trigger guard were all engraved in deep relief.

Type: Over-and-under
    shotgun
Origin: Browning
    (Fabrique Nationale,
    Herstal, Belgium).
Caliber: 12 gauge
Barrel length: 28in

Browning BPS Slide-action Shotgun

The BPS manufactured in Japan by B.C. Miroku features vent-ribbed barrels in various lengths, all of which are fitted for Invector screw-in chokes; calibers are 10, 12, and 20 gauge, and there is a five round tubular magazine. Barrels and action are of steel and the stock and forearm are of synthetic composition.

Type: Slide-action shotgun
Origin: Browning (B.C. Miroku, Japan)
Caliber: see text   **Barrel length:** see text

Browning Modified Trap Gun

This gun started as a standard Lightning over-and-under but little of that original weapon remains. The top barrel has been cut off and plugged and an elaborate (and unsightly) vented rib installed above the remaining barrel. The stock has also been altered by the addition of a 1.7 inch extension to the comb.

Type: Trap shotgun
Origin: Browning (Fabrique Nationale, Herstal, Belgium)
Caliber: 12 gauge   **Barrel length:** 32in

Browning Over-and-Under Shotgun

The .410 caliber over-and-under shotgun was made to a high standard by Fabrique Nationale in Belgium and then engraved by Master-Engraver Angelo Bee of Chatsworth, California. The action is decorated with, on the left, a quartet of quail in a prairie scene, all inlaid in gold and surrounded by gold inlaid vines. Gold wire and vines also decorate the tang, trigger guard and latch. The work is signed "A. Bee."

Type: Over-and -under shotgun
Origin: Browning (Fabrique Nationale, Herstal, Belgium).
Caliber: .410 gauge   **Barrel length:** 28in

Browning Citori 525 Field

A fine example of Browning craftsmanship where traditional build techniques such as "lampblack and file" are still used to achieve superlative fit of components. This multi-choke 28 Gauge shotgun has a 26 inch vented rib barrel, blued finish with contrasting silver nitride receiver with scroll engraving, checkered satin finish walnut stock and dayglo orange bead sights.

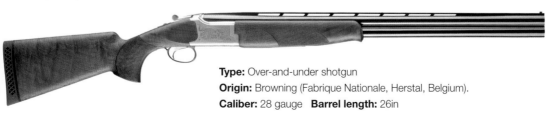

Type: Over-and-under shotgun
Origin: Browning (Fabrique Nationale, Herstal, Belgium).
Caliber: 28 gauge   **Barrel length:** 26in

Browning Cynergy Sporting Composite

This futuristic-looking shotgun has a composite stock with an adjustable comb, with rubber overmoldings in the grip areas. The Inflex recoil pad built into the butt reduces felt recoil to an agreeable level. The gun comes with 3 Invector "Diana" grade choke tubes. The Cynergy series comes with a Monoblock hinge which employs a greater surface area to reduce wear. This example is in black but other colors like yellow are particularly eye-catching.

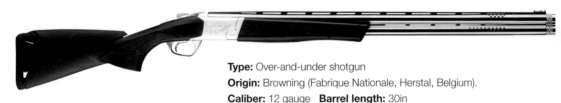

Type: Over-and-under shotgun
Origin: Browning (Fabrique Nationale, Herstal, Belgium).
Caliber: 12 gauge   **Barrel length:** 30in

Browning Silver Micro

Designed with the smaller or younger shooter in mind; the Browning Silver Micro features a compact stain finish walnut stock, and an aluminum receiver to minimise weight. It has a choice of three Invector Plus chokes; Full, Modified, and Improved Cylinder. The Magazine holds 4 rounds of 20 gauge ammunition. It is finished in matt silver with a vented rib barrel.

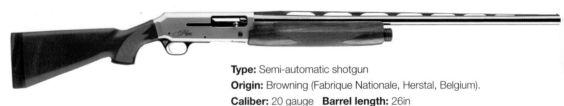

Type: Semi-automatic shotgun
Origin: Browning (Fabrique Nationale, Herstal, Belgium).
Caliber: 20 gauge   **Barrel length:** 26in

Browning Model BT-99 Single-Barrel Trap Gun

The BT-99, manufactured in Japan by B.C. Miroku, was introduced in 1968 and versions remain in production today. It is a boxlock, single-barrel, break-open trap gun, with either 32 or 34 inch vent-ribbed barrel, with the muzzle tapped for a screw-in choke. It is fitted with automatic ejectors. The example shown is a BT-99 Pigeon grade, with a 32 inch vent-ribbed barrel and an adjustable recoil pad assembly, and a triple X fancy walnut stock.

Type: Single-barrel shotgun
Origin: Browning (B.C. Miroku, Japan)
Caliber: 12 gauge   **Barrel length:** see text

Browning Gold Light Mossy Oak

A classic Turkey gun which is endorsed by the National Wild Turkey Federation.It has three interchangeable Invector choke tubes including a special "Full" Turkey grade. The 5 shot magazine is one of the largest of any 10 gauge shotgun. It has an alloy receiver and comes in a variety of camouflaged color schemes including this Mossy Oak break-up pattern.

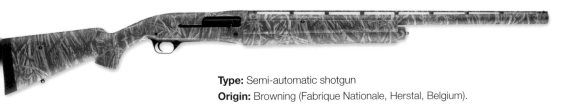

Type: Semi-automatic shotgun
Origin: Browning (Fabrique Nationale, Herstal, Belgium).
Caliber: 10 gauge   **Barrel length:** 28in

Browning Maxus

One hundred and five years on from John M. Browning's groundbreaking Auto-5 shotgun ,this new state-of-the-art autoloading shotgun offers a new Power Drive Gas System based on Brownings original but employing a greatly improved longer stroke gas piston and larger exhaust ports to dump excess gases. This results in appreciably less muzzle jump and felt recoil which as Browning say quite simply translates into more birds in the bag!

Type: Semi-automatic shotgun
Origin: Browning (Fabrique Nationale, Herstal, Belgium).
Caliber: 12 gauge   **Barrel length:** 26, 28in

Eastern Arms Single-Barrel Shotgun

This was another of the many shotguns produced by a major manufacturer for a hardware company, in this case by Iver Johnson for Sears & Roebuck, using the trade name "Eastern Arms." It is a 20 gauge weapon with a 27.75 inch barrel and, like all such "Hardware Guns," as they are called, it is simple, straightforward and robust.

Type: Single-barrel shotgun
Origin: Eastern Arms (Iver Johnson)
Caliber: 20 gauge   **Barrel length:** 27.75in

Federal Gas Riot Gun

Issued to the highways department of the Illinois State Police this gas gun was designed and made by Federal Gas Laboratories Inc, of Pittsburgh, Pennsylvania and operated on the "tip-up" principle to fire standard 37mm (1.5 inches) cartridges. There is a fixed sight on the breech marked "50 yards" and a folding sight on the receiver marked for 75 and 100 yards.

Type: Anti-riot shotgun
Origin: Federal Laboratories
     Incorporated of America
Caliber: 37mm
Barrel length: 12in

Fox Sterlingworth Double-Barrel Shotgun

The Sterlingworth shotguns, made from 1911 to 1946, were double-barreled weapons with 26, 28 or 30 inch barrels and extractors; automatic ejectors were also available, and double triggers were normally fitted. The example seen here is 12 gauge, with a 28 inch barrel, a walnut stock and, a single trigger. The owner of this weapon has added a 2 inch extension to the stock and a recoil pad.

Type: Double-barrel shotgun
Origin: A.H. Fox, Philadelphia, Pennsylvania
Caliber: 12 gauge   **Barrel length:** 28in

Fox Single-Barrel Trap Gun

This was one of some 570 single-barrel trap guns, designed in 1918-19 by A.H. Fox and made between 1919 and 1936. There were four grades: J, K, L and M. The example seen here is grade JE, with the E-suffix indicating that it is fitted with automatic ejectors. It has a 32 inch, 12 gauge barrel and has some fine engraving on barrel and action.

Type: Single-barrel shotgun
Origin: A.H. Fox, Philadelphia, Pennsylvania
Caliber: 12 gauge   **Barrel length:** 32in

Franchi Model 2004 Single-Barrel Trap Gun

Italian weapons manufacturer, Franchi of Brescia, exports a vast range of sporting guns to the United States. One of these was the Model 2004 (the model number has nothing to do with the calendar year), single-barrel trap gun, with a prominent ventilated rib, seen here.

Type: Single-barrel trap gun
Origin: L. Franchi, Brescia, Italy
Caliber: 12 gauge   **Barrel length:** 34in

Franchi Spas 12

Franchi is noted for its line of good quality sporting shotguns, but it also developed the SPAS (Special Purpose Automatic Shotgun} specifically for military or anti-riot duties. The first of a series of models was introduced in 1979 and the SPAS-12 is shown here. The SPAS is capable of operating either in the gas-operated, self-loading mode or in a manually-operated, slide-action mode, which are selected by a small two-position button.

Type: Anti-riot shotgun
Origin: Luigi Franchi Development, Brescia, Italy
Caliber: 12 gauge   **Barrel length:** 21.5in

Franchi Semi-Automatic Shotgun

Franchi has produced a series of semi-automatic shotguns and this one has been given the custom engraving treatment. It has a 28 inch vent-ribbed barrel which is fitted with an adjustable poly choke. The receiver has been engraved with silver lined scenes depicting pheasants on the left and ducks on the right.

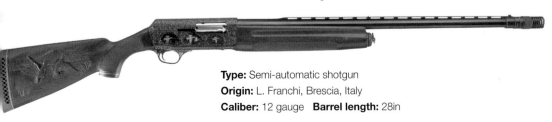

Type: Semi-automatic shotgun
Origin: L. Franchi, Brescia, Italy
Caliber: 12 gauge   **Barrel length:** 28in

Franchi AL-48

The Franchi AL-48 is a semi-automatic, long-recoil shotgun in 12 or 20 gauge, with 24 or 28 inch barrels, or in 28 gauge with a 26 inch barrel only. All are fitted with a five-round magazine. The example shown here has a 28 inch vent-ribbed barrel and is in the very stylish "Black Magic" finish.

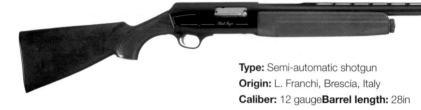

Type: Semi-automatic shotgun
Origin: L. Franchi, Brescia, Italy
Caliber: 12 gauge **Barrel length:** 28in

Francotte Double-Barrel Shotgun

The Auguste Francotte company has been in business in Liege since 1844, its main products being sporting shotguns and rifles. The very traditional example seen here is a double-barrel trap-shooting gun with 30 inch, 12 gauge barrels. It appears from markings on the gun that it was imported into the United States by Francotte's New York agents named von Lengerke & Detmold.

Type: Double-barrel trap shotgun
Origin: A. Francotte & Cie SA, Liege, Belgium
Caliber: 12 gauge   **Barrel length:** 30in

Frigon FT-1 Double-Barrel Shotgun

Frigon imports shotguns made by Marocchi of Brescia, Italy. The FT-1, which was introduced in 1986, is a 12 gauge, boxlock, single-barrel shotgun, with either 32 or 34 inch barrels. The example seen here has a 34 inch vent-ribbed barrel and its walnut stock is fitted with a "Kickeez" recoil pad.

Type: Double-barrel shotgun
Origin: Frigon, Clay Center, Kansas (Marocchi Armi, Brescia, Italy)
Caliber: 12 gauge   **Barrel length:** 34in

Gamba London Double-Barrel Shotgun

The Gamba London is a 12 or 20 gauge double-barrel shotgun with Holland & Holland type of sidelocks. There are a variety of barrel lengths and a selection of chokes. This particular weapon has a high grade finish with the action being engraved with tight English scrollwork and a good quality walnut stock in the straight "English" style.

Gamba Edinburgh Trap Gun

This series of guns is named after British cities, in this case Edinburgh. It is a double-barrel, side-by-side shotgun with two 31.5 inch barrels with 2.75 inch chambers. The action is Holland &c Holland-type sidelock, with cocking indicators, single trigger and tang safety. There is very tight scrollwork in the English arabesque style.

Type: Monoblock trap gun
Origin: Armi-Renato Gamba, Gardone V.T., Italy
Caliber: 20 gauge **Barrel length:** 26.75in

Harrington & Richardson Special Forces Shotgun

These shotguns were purchased from Harrington & Richardson by the Green Berets - for use in the Vietnam War. Their main use was to be given as gifts to the Montagnard people, who lived in the mountains, and were ultra-loyal, to the United States in their fight against Communism. They were actually inscribed "Special Forces Model."

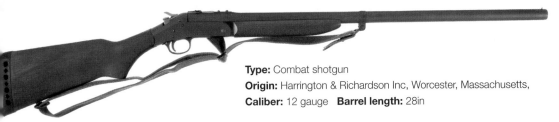

Type: Combat shotgun
Origin: Harrington & Richardson Inc, Worcester, Massachusetts,
Caliber: 12 gauge **Barrel length:** 28in

Huglu Over-and-Under Shotgun

Huglu Shotguns was formed as a co-operative and today there more than 100 separate workshops with an annual output of approximately 65,000 shotguns (15,000 over-and-unders, 10,000 side-by-sides, 15,000 slide-action, and 25,000 semi-automatics). The weapon seen here is an over-and-under with a customized upgrade with engraved scenes showing pairs of golden geese either side of the action and a profusely carved stock depicting hunting scenes.

Type: Over-and-under shotgun
Origin: Huglu Shotguns, Inc., Huglu-Beysehir-Konya, Turkey
Caliber: 12 gauge   **Barrel length:** 30in

Ithaca Single-Barrel Trap Gun

The original Ithaca single-barrel trap gun used a lock designed by Emil Flues of Bay City, Michigan and was in production from 1914 to 1922. It was then replaced by a new design by one of Ithaca's own staff, Frank Knickerbocker, which was produced from 1922 to 1988; this was a very popular weapon among champion trap shooters, by whom it was known, quite simply, as "The Knick."

Type: Single-barrel trap shotgun
Origin: Ithaca Gun Company, Ithaca, New York
Caliber: 12 gauge   **Barrel length:** 32in

Right: This is a Grade 5E weapon, with more intricate scrollwork and gold inlaid animal/bird figures.

The example of a "Knick" seen here being in Grade 4E, and which is engraved with scenes of an Indian archer and a trap shooter. These later guns with intricate engraving are highly collectible.

This example is a Grade 7E with full coverage oak leaf/acorn motifs engraved on the action, tang, and trigger guard, together with bird scenes on the action.

Jing An Over-and-Under Shotgun

The arms industry in China spent its formative years in producing military weapons for the Peoples' Liberation Army, but is now expanding rapidly into civilian, particularly sporting, weapons. This Jing An over-and-under shotgun is a typical recent example. It was imported into the United States by CAI. It is likely that these guns will occupy the budget end of the market at present.

Type: Over-and-under shotgun
Origin: People's Republic of China
Caliber: 16 gauge   **Barrel length:** 28in

W. Karl Double-Barrel Shotgun

This elegant and well-balanced double-barrel shotgun was made by a minor German gunsmith, Willi Karl of Luneberg, a small city about 30 miles south-east of Hamburg. It was then retailed by Stahl & Berger of Hamburg. The engraving is very intricate and covers both the action and the ends of the barrels. The butt has been fitted with a Mershon recoil pad.

Type: Double-barrel shotgun
Origin: Willi Karl, Luneberg, Germany
Caliber: 16 gauge
Barrel length: 25.25in

Krieghoff Combination

Krieghoff has set up a subsidiary in the United States, Krieghoff International, which imports the factory's products. This is a combination 7mm rifle and 16 gauge shotgun, fitted with a Carl Zeiss 4x telescopic sight on a claw sight for rapid removal. The stock has a cheek piece and is fitted with a recoil pad.

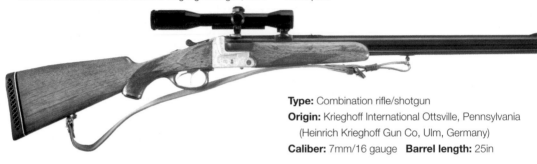

Type: Combination rifle/shotgun
Origin: Krieghoff International Ottsville, Pennsylvania
(Heinrich Krieghoff Gun Co, Ulm, Germany)
Caliber: 7mm/16 gauge   **Barrel length:** 25in

Krieghoff Over-and-Under Shotgun

The Krieghoff Model 32 was a series of superposed shotguns in 12, 20, 28 or .410 gauge with barrels ranging from 26.5 to 32 inches in length, which was discontinued in 1988. The first example seen here is in 12 gauge with a 32 inch vented-rib barrel, and with deep engravings on the receiver (duck on the right, bird and dog on the left). The furniture is walnut and the stock has a white line recoil pad.

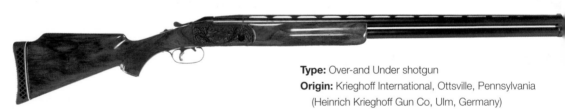

Type: Over-and Under shotgun
Origin: Krieghoff International, Ottsville, Pennsylvania
(Heinrich Krieghoff Gun Co, Ulm, Germany)
Caliber: see text   **Barrel length:** see text

Laurona Shotgun

Laurona is a Spanish gunmaker, located in Eibar, a major center for such industries in Spain. Laurona concentrates on sporting guns and this over-and-under is typical with 12 gauge, 28 inch barrels with ventilated ribs, and some delicate rose bouquet engraving on the action which is finished in Silver Nitrate contrasting with the dark blue of the barrel finish.

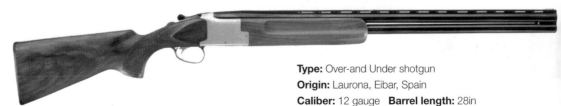

Type: Over-and Under shotgun
Origin: Laurona, Eibar, Spain
Caliber: 12 gauge   **Barrel length:** 28in

This second weapon, also by Laurona, is a side-by-side, .410 gauge shotgun with 28 inch barrels, three inch chambers, double triggers, and a recoil pad. There is light scrollwork on the action.

Linder (Charles Daly) Sextuple Model Single-Barrel Trap

This 12 gauge box-lock, also made in Germany by Linder for Charles Daly (see above) was produced at some time between 1933 and 1939. It is a single-barrel shotgun, which got its name of "sextuple" from the fact that it had six locking lugs. It was fitted with full-choke barrels, a full-length ventilated rib, and automatic ejectors. The action is scroll-engraved in various styles.

Type: Single barrel shotgun
Origin: Linder, Suhl, Thuringia (for Charles Daly, New York)
Caliber: 12 gauge   **Barrel length:** 34in

Miroku Model 90 Shotgun

B.C. Miroku is based in Kochi, Japan, with a workforce some 1,000 strong. Their products were aimed for some years at the domestic Japanese market, but also started to make weapons for sale on the U.S. market. Their first customer was Charles Daly and weapons bearing the latter label made between 1963 and 1976 were actually products of the Miroku factory in Japan. In 1976 FN of Belgium and Miroku combined to buy the U.S. Browning company, whereupon Miroku started producing Brownings. Miroku also exports a small number of weapons under its own name, such as this Model 90 shotgun which is a 12 gauge weapon with a 32 inch fully vent-ribbed barrel, blued finish, walnut stock and white line recoil pad.

Type: Single barrel, trap shotgun
Origin: B. C. Miroku Firearms Company, Kochi, Japan
Caliber: 12 gauge   **Barrel length:** 32in

Marlin Model 44A Slide-Action Shotgun

The Model 44 slide-action shotgun was produced between 1922 and 1933. It was a hammerless, 20 gauge, takedown weapon with a four-round tubular magazine beneath the barrel. The Model 44A was in plain finish, but there was also a Model 44S with a better grade walnut stock with checkering.

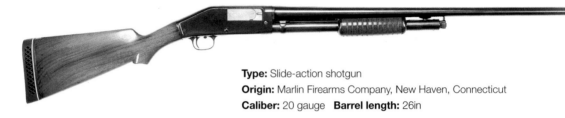

Type: Slide-action shotgun
Origin: Marlin Firearms Company, New Haven, Connecticut
Caliber: 20 gauge   **Barrel length:** 26in

Marlin Model 90 Over-and-Under Shotgun

The Model 90 was manufactured by Marlin between 1937 and 1963. One production run was for Sears, Roebuck as a "Hardware Gun" (see Eastern Arms entry page 211) and was marketed by them under the trades name "Ranger" up to 1941, and "J.C. Higgins" from 1946 onwards. The same weapon was also marketed by Marlin as the Model 90. The two shotguns shown here are both Marlin Model 90s.

Type: Over-and-under (superposed) shotgun
Origin: Marlin Firearms Company, New Haven, Connecticut
Caliber: see text
Barrel length: see text

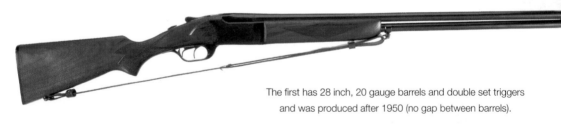

The first has 28 inch, 20 gauge barrels and double set triggers and was produced after 1950 (no gap between barrels).

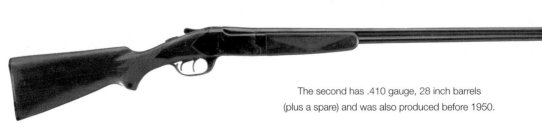

The second has .410 gauge, 28 inch barrels (plus a spare) and was also produced before 1950.

Mossberg Model 500

The Mossberg Model 500 pump-action shotgun has been in production for well over twenty years, during which time many millions have been sold. There have been at least seventeen variants, ranging from standard field models, through slug (including fully rifled), bantam for young shooters, turkey, waterfowl, security and combination models, and it has also been accepted by the U.S. army.

The Model 500 is marketed in a wide variety of barrel lengths, calibers and finishes, and the standard magazine holds five shells.

Type: Slide-action shotgun
Origin: O.F. Mossberg & Sons Inc, North Haven, Connecticut
Caliber: see text **Barrel length:** see text

Shown here is a Model 500 Crown Grade with 28.25 inch vent-ribbed barrel in 20 gauge.

This one is in 12 gauge with a 28 inch vent-ribbed barrel and a Woodlands camouflage pattern finish.

Finally we have a Model 500 ATP in 12 gauge, with plastic pistol grips and no stock butt.

Mossberg Model 835 Slide-Action Shotgun

The Mossberg Model 835 Ulti-Mag is a 12 gauge, pump-action shotgun, usually with a vent-ribbed barrel, and with a number of fully-camouflaged variants. We show a Model 835 with a 26 inch barrel and composition stock with a matte blue finish.

Type: Slide-action shotgun
Origin: O.F. Mossberg & Sons Inc,
    North Haven, Connecticut
Caliber: 12 gauge
Barrel length: 26in

Mossberg Model 9200 Semi-Automatic Shotgun

The Mossberg Model 9200 series semi-automatic shotguns are all in 12 gauge and, like most Mossberg models, include variants with camouflage finish. We show one with a 12 gauge 28 inch vent-ribbed barrel and green synthetic stock. This gun was replaced with the Model 935 which has proved a bigger success for the company.

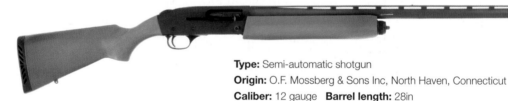

Type: Semi-automatic shotgun
Origin: O.F. Mossberg & Sons Inc, North Haven, Connecticut
Caliber: 12 gauge   **Barrel length:** 28in

Newport Double-Barrel Shotgun

"Newport" was yet another of the trade names used by Crescent, which was itself owned by H. & D. Folsom. The Newport weapons were made for the Chicago-based Hibbard, Spencer and Bartlett company. This particular example has two 16 gauge, 30 inches long barrels, side lock action with double triggers, and a tang safety.

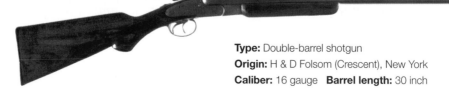

Type: Double-barrel shotgun
Origin: H & D Folsom (Crescent), New York
Caliber: 16 gauge   **Barrel length:** 30 inch

Parker Trojan Double-Barrel Shotgun

The Trojan was a boxlock, double-barreled (side-by-side) shotgun. It was made in 12, 16, or 20 gauge and in the usual variety of barrel lengths. The example shown has a 12 gauge, 30 inch barrel with 2.6 inch chambers, and extractors. The recoil pad is a post-factory addition by one of the owners.

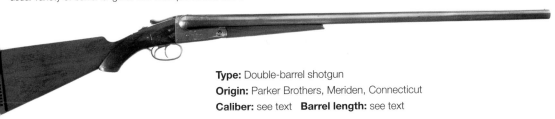

Type: Double-barrel shotgun
Origin: Parker Brothers, Meriden, Connecticut
Caliber: see text **Barrel length:** see text

Perazzi MX-7 Trap Gun

The MX-7 was introduced in 1993 and is available only in 12 gauge, but with either two 29.5 or 31.5 inch barrels in an over-and-under arrangement, or a single barrel which is either 32 or 34 inches in length. The version seen here has a single 34 inch vent-ribbed barrel.

Type: Over-and-under/single-barrel trapgun
Origin: Perazzi, Brescia, Italy
Caliber: see text
Barrel length: see text

Remington Model 10 Pump-Action

A 12 gauge weapon, the Model 10 had a short tubular magazine under the barrel loaded from underneath the breech. Empty shell cases were also ejected downward. It was originally sold in 8 grades, but more were added as time went on. There were sporting versions, hunters and riot guns, and in 1931 a Target Grade Model 10 was introduced with a ventilated top rib.

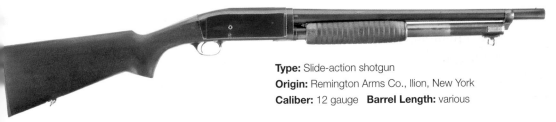

Type: Slide-action shotgun
Origin: Remington Arms Co., Ilion, New York
Caliber: 12 gauge **Barrel Length:** various

Remington Model 10 Trench Gun

Remington delivered 3,500 of these 23 inch Model 10 trench guns to the army during World War One. Another 1,500 were delivered with 20 inch barrels. Both had bayonet lugs and wooden handguards to protect the firers hand from barrel heat.

Type: Trench gun
Origin: Remington Arms Co., Ilion, New York
Caliber: 12 gauge
Barrel length: 23 and 20 in

Remington Model 11 Autoloading Shotgun

A John Browning design, this recoil-operated autoloader was first offered in 1906 as the Remington Autoloading Gun, but was renamed the Model 11 Autoloading Shotgun in 1911. For most of its life it was a 12 gauge weapon, but 20 and 16 gauge were introduced in 1931-32. It turned out to be a spectacular success for the company, with over 850,000 being made; and production only finally stopped in 1948.

Type: Semi-automatic shotgun
Origin: Remington Arms Co., Ilion, New York
Caliber: 12, 16 and 20 gauge   **Barrel length:** 26 in

Remington Army Model 11

The U.S. government purchased a number of Model 11s, particularly during World War Two where they were used in close combat situations, while others were bought by police departments for anti-riot duties. This one is a World War Two U.S. army Model 11, with a 26 inch, 12 gauge barrel.

Type: Semi-automatic shotgun
Origin: Remington Arms Co., Ilion, New York
Caliber: 12, 16 and 20 gauge   **Barrel length:** 26 and 20in

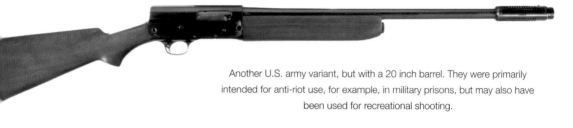

Another U.S. army variant, but with a 20 inch barrel. They were primarily intended for anti-riot use, for example, in military prisons, but may also have been used for recreational shooting.

This Model 11 was converted during World War Two for ground use by Army Air Corps air gunners to practice leading, against aerial targets. The weapon had threaded holes in the receiver, which enabled it to be attached to the simulated aircraft fuselage, and a Cutts compensator on the muzzle.

Left: The US War Department ordnance grenade stamp proves that these are genuine issue guns.

Remington Model 17 Pump-Action

Browning's next shotgun design for Remington was this neat slide-action weapon, which first went on sale in 1919, after prolonged development, and after some improvements from John Pederson. Only available in 20-gauge, it was light, at 5lbs 12 oz, and came with a takedown frame. The under-barrel tubular magazine was loaded from under the receiver, and shell cases were ejected the same way. The Model 17 came in 5 sporting grades plus a riot grade, and 72,644 were made before production stopped in 1941.

Type: Slide-action shotgun
Origin: Remington Arms Co., Ilion, New York
Caliber: 20 gauge   **Barrel length:** various

Remington Model 31 Pump-Action

The Model 31 was developed to replace the Model 17 and Model 29, and was Remington's first side-ejecting, repeating shotgun. The Model 31 held 5 shots in the tubular magazine, although a lightweight 3-shot version was also issued in 1931, as "The Sportsman." Another success for the company, the Model 31 remained in production from 1931 to 1949, during which time some 189,000 were made, in a multitude of grades and variations. Another 179,000 or so Sportsman shotguns were also sold during this time.

Type: Slide-action shotgun
Origin: Remington Arms Co., Ilion, New York
Caliber: 12, 16, 20 gauge
Barrel length: various

This image shows a Model 31-TC (Trap or Target Grade C), with a ventilated top rib for rapid, instinctive aiming.

The 20 inch example seen here is one of these. It bears the "US Property" stamp, and is also marked "ISP" on the right side of the receiver, which suggests that it may once have belonged to a police department, possibly "Illinois State Police."

Remington Model 32 Over-and Under

A simple break-open shotgun, the Model 32 was Remington's first attempt at an over-and-under configuration. Launched in March 1932 it was well-made, with machine engraving on the receiver and high-grade wood with checkered fore-end and wrist. Initially it came with two triggers but from 1934 had a single selective trigger. We show the Model 32 TC Target Grade, with a raised, ventilated top rib and recoil pad.

Type: Double-barrel over-and-under shotgun
Origin: Remington Arms Co., Ilion, New York
Caliber: 12 gauge   **Barrel length:** various

Remington Model 870

The Remington Model 870 slide action shotgun was introduced in 1950, offered with a variety of barrels -20, 26, 28 or 30 inch With this weapon Remington hit on a combination of simplicity, robustness, balance and effectiveness that is world-beating and it is still one of their main product lines; and over six million have been made, it is the most popular shotgun of any type in history. Variants include straightforward hunting shotguns, skeet, target-shooting and competition models, "Express" models, heavy duty "Magnum" versions for heavier loads, rifled "slug" guns for big game targets, folding stock versions and specialist military and police models.

Type: Slide-action shotgun
Origin: Remington Arms Co., Ilion, New York
Caliber: 10, 12, 16 or 20 gauge
Barrel length: 20, 26, 28, and 30in

A Model 870 "Competition" target shooter with wooden furniture, checkered at the wrist and foregrip, a short magazine, long barrel and ventilated top rib.

This Model 870 Express has a short magazine and ventilated top rib.

A Model 870 with dulled green finish on the metalwork but a standard wooden stock and grip. This one comes with a shorter and choked second barrel.

This Model 870 sports a longer 30 inch barrel, complete with ventilated top rib.

Remington Model 870 Magnum and Slug Guns

When larger game is hunted, users normally want a more powerful cartridge than the normal "buckshot" type. Magnum cartridges are longer than standard, with a more powerful charge and heavier load. Magnum variants of the M870 have longer chambers and often quite short barrels (20 or 26 inch). For some targets such as deer etc, a heavy single slug is often used rather than the multiple projectiles in normal shotgun ammunition. Slug barrels are usually rifled, and many shotguns have sets of interchangeable barrels to allow the owner to set the gun up with the right kind of ammunition for a particular job.

Type: Slide-action shotgun
Origin: Remington Arms Co., Ilion, New York
Caliber: 10, 12, 16 or 20 gauge
Barrel length: 20,26, 28, and 30in

A Model 870 Magnum Special Purpose, with dull green finish to metalwork and green synthetic stock and foregrip. The stock has an integral cheek pad, while on the receiver is a mounting rail for fitting various optical and night vision sights.

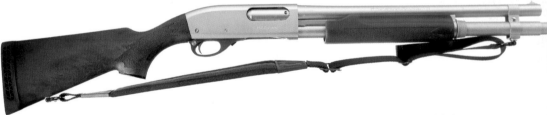

This Model 870 Magnum is the "Marine" type, where the bright satin finish on the metalwork helps prevent corrosion in salt environment. It also has a green synthetic stock and foregrip, and rubber recoil pad.

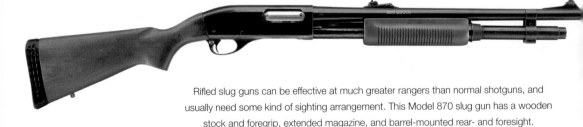

Rifled slug guns can be effective at much greater rangers than normal shotguns, and usually need some kind of sighting arrangement. This Model 870 slug gun has a wooden stock and foregrip, extended magazine, and barrel-mounted rear- and foresight.

Remington Model 870 Military/Police

Model 870s used for military and police work usually have shorter barrels, making them handier for rapid aiming and easier to get in and out of vehicles. The versatile shotgun can be used for a range of ammunition types, including buckshot, solid slugs (for forcing doors open), non-lethal baton rounds and irritant gas projectiles.

Type: Slide-action shotgun
Origin: Remington Arms Co., Ilion, New York
Caliber: 10, 12, 16 or 20 gauge
Barrel length: 14, 18, 20in

A Model 870 modified for police and military use, with synthetic pistol grip, short barrel, camouflaged detachable skeleton stock and dull green metalwork. Note that the foregrip remains checkered wood.

A Model 870, with dull green finish to the metalwork and a green synthetic stock and foregrip. It also has a short barrel and extended magazine.

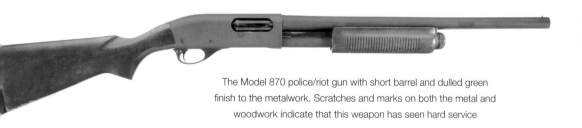

The Model 870 police/riot gun with short barrel and dulled green finish to the metalwork. Scratches and marks on both the metal and woodwork indicate that this weapon has seen hard service

Remington Model 1100 Autoloading Shotgun

Introduced in 1963, the Model 1100 was Remington revisiting the autoloading shotgun and producing a weapon to fill the gap left by the now out-of-production Model 11. Using Remington's signature smooth outline and styling, it was another success for the company. Since introduction, over 3 million have been made, and solid and reliable, it comes in a range of gauges, including 12, 12 Magnum, 16 and 20 gauges. A lightweight version is also available in 28 and .410m gauges. The two shown here have similar levels of finish, with fine scrollwork on the receiver and bolt. The first one shows the signs of hard usage - exactly what these fine, practical guns were intended for.

Type: Autoloading shotgun
Origin: Remington Arms Co., Ilion, New York
Caliber: see text
Barrel length: 28in and 30in

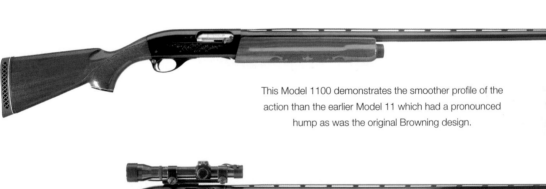

This Model 1100 demonstrates the smoother profile of the action than the earlier Model 11 which had a pronounced hump as was the original Browning design.

A complete shotgun "set," this Model 1100 comes with two extra barrels, on choked, and one a heavy slug or deer barrel with fore- and rearsights. The weapon also has a mounting rail above the receiver which is carrying an optical sight.

Remington Model 3200

The Model 3200 was introduced in 1973, the first Remington over-and-under shotgun since the Model 32, which ended production in 1941. It bears a close visual and engineering resemblance to the earlier weapon although modern production methods allow it to made quicker, more efficiently and comparatively cheaper. It was available in a range of gauges and grades.

Type: Autoloading shotgun
Origin: Remington Arms Co., Ilion, New York
Caliber: see text   **Barrel length:** 28in and 30in

Remington Parker AHE

Remington introduced this in 1988, and it is handcrafted in the Parker Gun Works division of Remington. It represents a double-barreled Parker shotgun of yesteryear, and is made to the same exacting standards as before. It has ribbed side-by-side barrels, a smooth, fast-acting single selective trigger, and fine engravings on the receiver. Only a few of these very expensive collectors items were made.

Type: Double-barrel shotgun
Origin: Remington Arms Co., Ilion, New York
Caliber: 20 gauge   **Barrel length:** 28in

Richland Arms Model 7 11 Magnum Double-Barrel Shotgun

The Richland Arms Company imported Spanish-made shotguns, but ceased trading in 1986. This Model 711 Magnum is a double-barreled gun with two 10 gauge, 32 inch, solid rib barrels and 3.5 inch chambers. It has double triggers and automatic ejectors and the action is decorated with fine English scrollwork.

Type: Double-barrel shotgun
Origin: Richland Arms Company, Blissfield, Michigan
Caliber: 19 gauge   **Barrel length:** 32in

Ruger Red Label Over-and-Under Shotgun

Sturm, Ruger introduced the Red Label high quality, boxlock over-and-under shotgun range in 1977 in 20 gauge only and it was not until 1982 that the 12 gauge version appeared.

This is one of those early examples, with 28 inch vent-ribbed barrels in 20 gauge.

Type: Over-and-under shotgun
Origin: Sturm, Ruger & Co, Southport, Connecticut
Caliber: see text
Barrel length: see text

Ruger Gold Label Shotgun

Made at the manufacturing plant at Newport, New Hampshire, this traditional English style side-by side has the benefit of modern technology and materials. It has a stainless steel receiver and blued barrels which combined with the

grade AAA American walnut stock and forend makes for an attractive gun. It has a single selective trigger, changeable chokes and is chambered for up to 3 inch long cartridges.

Type: Double-barrel shotgun
Origin: Sturm, Ruger & Co, Southport, Connecticut
Caliber: 12 gauge **Barrel length:** 28in

Savage Model 430 Superposed Shotgun

The Savage Model 420 and 430 superposed shotguns were produced between 1937 and 1943 in 12, 16 or 20 gauge and 26, 28, or 30 inch barrels. The 430 differed from the 420 only in having a checkered stock and a solid ribbed barrel.

Both models were available in single- or double-trigger versions. The example shown here is a Model 430 with a 28 inch barrel with double triggers.

Type: Over-and under shotgun
Origin: Savage Arms Corporation, Chicopee Falls, Massachusetts
Caliber: 12 gauge   **Barrel length:** 28in

Savage Model 440 T Superposed Shotgun

The Model 440T was made in Italy between 1968 and 1972 and marketed in the United States under the Savage label. It has two 12 gauge over-and-under 30 inch barrels and a walnut, trap-style stock. It is finished in blued steel both for the action and the barrels.

Type: Over-and under shotgun
Origin: Savage Arms Corporation, Chicopee Falls, Massachusetts
Caliber: 12 gauge
Barrel length: 30in

Savage Model 720 Semi-Automatic Shotgun

The Model 720 was a semi-automatic shotgun made in the United States between 1930 and 1949. It was available in either 12 or 16 gauge, with barrels ranging from 26 to 32 inches. The example shown here has a 16 gauge, 28 inch barrel, with a modified choke.

Type: Semi-automatic shotgun
Origin: Savage Arms Corporation, Chicopee Falls, Massachusetts
Caliber: 16 gauge   **Barrel Length:** 28in

SKB Shotgun

SKB is a Japanese company, its title being derived from the family's name of Sakaba, with the vowels removed. Their shotguns have been imported into the United States by several well-known companies, but are now imported under their own name, as SKB Shotguns of Omaha, Nebraska. Shown here is a Model 605 with 12 gauge 28 inch barrels, engraved action, walnut stock and a white line recoil pad.

Type: Over-and-under shotgun
Origin: SKB,Omaha, Nebraska
Caliber: see text
Barrel length: see text

Here is an SKB Model 7300 slide-action shotgun in 12 gauge with a 28 inch barrel

This is the XL 900MR semi-automatic also in 12 gauge with 28 inch barrels.

Franz Sodia Over-and-Under

This is a twin barrel shotgun in an over-and-under configuration, with a three-piece forearm and a very blond walnut butt stock with a white line recoil pad. The action is covered with deep-relief engraving, with a rabbit scene on the left side and a capercaillie on the right, and a woodcock on the bottom.

Type: Over-and-under shotgun
Origin: Franz Sodia Jagdgewehrfabrik,Ferlach, Austria
Caliber: 16 gauge   **Barrel length:** two 28 inch

Franz Sodia Combination Rifle/Shotgun

This is a combination 6.5mm caliber rifle and a 16 caliber shotgun, with cocking indicators on top of the action. There is a bead sight on the muzzle and a two-leaf rearsight - one standing, one folding. There is deep-relief engraving with much scrollwork; there are game scenes on the side plates.

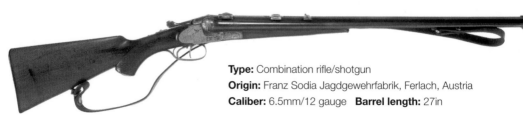

Type: Combination rifle/shotgun
Origin: Franz Sodia Jagdgewehrfabrik, Ferlach, Austria
Caliber: 6.5mm/12 gauge   **Barrel length:** 27in

Franz Sodia Single –Barrel Trap Shotgun

This beautifully finished single-barrel shotgun has a vent-ribbed 34 inch barrel and highly polished walnut stock and forearm. The box lock action is engraved with game scenes - dog and pheasants on the left and ducks on the right. The stock has a high comb, ideal for trap shooting, and is fitted with a Pachmayr white-line recoil pad.

Type: Single-barrel trap shotgun
Origin: Franz Sodia Jagdgewehrfabrik, Ferlach, Austria
Caliber: 12 gauge
Barrel length: 34in

Stevens Model 94B Single-Shot Shotgun

There have been at least 26 Stevens single shot shotguns in the usual variety of gauges and barrel lengths. This Model 94B is typical with a 12 gauge, 21 inch barrel and a plain walnut stock. It differs only in having had a bayonet lug welded to the underside of the barrel, about 4 inches from the muzzle, which suggests a possible military link in its past.

Type: Single-shot shotgun
Origin: Stevens Arms Company, Chicopee Falls, Massachusetts
Caliber: 12 gauge   **Barrel length:** 21in

Stevens Model 311-A Double-Barrel Shotgun

The Model 311 is one of the long line of double-barrel designs produced by Stevens and there were at least thirteen different variants within the 311 series. This is a Model 311-A hammerless boxlock in 12 gauge, with a 28 inch barrel.

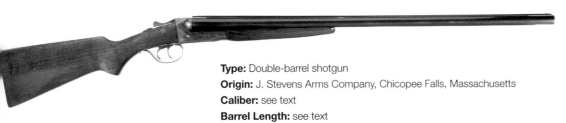

Type: Double-barrel shotgun
Origin: J. Stevens Arms Company, Chicopee Falls, Massachusetts
Caliber: see text
Barrel Length: see text

Stevens Utility Grade Pump-Action Shotgun

Over the years, the J. Stevens Arms Company, Chicopee Falls, Massachusetts, has manufactured a number of basic slide-action shotguns, with a variety of barrel lengths, gauges and chokes. They have blue metalwork and walnut stocks, with minimal decoration. These utility-grade weapons include Models 520, 522, 620, 621, 67, 77, an 820 and an example is shown here.

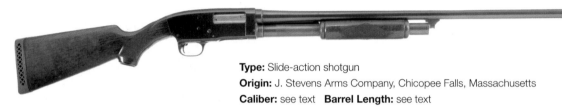

Type: Slide-action shotgun
Origin: J. Stevens Arms Company, Chicopee Falls, Massachusetts
Caliber: see text   **Barrel Length:** see text

Stevens Model 520-30 Trench Gun

During World War One a number of trench gun conversions were ordered by the U.S. Government to meet the demand for an effective weapon for close combat in the trenches in France. Other famous shotgun manufacturers like Remington and Winchester were already engaged in production and Stevens' Model 520 combat shotgun (seen here) was already in service with the U.S. Army.

Type: Trench gun
Origin: J. Stevens Arms Company, Chicopee Falls, Massachusetts
Caliber: 12 gauge   **Barrel length:** 20in

To meet new requirements Stevens modified his existing design to produce the new Model 520-30. This had a 20 inch barrel, which, like the other trench guns, fired 12 gauge shot. The magazine held five rounds, which with one already chambered, gave a combat load of six. Also like the others, it was fitted with a muzzle-mounted bayonet adaptor and a barrel handguard, although, unlike the Remington, this was made of perforated metal.

Stevens Model 620 Trench Gun

Production of World War One trench guns ceased almost as soon as the war ended; of those already completed, some were retained in store and others sold off on the civilian market. On the outbreak of World War Two, however, a new need for shotguns was foreseen and what remained of the military stocks were reissued. This still left a shortfall and among the new weapons ordered was the Stevens Model 620 riot gun seen here.

Type: Trench gun
Origin: J. Stevens Arms Company, Chicopee Falls, Massachusetts
Caliber: 12 gauge
Barrel length: 20in

Another trench gun conversion was also produced, the Model 620A. Both shotguns fired 12 gauge and had 20 inch barrels.

Stevens Model 77E Combat Shotgun

As soon as large numbers of U.S. troops were committed to the war in Vietnam, requests began to filter back to Washington for combat shotguns. Having failed to learn the lesson from the aftermath of World War One, most of the stock of World War II weapons had been sold off to civilians, so the Government turned towards two companies for new models. As a result barrel, fired 12 gauge and could be loaded with seven rounds (six in the magazine and one already chambered). Some 70,000 Stevens Model 77Es were procured and supplied to the troops. The Model 77E had a 20 inch barrel, fired 12 gauge and could be loaded with seven rounds (six in the magazine and one already chambered).

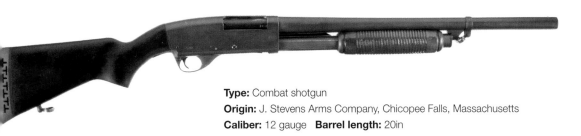

Type: Combat shotgun
Origin: J. Stevens Arms Company, Chicopee Falls, Massachusetts
Caliber: 12 gauge   **Barrel length:** 20in

Montgomery Ward Shotguns

Montgomery Ward, founded in 1872, was a Chicago-based retail and mail-order giant which went bankrupt in 2000 after 128 years in business. Like similar businesses it included firearms among its wares, which were made to Ward's specification by established manufacturers, such as Stevens, and then sold under a variety of trade-names. Sears used "Craftsman" and "J.C. Higgins," while Montgomery Ward used "Western Field" and "Hercules."

This first Ward shotgun is a 12 gauge, 24 inch barrel double-barrel, side-by-side shotgun, with twin triggers by an unknown manufacturer.

This however, is a 30 inch, 16 gauge single-barrel shotgun, which was made for Ward by Iver Johnson, based on their Champion model.

A Western Field Model 30 slide-action shotgun by an unknown maker with a 12 gauge, 28 inch barrel.

Another Western Field shotgun, this time a rebadged Marlin Model 90.

This one is a Western Field M550C slide action fitted with a C-Lect choke.

Weatherby Centurion Semi-Automatic Shotgun

Weatherby was founded in 1945 and much of their earlier production effort was concentrated on high-power rifles. The Centurion, introduced in 1972, was the first shotgun, and was a gas-operated, semi-automatic, but various barrel lengths and chokes were offered. There was also a Centurion deluxe which had a vent-ribbed barrel, better quality walnut and a limited amount of engraving. The weapon seen here is a standard Centurion, with a vent-ribbed, 30 inch barrel. Production of the Centurion ended in 1981.

Type: Semi-automatic shotgun
Origin: Weatherby Corporation, Atascadero, California
Caliber: 12 gauge   **Barrel length:** 30in

Weatherby Athena Over-and-Under Shotgun

This gun belonged to the famous singer Conway Twitty (1933-93) who had fifty-five singles reach Number 1 in the United States during the 20th century, more than any other singer, including Elvis. When he died in 1993 his various ex-wives had a public dispute about his assets and his goods had to be auctioned off, including this shotgun. It is a Weatherby Athena that was custom-made for the singer, with 12 gauge, 28 inch barrels, which are both vent-ribbed and side-ribbed, and a high-grade Claro walnut stock. The side-plates have rose and scroll engraving, and the forearm and stock have fine checkering. At the time of the auction it was proved to have been virtually unused, a sad fate for such a splendid example of the gunmaker's art.

Type: Over-and-under shotgun
Origin: Weatherby Corporation, Atascadero, California
Caliber: 12 gauge   **Barrel length:** 28in

Winchester Model 1887 Lever-Action Shotgun

Winchester bought the patent for a lever-action design from John Browning and put it into production as the Model 1887 shotgun, of which some 65,000 had been sold by the time production ended in 1901. The Model 1887 was made in 10 and 12 gauges with either 30 or 32 inch barrels, with a Riot Gun variant with a 20 inch barrel.

Type: Lever-action shotgun
Origin: Winchester Repeating Arms Company, New Haven, Connecticut
Caliber: 10 gauge
Barrel length: 30.25in

Winchester Model 1893 Slide-Action Shotgun

The Model 1893 slide-action, Winchester's first, was based once again on a John M. Browning design. Although some 35,000 were sold between 1893 and 1897. The Model 1893 was produced in 12 gauge only, with either 30 or 32 inch barrel. The example seen here is a special order Model 1893 with a Damascus barrel, deluxe flame grain walnut and checkered pistol grip.

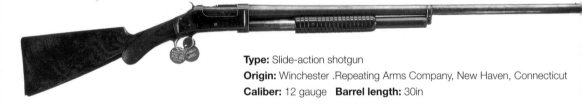

Type: Slide-action shotgun
Origin: Winchester .Repeating Arms Company, New Haven, Connecticut
Caliber: 12 gauge   **Barrel length:** 30in

Winchester Model 1897 Pump-Action Shotgun

The Model 1893 was Winchester's first slide-action shotgun and was soon followed by the much improved Model 1897, which had a stronger frame and longer, better-angled stock. Most had walnut stocks with steel butt plates. It was produced in a variety of model such as Standard, Trap, Pigeon,Tournament ,Brush, Brush Takedown, Riot and Trench. The Riot and Trench-gun versions are described separately. Here we show a Standard version with 30 inch barrel in 12 gauge.

Type: Slide-action shotgun
Origin: Winchester .Repeating Arms Company, New Haven, Connecticut
Caliber: 12 gauge   **Barrel length:** 30in

Winchester Model 1897 Trench Gun

When, in 1917, the commanders in France demanded a trench gun, the first to be selected by the Ordnance Department was the Model 1897 which was readily available. With a 20 inch barrel and solid frame, it had a useful capacity of five rounds in the magazine plus one in the chamber. However, the Ordnance Department stipulated that the weapon must have a bayonet, which caused a difficulty, since the normal bayonet had a guard ring which fitted over the muzzle of .30-30 barrel, but would not fit over the greater diameter 12 gauge barrel. This was resolved by the use of an attachment, designed at the Springfield Armory, which went over the muzzle.

Type: Slide-action shotgun
Origin: Winchester .Repeating Arms Company,
   New Haven, Connecticut
Caliber: 12 gauge
Barrel length: 20in

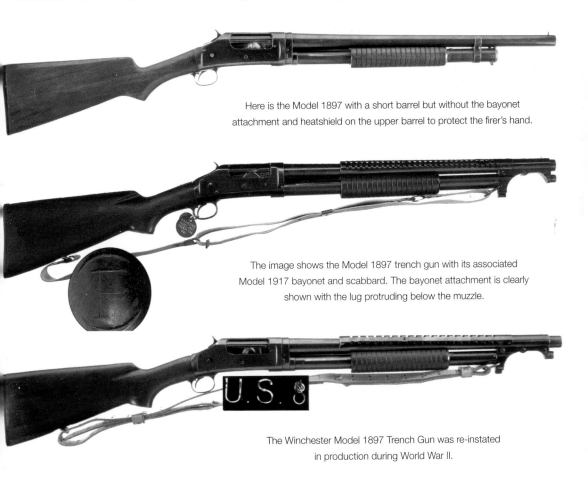

Here is the Model 1897 with a short barrel but without the bayonet attachment and heatshield on the upper barrel to protect the firer's hand.

The image shows the Model 1897 trench gun with its associated Model 1917 bayonet and scabbard. The bayonet attachment is clearly shown with the lug protruding below the muzzle.

The Winchester Model 1897 Trench Gun was re-instated in production during World War II.

Winchester Model 12 Pump-Action Shotgun

The Winchester Model 12 pump-action shotgun was designed by the legendary T.C. Johnson and having been introduced in 1912 it remained in production until 1963, by which time just under two million had been sold. It was produced in eight basic models, most of them being available in various gauges-12, 16, 20, and 28 and barrel lengths of 26, 28, 30, and 32 inches.

Type: Slide-action shotgun
Origin: Winchester .Repeating Arms Company, New Haven, Connecticut
Caliber: see text
Barrel length: see text

A Model 12 in 12 gauge, with a 26 inch barrel.

Another 12 gauge Model 12 shotgun, this time with a 30 inch barrel and extra barrel assembly.

This one has a 26 inch barrel in the rare 28 gauge.

This is the riot gun version, which was only available in 12 gauge and with a 20 inch barrel, marked in this case "Illinois Tollway."

The U.S. Army bought a number of Model 12 Trench Guns during World War II, which were also in 12 gauge with 20 inch barrels. This example is missing the heatshield and bayonet attachment.

Next came the Skeet Grade, shown here with a 26 inch barrel which is vent-ribbed with round posts: it is in the relatively unusual 28 gauge and was made in 1955.

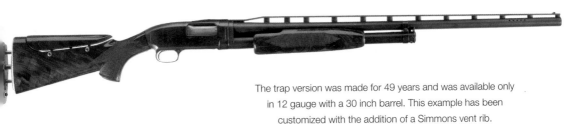

The trap version was made for 49 years and was available only in 12 gauge with a 30 inch barrel. This example has been customized with the addition of a Simmons vent rib.

Winchester Model 12 Special Finishes

We show a range of special finishes that the Model 12 has appeared in, from a spectacular hand-crafted museum-quality one-off to simpler weapons with a little engraving. All the weapons shown are in 12 gauge, with 30 inch barrels. There could be nothing finer than a set made for the Company President's personal collection by Winchester's own engraving shop. This one-of-a-kind "Presidential Model 12 Pigeon Grade" set has three barrels, all 12 gauge and 30 inches long, one each for skeet, trap and field shooting. The whole set is housed in a custom-made black Winchester hardwood case.

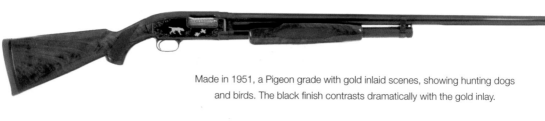

Made in 1951, a Pigeon grade with gold inlaid scenes, showing hunting dogs and birds. The black finish contrasts dramatically with the gold inlay.

A vent-ribbed barrel Model 12 , made in 1959, where the engraved scenes are more elaborate, while the stock and forearm are carved with oak leaves and flower motifs. The butt and pistol grip have been customized by the addition of layers of different colored woods.

Still decorated to a high standard, this Model 12 is adorned in a much simpler style with single dog and bird motifs.

Winchester Model 12 Miscellany

This is the collector's corner of the Model 12 section. The guns here are pretty particular models featuring some of the more unusual versions of the gun. These would be of special interest to collectors.

We showed earlier the Company President's very special set with three barrels, but many owners bought more than one barrel. This one is a 12 gauge with two barrels, both serial numbered to the gun, one 30 inches long (on the gun) the other 26 inches.

Owners could also have accessories added, as this one, which has a Power-Pac compensator attached to the muzzle.

A very rare version of the Model 12, made in 1927, with a stainless steel barrel.

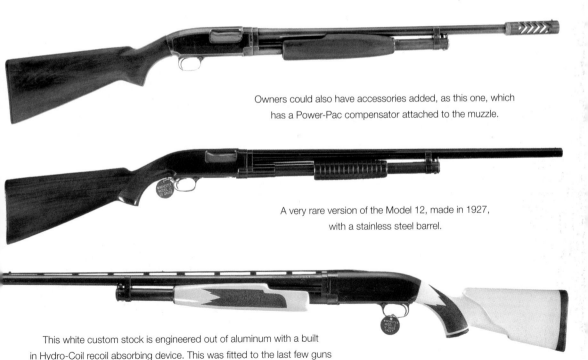

This white custom stock is engineered out of aluminum with a built in Hydro-Coil recoil absorbing device. This was fitted to the last few guns and did not prove to be popular.

Winchester Model 12 Combat

A riot gun version of the Model 12 was introduced in 1918 and was periodically put into production to meet specific orders, until finally withdrawn in 1963.

Type: Combat shotgun
Origin: Winchester Repeating Arms Company, New Haven, Connecticut
Caliber: 12 gauge   **Barrel length:** 20in

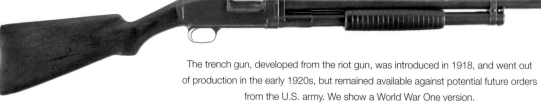

The trench gun, developed from the riot gun, was introduced in 1918, and went out of production in the early 1920s, but remained available against potential future orders from the U.S. army. We show a World War One version.

It was put back into production during World War Two and then remained in service through the Korean War until Vietnam.

Winchester Model 20 Single-Barrel Shotgun

The Winchester Model 20 was made at the end of World War I to soak up a glut of production, labour and materials from wartime. There were severe limits to the range, in order to simplify production and keep the price down,

it being made only in .410 gauge with a 26 inch barrel, while the walnut stock was of the simplest shape and had a hard rubber butt plate.

Type: Single-barrel shotgun
Origin: Winchester Repeating Arms Company, New Haven, Connecticut
Caliber: .410 gauge   **Barrel length:** 26in

Winchester Model 22 Double-Barrel Shotgun

The Winchester Model 22 is hard to find in the United States as it was made for Winchester by Laurona in Spain and then sold only in Europe and in U.S. Armed Forces Post-Exchanges overseas. It was never sold in the United States and the example seen here is from the Winchester company's own collection, in 12 gauge with a 28 inch barrel. See also the other Laurona Models on page 218.

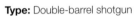

Type: Double-barrel shotgun
Origin: Winchester Repeating Arms Company, New Haven, Connecticut
Caliber: 12 gauge   **Barrel length:** 28in

Winchester Model 23 Double-Barrel Shotgun

The Model 23 was a double-barrel, side-by-side, box-lock shotgun in either 12 or 20 gauge, with barrels of 25.5, 26, 28 or 30 inch lengths and was produced in seven main grades.

Type: Double-barrel shotgun
Origin: Winchester Repeating Arms Company, New Haven, Connecticut
Caliber: see text
Barrel length: see text

Winchester Model 24 Double-Barrel Shotgun

The Model 24 double-barrel, side-by-side shotgun was intended to meet a gap in the medium-priced market and achieved a fair measure of success, with approximately 116,000 sold between its introduction in 1939 and its withdrawal in 1957. It was made in 12, 16 and 20 gauge, with 26, 28 and 30 inch barrels, but was available in only one grade.

Type: Double-barrel shotgun
Origin: Winchester Repeating Arms Company, New Haven, Connecticut
Caliber: see text   **Barrel length:** see text

This is a 20 gauge example with a 26 inch barrel and has
a white line recoil pad.

Winchester Model 25 Slide-Action Shotgun

The Model 25 entered the product line in 1949. It was an attempt to produce a cheaper version of the very successful Model 12, to which it bore many similarities, but it was a solid-frame weapon, which could not be taken down. It was not a great success and production ceased after only five years, with some 88,000 sold -not a major success by Winchester standards. The example shown here, which has a 28 inch barrel, shows the simplicity of design and the plain, but perfectly adequate, finish.

Type: Slide-action shotgun
Origin: Winchester Repeating Arms Company, New Haven, Connecticut
Caliber: 12 gauge **Barrel length:** 26 or 28in

Winchester Model 36 Single-Barrel Shotgun

Like the Model 20, the Model 36 was rushed into production in 1920 to help occupy the machinery that had fallen silent with the ending of the wartime contracts. Production started in 1920 and ended in 1927 after some 20,000 had been sold. It was a bolt-action breech-loader and was cocked by a rearward pull on the firing-pin head. The company referred to it as the "Garden gun" to promote its use around the house and barn to control pests. It could fire 9mm Long shot, 9mm Short shot or 9mm Ball.

Type: Single-barrel "Garden" shotgun
Origin: Winchester Repeating Arms Company, New Haven, Connecticut
Caliber: 9mm RF **Barrel length:** 17.5in

Winchester Model 37 Single-Barrel Shotgun

The Model 37 entered production in 1936 and remained in the company catalog until 1963, by which time over one million had been sold. It was designed to be a simple weapon at a low price which would give it mass appeal. It was produced in various popular gauges and with barrels from 26 to 30 inches in length, but there were no variations in finish.

Type: single-barrel shotgun
Origin: Winchester Repeating Arms Company, New Haven, Connecticut
Caliber: see text
Barrel Length: see text

A Model 37 Red Letter in 20 gauge with a 26 inch barrel and modified choke.

A very rare Model 37 Red Letter in 28 gauge with a 28 inch barrel and Winchester in red lettering on the bottom of the action.

Winchester Model 42 Slide-Action Shotgun

The Model 42 was designed by William Roehmer around the .410 bore, and was, in many respects, a slightly scaled-down Model 12 It was produced in five basic models, with some 164,000 made in a production run lasting from 1933 to 1963. The Model 42 was made in only one calibre, .410 gauge, and with only two barrel lengths, 26 inch and 28 inch.

Type: Slide-action shotgun
Origin: Winchester Repeating Arms Company, New Haven, Connecticut
Caliber: .410 gauge   **Barrel length:** 26 or 28in

Winchester Model 50 Semi-Automatic Shotgun

The Model 50 used a short recoil system with a floating chamber and some 200,000 sold by the time production ended in 1961. The Model 50 was produced in either 12 or 20 gauge and in a variety of barrel lengths. It was made in four grades -Standard, Skeet, Trap and Pigeon, and a lighter "Featherweight" version was available in all except the Trap grade.

Type: Semi-automatic shotgun
Origin: Winchester Repeating Arms Company, New Haven, Connecticut
Caliber: 12 or 20 gauge   **Barrel length:** see text

Winchester Model 59 Semi-Automatic Shotgun

The Model 59 was marketed between 1960 and 1965 and had a barrel made of steel-lined fiberglass that was available in lengths between 26 and 30 inches, but only in 12 gauge. A variety of chokes could be fitted and there were two grades, Standard, in plain walnut, and Pigeon in high grade walnut, both with checkering. The example shown here is a post-1961 model fitted with a Winchester VersaLite choke tube on a 28 inch barrel.

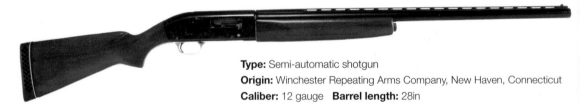

Type: Semi-automatic shotgun
Origin: Winchester Repeating Arms Company, New Haven, Connecticut
Caliber: 12 gauge   **Barrel length:** 28in

Winchester Model 101 Over-and-Under Shotgun

Made by Classic Doubles of Tochigi City, Japan, this gun is then imported into the United States as the Winchester Model 101. It is a double-barreled, over-and-under shotgun in 12, 20, 28 gauges. This one is a Model 101 Field Grade in 12 gauge with 26 inch barrels and a vented-rib to the top. It is in the basic finish apart from an added white line recoil pad.

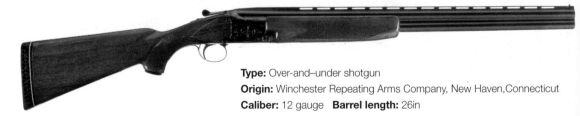

Type: Over-and–under shotgun
Origin: Winchester Repeating Arms Company, New Haven,Connecticut
Caliber: 12 gauge   **Barrel length:** 26in

Winchester Model 1200 Slide-Action Shotgun

The Model 1200 slide-action shotgun was made between 1964 and 1981 in 12, 16 or 20 gauges, with 26, 28 or 30 inch vent-ribbed barrels, and an alloy receiver.

Type: Slide-action shotgun
Origin: Winchester Repeating Arms Company, New Haven, Connecticut
Caliber: see text
Barrel length: see text

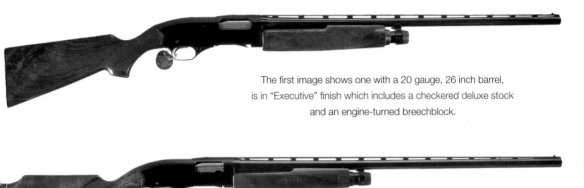

The first image shows one with a 20 gauge, 26 inch barrel, is in "Executive" finish which includes a checkered deluxe stock and an engine-turned breechblock.

A version made for clay pigeon shooting in 12 gauge, with a 28 inch barrel.

Winchester Model 1200 Trench Gun

This weapon was based almost entirely on civilian sporting shotgun components, with a 12 gauge, 18 inch barrel, an overall length of 39 inches and a capacity of five rounds (four in the magazine, one in the chamber). The Model 1200 underwent tests by the army, air force and marines resulting in an order in 1968 for a large quantity of a 20.1 inch barreled version, with a vented metal handguard.

Type: Combat shotgun
Origin: Winchester Repeating Arms Company, New Haven, Connecticut
Caliber: 12 gauge
Barrel length: 20.1in

Winchester Model 1300 Slide-Action Shotgun

The Model 1300 was introduced in 1978 and remains Winchester's current production slide-action shotgun. It has been made in some 37 different grades/configurations, not all of them concurrently available. It is a takedown weapon, in either 12 or 20 gauge, but with a wide variety of barrels and chokes. We show a Model 1300 Stainless Marine in 12 gauge, with an 18 inch barrel and seven-round magazine. All the working parts are made of stainless steel, while the stock forearm and stock butt are made of a black synthetic material, with the latter having an added recoil pad.

Type: Over-and-under shotgun
Origin: Winchester Repeating Arms Company, New Haven, Connecticut
Caliber: see text
Barrel length: see text

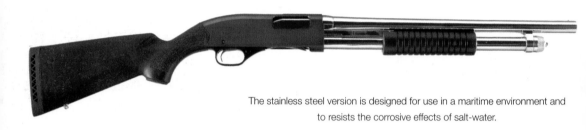

The stainless steel version is designed for use in a maritime environment and to resists the corrosive effects of salt-water.

A Model 1300 Defender Pistol Grip in 12 gauge with an 18 inch barrel and an eight-round magazine.

The Model 1300 Slug Hunter with a full rifled barrel for 3 inch/12 gauge shells; the camouflage-pattern canvas sling is part of the outfit.

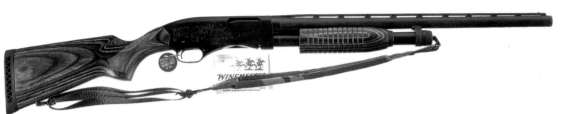

This is a Model 1300 Turkey Model with a 22 inch barrel
incorporating the WinChoke system.

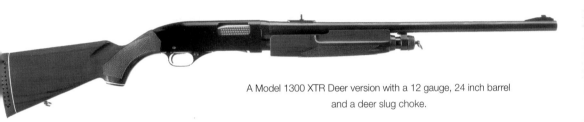

A Model 1300 XTR Deer version with a 12 gauge, 24 inch barrel
and a deer slug choke.

Winchester Super X Model 1 Semi-Automatic Shotgun

The Super X Model 1, produced 1974-81, was a gas-operated semi¬automatic shotgun in 12 gauge only, but with 6, 28 or 30 inch barrels. It was of all-steel construction with a vented top rib to the barrel and walnut stock with checkered pistol grips. The example shown here has a 26 inch skeet choked barrel and a white line recoil pad. Finish is blued steel throughout.

Type: Semi-automatic shotgun
Origin: Winchester Repeating Arms Company, New Haven, Connecticut
Caliber: 12 gauge.
Barrel length: 26in

Index